Sir Arthur Evans

The Horsemen of Tarentum

Sir Arthur Evans

The Horsemen of Tarentum

ISBN/EAN: 9783337034467

Printed in Europe, USA, Canada, Australia, Japan

Cover: Foto ©ninafisch / pixelio.de

More available books at **www.hansebooks.com**

THE "HORSEMEN" OF TARENTUM.

A CONTRIBUTION TOWARDS THE NUMISMATIC HISTORY OF

GREAT GREECE.

INCLUDING AN ESSAY ON ARTISTS', ENGRAVERS', AND
MAGISTRATES' SIGNATURES.

BY

ARTHUR J. EVANS, M.A., F.S.A.,
KEEPER OF THE ASHMOLEAN MUSEUM, OXFORD.

WITH WOODCUTS AND ELEVEN AUTOTYPE PLATES ILLUSTRATIVE OF THE
EQUESTRIAN COIN-TYPES OF TARENTUM.

REPRINTED FROM THE NUMISMATIC CHRONICLE,
WITH INDICES AND ANALYSIS OF CONTENTS.

LONDON:
PUBLISHED BY BERNARD QUARITCH, 15, PICCADILLY.
1889.

ANALYSIS OF CONTENTS.

	PAGE
INTRODUCTION	1—29
EARLY TARENTINE COINAGES AND THEIR CHRONOLOGY.	1—4
Incuse types, &c.	1, 2
The seated Dêmos	3
THE EQUESTRIAN TYPES ("HORSEMEN") OF TARENTUM	4
Their long duration	4
Previous records and classifications of these types	5
Fresh evidence acquired by author from recent finds, &c.	6
EQUESTRIAN DIDRACHMS OF TARENTUM DIVIDED INTO TWO CLASSES OF FULL AND REDUCED WEIGHT.	7
REDUCTION OF WEIGHT COINCIDES WITH PYRRHUS' EXPEDITION	7
CONTINUANCE OF TARENTINE COINAGE AFTER ROMAN OCCUPATION OF 272	7
ORIGINAL VICTORIATE STANDARD ADOPTED AT TARENTUM IN HANNIBAL'S TIME	7
CHRONOLOGICAL ARRANGEMENT OF EQUESTRIAN TYPES INTO TEN PERIODS	8, 9
Pollux's citation from Aristotle touching "Nummos" of Tarentum	9—11
Tarentum as an adherent of Achæan Monetary Convention	11
Earliest coinage silver staters or didrachms only	11
LATER TARENTINE MONETARY SYSTEM COMBINES ATTIC DRACHM WITH SYRACUSAN LITRA	11
Issue of Federal diobols with Hêrakleian types	11
SIGNIFICATION OF HORSEMAN TYPE AT TARENTUM	11—22
Earliest Equestrian types purely agonistic	12
Tarentine polity originally modelled on Spartan Mother-City	12
Influence of Archytas' Stratêgia on Civic Government	13
Absence of names of Stratêgoi upon the Coins	13
Full-length signatures to be referred to Ephor Epônymos	14
CONNEXION OF HORSEMAN TYPES WITH CULT OF LOCAL HEROES AND STATE PATRONS—TARAS, POSEIDÔN, PHALANTHOS, HYAKINTHOS	14—16
Phalanthos and Taras interchanged in local myth	15

	PAGE
Phalanthos on Tarentine coins	15, 16
Dioskuri on these Equestrian types	17
Inscription referring to Hippic Deities of Tarentum	17
Parallels to Equestrian coin-types presented by terra-cotta figures from votive deposit on site of a Chthonic Sanctuary recently discovered at Taranto	17
CHTHONIC AND FUNEREAL CONNEXION OF SYMBOLS ASSOCIATED WITH THESE COIN-TYPES	18
Comparison between seated figure of Taras (Dêmos) holding *kantharos* on archaic coin and Spartan sepulchral relief	19
Illustrations of Tarentine Religious Games from Equestrian types	20
Torch-racers, ἀποβάτης and ἀμφιππος	20
Illustrations of military exercises of Tarentine cavalry	20—22
Historical allusions on Tarentine coins	22—24
SYMBOLS ON EARLIER COINAGE AN INTEGRAL PART OF TYPE	24
Symbols and signatures compared with those of Hêrakleian Tables	25—26
Types parlants and "canting" badges of Tarentine magistrates	25—26
Allusions to religious festivals	27
DISTINCTION TO BE DRAWN BETWEEN SIGNATURES OF DIFFERENT PERIODS	28
EARLIER SIGNATURES THOSE OF ENGRAVER OR MONEYER	28
The same engravers employed by other Magna-Graecian cities	28
LATER FULL-LENGTH SIGNATURES THOSE OF MAGISTRATES	29

PERIOD I. TRANSITIONAL (B.C. c. 450—c. 430)   . 29—35

Overlapping of "horseman" class with that displaying seated Dêmos	29, 30
Archaic characteristics of early equestrian types	30, 31
The inscription TAPANTINΩNHMI	31, 32
Numismatic landmark supplied by Rhêgian coinage of 466	32—34
Types of Period I.	34, 35

PERIOD II. (B.C. c. 420—c. 380)   . . . . . 35—45

Evidences of interval between Periods I. and II.	35, 36
Characteristics of coinage of Period II.	36, 37
Coin representing Phalanthos	37, 38
Comparison with Thracian and Macedonian types	38
Chronological evidence derived from Paestum Find of 1858	39—41
Corroborated by Naples hoard (1888)	41, 42
Types of Period II.	42—45

PERIOD III. THE AGE OF ARCHYTAS (B.C. c. 380—345) 45—63

Evidences of peaceful activity	46

CONTENTS.

	PAGE
FEDERAL CURRENCY NOW INSTITUTED	46, 47
Characteristics of coins of this Period	47, 48
Two classes of fabric—compact and broad	47
Influence of sculpture and painting	48
Coins signed by engraver Lo	50
Taras represented spearing fish	50
Engraver's signature ΣΩΚ on oblong tablet	50, 51
Group of engravers' signatures ΚΑΛ ΦΙ and ΑΡΙ	51—55
Influence of Hêrakleian type at Tarentum	52—54
The Hêrakleian and Metapontian engraver, Aristoxenos, at Tarentum	54, 55
Coins of this Period of broader fabric	55—57
Treatment of hair and horses' manes	56, 57
Types of Period III.	57—63

PERIOD IV. ARCHIDAMOS AND THE FIRST LUCANIAN WAR (344—334 B.C.) . . . . . 64—80

Employment by Tarentines of foreign *Condottieri*	64
Landing of Spartan King Archidâmos	64
TARENTINE GOLD COINS NOW FIRST ISSUED	65—67
Gold stater representing Taras supplicating Tænarian Poseidôn	66, 67
Allusion to Tarentine invocation of Spartan help	67
Characteristics of didrachm types of Period IV.	68, 69
Example of pictorial design	69
Noble group of coins signed ΚΑΛ, ΑΡΙ, & ΦΙ	70
Picturesque compositions of the engraver ΚΑΛ	71
The horseman received by Nikê, an Ephêbos, or a boy	71
Hêrakleian and Metapontian designs of engraver ΚΑΛ	72, 73
First appearance of scheme of horseman lancing downwards	73
Pensive figure of Taras holding helmet between stars of Dioskuri	74
Possible allusion to heroic death of Spartan King	75, 76
Types of Period IV.	76—80

PERIOD V.—FROM THE MOLOSSIAN ALEXANDER TO THE SPARTAN KLEONYMOS (334—302 B.C.) . 80—105

Arrival and Italian career of Alexander, the son of Neoptolemos	80, 81
Influence of his expedition on Tarentine and S. Italian coinage	81—89
Coins struck by Alexander in Italy	82, 83
Metapontian and Locrian moneyers of the Molossian	82, 83
ALLIANCE PIECES OF TARENTINES, RUBASTINES, AND EPIROTE KING	84, 85
TARENTINE GOLD STATERS STRUCK AT THIS TIME	85, 86
Their close analogy with some didrachm types	86

CONTENTS.

	PAGE
Appearance of Molossian symbol, the seated eagle, on Tarentine didrachms	87, 88
Fat infantile figure of Taras as assimilated to Iacchos of Mysteries	89—92
Chronological evidence supplied by Benevento Find	92—94
Remarkable type reading ΣYM, perhaps ΣYMMAXIKON	95—97
Numismatic allusions to Sicilian expedition under Spartan Akrotatos	96—100
Hoard of Tarentine and Macedonian Gold Staters found at Taranto in 1883	97—100
Warlike design of Taras as an archer, reproduced at time of Pyrrhus' arrival	100, 101
May here refer to arrival of Spartan Kleonymos in 302	101
Types of Period V.	101—105

ARTISTS', ENGRAVERS', AND MAGISTRATES' SIGNATURES . . . . 105—124

Groups of coins of first four Periods presenting engravers' signatures	105, 106
Group of coins of Period V. with signatures, ΦI, ΦIΛI, ΦIΛIΣ	106
Microscopic character of some of these signatures	107—109
Characteristics of gem engraver employed as die-sinker	107—109
Range of engraver Philis ... in composition and design	109
Contemporary appearance of a Tarentine type and signature ΦIΛIΣTI at Terina	110, 111
Circumstantial evidence that Tarentine Philis ... is the same engraver as the Velian Philistiôn	111—114
Tarentine, Hêrakleian, and Metapontian details introduced by Philistiôn on Velian dies	112—114
Groups of Equestrian types with signatures ΣA, ΣIM, and BY	114, 115
First Appearance of full-length Signatures of Magistrates on Tarentine Coins	116
Engravers' Signatures now relegated to secondary position	116
Theory that engravers necessarily signed in microscopic characters disproved by Syracusan examples	116, 117
Regular Transition from minute to conspicuous Signatures observable in Practice of Thurian Engravers	117, 118
Both methods employed by same engraver on a single coin	118, 119
Little facilities for interweaving signatures with design on Tarentine coins	119, 120
Ancient engravers also frequently moneyers	120
Coinage in hands of private individuals as at Antioch in Antiochos Epiphanês' days	120, 121
Associations of engravers and moneyers in the same *bottega*	121

CONTENTS. vii

	PAGE
Such a practice best accounts for grouping of Tarentine signatures	122
THE SAME ARTISTIC ENGRAVERS EMPLOYED BY SEVERAL MAGNA-GRÆCIAN CITIES	122, 123
Engravers' signatures not necessarily artists' . . .	124

PERIOD VI.—FROM KLEONYMOS TO PYRRHUS (302—281 B.C.) . . . . 124—135

All full-weight didrachms with signatures at full-length included in this period	124, 125
APPEARANCE OF DRACHMS OF FEDERAL TYPE OF REDUCED WEIGHT	125—127
Find of Tarentine and Magna-Græcian coins near Oria	126, 127
Litræ and Hêmilitra still struck of full weight . .	128
Engravers' and magistrates' signatures together on coins of Period VI.	129, 130
The engravers' signatures ΞΙ and ΕΥ	130
The signature ΞΟΡ on gold and silver coinage of this Period	130, 131
CAMPANO-TARENTINE DIDRACHMS NOW FIRST ISSUED .	131
THESE PIECES STRUCK FOR CIRCULATION IN APULIA AND SAMNIUM	131
NOT FOUND IN THE NEIGHBOURHOOD OF TARANTO .	131
Types of Period VI.	132—135

PERIOD VII.—THE PYRRHIC HEGEMONY (B.C. 281—272) . . . . 135—163

Historical sketch of period preceding Pyrrhus' arrival .	136—138
Tarentine independence threatened by Agathoklês .	136, 137
Outbreak of hostilities with Rome . . .	137, 138
Pyrrhus called in by the Tarentines . . .	138
REDUCTION OF DIDRACHM AND LITRA STANDARD AT TARENTUM	139
APPEARANCE OF PYRRHIC BADGES ON TARENTINE COINS .	139
THE ELEPHANT SYMBOL ON DIDRACHMS	139
ATHÊNÊ ALKIS ON GOLD STATERS	139, 140
Eagle, thunderbolt, and spearhead on Tarentine gold .	140—142
Spearhead, Æakid badge	142
Appears on latest full-weight didrachms . . .	143
ATHÊNÊ ALKIS ON LATEST FULL-WEIGHT LITRAS . .	144
LITRAS OF REDUCED WEIGHT ISSUED WITH ELEPHANT SYMBOL	145
EVIDENCE THAT REDUCTION OF WEIGHT TOOK PLACE AT TIME OF PYRRHUS' EXPEDITION	145
Late full-weight didrachms with anchor . . .	146
Anchor at Tarentum symbol of maritime victory . .	147
Sinking of Roman fleet probable occasion of type . .	147
Tarentine didrachms of Pyrrhic epoch with thunderbolt and prow	148
Taras assimilated to Seleukid Apollo . . .	149, 150

viii   CONTENTS.

                                                                                           PAGE

Complimentary allusion to pecuniary aid supplied by
    Antiochos I. . . . . 150—152
Signatures on Pyrrhic coinage of Tarentum 152
RESULTS CORROBORATED BY HOARD RECENTLY DISCOVERED IN
    CALABRIA . . . . 153—155
Drachms belonging to Pyrrhic epoch 154
Some rare types of this Period 155, 156
Inscription ϹΙϹ of shield on horseman 156
Types of Period VII. . . . . . . 156—163

TARENTUM AS A CIVITAS FŒDERATA . . . 163—169
    UNFOUNDED ASSUMPTION THAT TARENTINE COINAGE CEASED
        ON ROMAN OCCUPATION OF 272 B.C. 163
    Tarentum recognised as "Free and Allied City" . . . 164
    EVIDENCE OF CONTINUANCE OF COINAGE SUPPLIED BY GREAT
        HOARD FOUND AT TARANTO IN 1883 . . . 165
    Summary account of Taranto hoard . . . . 165—169
    The types later than those of Calabrian hoard . . . 166
    Symbols and signatures on coins of smaller denominations 166, 167
    Coins of Taranto Find divided into earlier and later class 168, 169

PERIOD VIII. THE ROMAN ALLIANCE I. (B.C. 272—
    c. 235) . . . . 169—182
    Bulk of Taranto hoard belongs to this Period . . . 169
    Evidence of continued material prosperity in prolific coinage . 169
    Campano-Tarentine coinage also abundant 170
    View that Neapolitan silver coinage ceased on first emission
        of Roman denarii in 268 untenable 171
    SCHEME AND STYLE OF BULK OF CAMPANO-TARENTINE COINS
        RESEMBLE REGULAR DIDRACHM TYPES OF THIS PERIOD 171, 172
    Large proportion of symbols the same in both series . 172, 173
    Several of these symbols "canting" badges of magistrates 173, 174
    Symbols on Campano-Tarentine coins referring to Tarentine
        magistrates of the post-Pyrrhic epoch . . . 175
    EVIDENCE OF MONETARY ALLIANCE BETWEEN TARENTUM,
        TEATÈ IN APULIA, AND NEAPOLIS 176
    Types of Period VIII. . . . . . . 176—182

PERIOD IX. THE ROMAN ALLIANCE II. (B.C. c. 235—
    228) . . . . 183—196
    Latest coins of great Taranto hoard belong to separate and
        well-marked class 183
    Characteristics of this group of coins 183
    Careful execution of coins of this Period as compared with
        preceding 183
    Occurrence of sensational subjects: horse-racing types . 183

	PAGE
Epigraphic characteristics: c for ε, &c.	184
Appearance of complicated monograms	184
Elaboration of military equipment, dress of riders, &c.	185
Evidence supplied of Agonistic revival	186
Connexion of this with festival of Hyakinthia	186—189
Torch-racing types of Hèraklêtos and Daïmachos	188, 189
THESE LATE TARENTINE TYPES REPRODUCED ON DENARII OF CALPURNIAN FAMILY ASSOCIATED WITH HEAD OF APOLLO,	189—191
These denarii commemorate importation of Ludi Apollinares to Rome by Prætor Calpurnius	189—191
Ludi Apollinares, celebrated "according to the Greek rite," shown to have been taken from Tarentum	190, 191
INTERRUPTION OF TARENTINE COINAGE BETWEEN CLOSE OF THIS PERIOD AND HANNIBALIC OCCUPATION	191, 192
FIND OF EARLY VICTORIATI ON TARENTINE SITE	192
Occasion of interruption of autonomous coinage to be sought in events of 228 B.C.	192—194
Victoriate currency adopted by Dyrrhachium, Apollonia, and Corcyra	192
Now issued by Kroton, Luceria, and other cities of S. Italy	193
Types of Period IX.	194—196

PERIOD X. THE HANNIBALIC OCCUPATION (212—209 B.C.) . . . . 196—211

STANDARD AND FABRIC OF THIS CLASS DIFFERENT FROM ALL PRECEDING	196, 197
Sambon's view that these coins represented halves of full-weight didrachms shown to be untenable	197
NO DIDRACHMS OF SIMILAR TYPES	197
Reasons for believing that these coins were struck at time of Hannibal's protectorate	198
Original Roman Victoriatus much reduced at this time	199
STANDARD OF THESE COINS ANSWERS TO THAT OF ORIGINAL VICTORIATUS	200
Original Victoriate standard preserved by Illyrian cities	200—201
Half of unit struck by magistrate Sōkannas	202
Types of present class imitated from coins of Period IX.	202
Epigraphic style more conservative than preceding class	202, 203
Evidences of chronol gical gap between Periods IX. and X.	203
Non-Hellenic character of some of the magistrates' names	203, 204
These names not, however, Messapian	203, 204
Absence of names of the revolutionary leaders	205
Plebeian character of the Tarentine Revolution	205
ALLIANCE COINS OF METAPONTINES AND LUCANIANS ALSO NOW STRUCK ON SAME VICTORIATE STANDARD	206, 207
Historic record of defection of Metapontines and Lucanians to Hannibal	207, 208

x   CONTENTS.

	PAGE
TARENTINE GOLD STATERS AND THIRDS STRUCK DURING HANNIBALIC PERIOD	208, 209
Types of Period X.	210, 211

APPENDIX A.
COINS FROM THE BENEVENTAN FIND .   212—215

APPENDIX B.
CALABRIAN FIND .   216—218

APPENDIX C.

TARANTO FIND	219—228
Tarentine didrachms	219, 220
Tarentine drachms	221
Tarentine litræ	222
Tarentine hêmilitra	223
Tarentine diobols (Pallas type)	224, 225
Tarentine obols (diota type)	226
Tarentine obols (horse's head)	227
Tarentine hêmiobolia	227
Thurian didrachms	228
Summary of hoard	228

INDEX I.
ATTRIBUTES AND SYMBOLS IN TARAS' HANDS .   229

INDEX II.
SYMBOLS AND OBJECTS IN THE FIELD   230

INDEX III.
SIGNATURES .   233

ERRATUM AND ADDENDUM.

P. 200, l. 14, 15—*for* "Corinthian tridrachms" *read* "Corcyræan staters."

P. 203, add to note 232—A Sêrambos is mentioned by Pausanias (VI. 10, 9) as a sculptor of Ægina.

THE "HORSEMEN" OF TARENTUM.

The general order of the early Tarentine coinages is fairly ascertained. The conformity both in weight and fabric existing between the first incuse pieces of the Dorian city and the earliest coins struck by the Achæan colonies of the Ionian and Tyrrhene shores, tends to show that already before the days of Pythagoras' sojourn within their walls the Italiote Greeks had learnt to federate for their common weal. But while at Metapontion, and perhaps some other cities, these broad-spread incuse pieces, which seem to have owed their origin to a definite monetary convention between the Magna-Græcian Commonwealths, continued to be issued for some time after the destruction of Sybaris, their adoption by the Tarentines was comparatively short-lived. The incuse coins of this city are in fact of excessive rarity. They are of two main types: in the one case [Pl. I. 1] presenting an early version of Taras on his dolphin, in the other [Pl. I. 2] a nude figure of a youth in a half-kneeling pose, holding a lyre and flower, who has with great probability been identified by the Duc de Luynes[1] with the Hyakinthian Apollo. Both these types,

---

[1] *Annali dell' Instituto, &c.*, vol. ii. p. 340. In rare instances (*Cab. des Médailles*, 1212; Sambon, *Monnaies de la presqu'île Italique*, Pl. xvii. 5) both types are combined, the Apollo in relief, Taras incuse.

if we may judge from the primitive form of the Assyrian
border that encircles the design,[2] go back at least to the
close of the period covered by the earliest class of Sybarite
coins. And inasmuch as the coinage of Sybaris had begun
some time previous to the overthrow of Siris, which city
in alliance with Pyxoeis or Buxentum struck incuse pieces
on the Sybarite model, we are at liberty to suppose that
these earliest Tarentine coins were first issued not long
after the approximate date of 560 B.C., when Siris was
laid waste by the neighbouring Achæan cities.[3]

At Tarentum, however, as already remarked, the issue
of the incuse pieces must have been of but short duration.
From the evidence of finds there can be but little doubt
that the first Tarentine types of double relief, those,
namely, which exhibit a wheel on one side [Pl. I. 3], were
in existence some years before the destruction of Sybaris
in 510, and that the first issues of the succeeding class on
which a hippocamp appears must have been more or less
contemporary with that event.[4] Next in chronological order

---

[2] This primitive rope or guilloche border occurs on some but not on all the coins representing the Hyakinthian Apollo. On the type with Taras on his dolphin it is always found.

[3] Justin, *Hist.* l. xx. c. 2.

[4] In the find made at Sava, not many miles from Taranto, in 1856 (Sambon, *Recherches sur les anciennes Monnaies de l'Italie Méridionale*, Naples, 1863, p. 11), incuse Sybarite coins, fresh from the mint, occurred in great abundance. With these were associated Tarentine coins of the wheel type, both obols and didrachms, some worn, but a great number equally fresh; a quantity of didrachms of the hippocamp type all *fleur de coin*, and two with the head of a nymph also fresh from the die. No incuse Tarentine coins occurred in this hoard, but the coins of Metapontion and Kroton, found with the others, were all of incuse types. On the other hand, in the Cittanova find, Provincia di Reggio, buried at latest before the end of the sixth century (F. v. Duhn, *Zeitschr. f. Numismatik*, vii. p. 309), we find the relief coinage of Kroton, Kaulonia, and Laos already beginning. In

come the didrachms [Pl. I. 6], presenting on the side opposed to the youthful hero on the dolphin the head in all probability of the local nymph Satyra, the mother of Taras,[5] eponymic perhaps of an earlier indigenous element than that personified by Taras himself, who, on his father's side at least, was sea-born. At other times the head of Satyra is replaced by that of Taras himself [Pl. I. 5].

The democratic revolution effected in Tarentum in 473 left its mark in a new type exhibiting the Dêmos of the city, impersonated as a seated male figure. This latter class of coins, which includes some of the finest products of the Tarentine mint, has been admirably discussed by Raoul Rochette.[6] With regard to their chronological arrangement grounds will be adduced in the course of the present study[7] for dividing them into three main categories, which may be summarised as follows:—

    Class I.—Of archaic character (guilloche border), B.C. 473 —466. [Pl. I. 7.]

---

the Cittanova find Tarentum was only represented by two incuse pieces, but it by no means follows that the coinage of double relief had not begun there before the date of its deposition, which from the abundance of freshly struck Sybarite coins could hardly have been later than 510. It is a significant fact that though found in the neighbourhood of Rhêgion no Rhêgian coins occurred in this hoard.

  [5] Schol. ad Virg. *Georg.* ii. 197. Cf. Pausanias, x. 10. "Τάραντα τε τὸν ἥρωα Ποσειδῶνός φασι καὶ ἐπιχωριάς νύμφης παῖδα εἶναι." Satyrion was the name of a locality near Tarentum (Diodoros, viii. 21). There can be no question as to the female character of most of the heads on this group of coins (cf. Carelli, *N. I. V.*, Tav. cv. 46, 48; Garrucci, *Le Monete dell' Italia Antica*, Tav. xcvii. 20, 22. Sambon, *Monnaies de la presqu'île Italique*, Pl. xvii. 6, &c.).

  [6] "Essai sur la Numismatique Tarentine" (in *Mémoires Numismatiques*, p. 167, seqq.).

  [7] See p. 32.

Class II.—B.C. 466—460. The seated Dêmos, surrounded by a wreath in conformity with the similar issue struck at Rhêgion to commemorate the triumph of the Democracy there, in all probability with Tarentine help, in 466 B.C. [Pl. I. 8.]

Class III.—The concluding series which seems to have alternated with the earliest equestrian types, and may have extended from B.C. c. 460 to c. 420. [Pl. I. 9—12.]

On the present occasion it is with the more familiar series of the equestrian types which finally superseded the "democratic" class, that I propose more especially to deal. These Tarentine "horsemen," as for convenience they are here designated, number among them the most varied, the most abundant, and in many respects the most beautiful of the Tarentine coinages, and show us the numismatic art of this city in its freest and most congenial developments. This prolific issue, covering two centuries and a half of civic history, exceeds that of all the other Greek coinages of Italy, and is itself a striking witness to the high degree of commercial prosperity attained by Tarentum in days when barbarian inroads and fratricidal enmities were dealing widespread ruin amongst the once flourishing communities that went to make " Great Greece." Here, too, as at Athens and at Corinth, the continuity of type maintained, despite in this case infinite variation of details, throughout so long a period of years, must be regarded as in great measure owing to the conservative instincts of citizens engaged in a widely ramifying trade with distant parts, which led them to adhere to designs that had once secured a currency in the commercial world.

This general unity of type, however, combined with the multiplicity of issues presenting continued variations of pose, attributes, and symbols, has surrounded the study of these equestrian types of Tarentum with peculiar difficulties. For the best existing record of the types themselves we still turn to the full and generally accurate plates of Carelli's monumental work, which stand out in favourable contrast to the incomplete and inexact representations contained in the posthumous volume recently published in the name of Garrucci.[8]

Owing, however, to the great complexity of the problem and the absence of exact data, no detailed attempt has been made to arrange this long didrachm series into definite chronological periods. Ground has certainly been broken in this matter by Sambon in his researches into the Coinages of Southern Italy,[9] and by the author of the *Historia Numorum*, so far as

---

[8] *Le Monete dell' Italia Antica.* Roma, 1885. It is difficult to condemn sufficiently the gross negligence displayed by those responsible for bringing out Garrucci's book in its present form. Tav. xcviii., which deals with the equestrian types of Tarentum, presents the following errata: 1. *Obv.* Taras holds a plant in place of akrostolion; *rev.* Ɪ for Λ. 4. *Obv.* T in f. omitted. 5. ⊢E beneath horse converted into a bulrush (!). 6. *Rev.* Λ beneath horse omitted. 7. *Rev.* ΓY for ΓY in f. 9. T. holds egg? instead of fish. 10. ΚΑΛΛΙΧ, for ΣΑΛΩΝΟΣ. 12. *Rev.* Μ FE ΑΓΟΝ, for ΙΩ Η ΑΓΟΛΛΩ. 13. *Rev.* ΗΕΡΑΚΗΝ, for ⊢ΗΡΑΚΛΗΙ. 16. *Rev.* ΤΑ, for ΣΑ. 20. Λ, for ⊢; *Rev.* Δλ, for ΔΑΙ. 26. *Rev.* Κ in f. omitted. The proofs of the letterpress seem also to have been left uncorrected. All this is the more to be regretted since the engraving of the plates is often exquisite *per se*.

[9] *Recherches sur les anciennes Monnaies de l'Italie Méridionale.* Naples, 1863, p. 108, *et seqq.* Signor Sambon seems to have been the first to recognise the early date of some of the equestrian types; in several respects, however, it is impossible to follow his general arrangements. The Campano-Tarentine coins, for example, which form a class by themselves, are interpolated as filling a separate Period in the regular didrachm series: and the coins of the time of the Hannibalic occupation are referred to a time previous to the reduction of the didrachm weight, in other words, to a date anterior to Pyrrhus' expedition.

the scope of his work would allow, but some of the most essential chronological stand-points, such as, for instance, the date of the reduction of the didrachm standard, have been hitherto involved in uncertainty. In the course of repeated visits to Taranto itself and other ancient sites of Great Greece, I have had the good fortune to come across several new finds of Tarentine coins, both alone and in association with those of other cities, the comparative study of which has supplied some new data for fixing the chronological succession of the equestrian series. The results thus arrived at have been supplemented by an examination of the Tarentine series in the cabinets of Paris, Berlin, Naples, of our National Museum, and of several other public and private collections, including the rich Hellenic treasury of Dr. Imhoof-Blumer, at Winterthur, to whom, as to many other numismatists and curators, my sincere thanks are owing. The copiousness of the material thus collected has facilitated morphological studies of the numerous varieties of these equestrian types, enabling me in many cases to trace the transformation of the scheme of Taras on his dolphin through regular gradations of change—a form of evidence which often throws a welcome light on the succession of the different issues. In several instances, moreover, it has been possible to bring these didrachm types into direct relation with the gold coinage of the city, as well as with the silver coinage of lesser denominations, and these correspondences have also supplied more than one valuable clue to the chronology of the "horsemen" themselves. In particular, as I hope to show, they enable us to assign a definite date for the reduction of the didrachm standard.

It has been already noticed by numismatists that the

standards of the coins themselves afford a safe criterion for dividing this didrachm series into two main classes. The issues belonging to the first division are all of the full weight of c. 123—120 grains (7·97—7·77 grammes), which answers to that of the earliest incuse coins of the city, while an exceptional piece is said to have been found as heavy as 128 grains.[10] In the second group the weight suddenly falls to c. 102—98 grains, but the date of the reduction of the standard, which marks off this latter series from the others, has hitherto been only approximately fixed.[11] Under Period VII., what I believe to be conclusive reasons will be brought forward for believing that the reduction of the didrachm weight coincides in fact with Pyrrhus' expedition in 281 B.C.; and that, further, the silver coinage of Tarentum, so far from breaking off with the Roman occupation of 272, continued without interruption to the period that succeeded the conclusion of the first Punic War. In Hannibal's time the Tarentine silver coinage was once more temporarily revived, with the same equestrian types;[12] the standard adopted, however, being no longer that of the preceding didrachm series, but in all probability that of the original Victoriatus, from which Rome herself had now fallen away, but which was still maintained by the Greek commercial cities on the other side of the Adriatic and elsewhere. In adopting this

---

[10] Cf. Carelli, *op. cit.*, Descr. No. 113=128·325 gr. (8·314 grammes). 198 and 209=124·365 gr. (8·06 grammes).

[11] Mr. Head, in his *Historia Numorum*, places it on general grounds at about 300 B.C.

[12] My own conclusions on this matter entirely coincide with those expressed by Mr. Head (*Hist. Num.* p. 54), so far as the Hannibalic dates of these late types are concerned. I have ventured to differ from him, however, as to the character of the standard adopted.

standard, the Tarentines seem to have associated themselves with other Magna-Græcian communities attached to the Hannibalic alliance, and attention will be called to a small group of coins of the same weight which seem to have been issued at this time by the Metapontines and Lucanians.

The general results arrived at by the evidence thus brought together have emboldened me to distribute the long array of the Tarentine "horsemen" for the first time into successive chronological divisions. No one, indeed, is better aware than myself of the extreme difficulty of the undertaking. In many cases it is impossible to assign more than approximate time-limits to the several classes; while, on the other hand, it is obvious that any grouping of types growing out of each other by gradual stages of evolution involves a constant temptation to cross divisions, the last issues of one period and the earliest of another often overlapping. Arbitrary lines have thus occasionally to be drawn where all in fact is transition. With these qualifications, however, and allowing for the slight overlapping of some of the classes, I venture to believe that future investigators will not find much cause to quarrel, either with the general order of the Periods that I have laid down, or, approximately at least, with their chronological limits. These Periods are as follows:—

FULL-WEIGHT STANDARD, 123—120 GR.

		B. C.
I. Transitional	. . .	c. 450—c. 430
II.	. . . . .	c. 420—c. 380
III. Age of Archytas	. .	c. 380—345
IV. Archidâmos and the First Lucanian War	. . .	c. 344—334
V. From the Molossian Alexander to the Spartan Kleonymos	. . . .	334—302
VI. From Kleonymos to Pyrrhus		302—281

REDUCED STANDARD, 102—98 GR.

VII. THE PYRRHIC HEGEMONY . 281—272
VIII. THE ROMAN ALLIANCE, I. . 272—c. 235
IX. THE ROMAN ALLIANCE, II. . c. 235—228
X. THE HANNIBALIC OCCUPATION . 212—209

Pollux, as is well known, quotes Aristotle as stating, in his *Tarentine Commonwealth*, that there was at Tarentum a coin called a "nummos," impressed with a figure of Taras riding on a dolphin [13]; and Mommsen [14] has assumed that the description applies to the silver staters or didrachms with which we are principally concerned. It has, however, been suggested by Professor Gardner [15] that Aristotle's description may, with more fitness, be applied to some Tarentine diobols presenting the same type; and the fact that the Romans applied the name of "nummus" to their sestertius, the weight of which was almost identical with the diobol, may certainly be regarded as pointing to this conclusion. There seems to me, however, to be a fatal objection to this interpretation, plausible as it may appear. It is, in fact, almost certain that the silver

---

[13] Pollux, ix. 80. "Ἀριστοτέλης ἐν τῇ Ταραντίνων πολιτείᾳ καλεῖσθαί φησι νόμισμα παρ' αὐτοῖς νοῦμμον ἐφ' οὗ ἐντετυπῶσθαι Τάραντα τὸν Ποσειδῶνος δελφῖνι ἐποχούμενον."

[14] *Hist. de la Monnaie Romaine* (ed. Blacas, i. 141).

[15] *Num. Chron.* 1881, p. 296. The Tarentine "nummos" is probably the "nomos" of the Hêrakleian Tables, and one objection urged is that the fine of ten νόμοι incurred according to these for failing to plant an olive-tree in place of one that had died on sacred land rented from the State, would be excessive if a "nomos" = a didrachm. But the argument does not seem to me to be conclusive. A good olive-tree is a valuable possession, and may be estimated in present money at over £4. It must also be observed that the scale of the fines is distinctly high and meant to be deterrent. For constructing a "chaff-store" (ἀχυρίον) of wrong dimensions on the sacred land, the fine was 4 minæ = 400 drachmæ; and for the same transgression in the case of an ox-stall 10 minæ = 1,000 drachmæ.

diobols referred to, with, perhaps, one unique exception,[16] were not struck till after Aristotle's time. Among the smaller denominations of Tarentine coins, the type of Taras riding on the dolphin, though always unusual, is not confined to diobols. It appears on litræ [17] and hêmilitra, but all of them struck after the reduction of the didrachm standard, which, as I hope to show, took place at the time of Pyrrhus' expedition. The diobols with which this type is associated are of two standards, the one [18] answering to the sixth of the full-weight didrachm of c. 122 grains, the other [19] to the same fraction of the reduced didrachm of c. 100 grains. Both classes are of great rarity. From their type and style they must date from about the same period; and the fact that the lighter obol of the two was struck in all probability after 300 B.C. makes it impossible to refer the earlier diobols exhibiting Taras on his dolphin to a much earlier date. The diobols presenting this type are altogether exceptional pieces, and had any of them been struck at the time when Aristotle wrote, they could never certainly have been cited as typical examples of the standard coin of Tarentum. His description of the Tarentine "nummos" (*if rightly reported by Pollux*) can only refer to the silver staters, by which alone the effigy of the

---

[16] The diobol presenting the signature ΣΩ. See p. 50, *note*.
[17] Cf. Car. T. cxvii. 287, wt. 8·713 gr. *B. M. Cat.* 394, wt. 9 gr. (·583 gramme). Another coin of the same type in my own collection weighs 10 gr. (·648 gramme). This type, with ℞ · ⋔, is no doubt contemporaneous with a didrachm of Period IX. presenting the same monograms: Car. cxvii. 288, wt. 102·9 gr.; *B. M. Cat.* 392, wt. 99 gr. A hemilitron of the same type, on which Taras is seen holding out a bunch of grapes, is in my own collection. It is somewhat chipped, and weighs only 2·25 gr.
[18] Cf. Car. T. cxvii. 324. Wt. 19·011 gr. (1·23 grammes).
[19] Cf. *B. M. Cat.* 381. Wt. 15·6 gr. (1·01 grammes). Car. cxvii. 325. Wt. 13·466 gr. (·842 gramme).

eponymic hero on the dolphin was rendered familiar to the Greek commercial world.

It must also be borne in mind, as offering a possible explanation of the name of *nomos* or *nummos* being here attached to the silver stater, that in the earliest incuse coinage struck by Tarentum as an adherent of what seems to have been a Monetary Convention amongst the Achæan cities of South Italy, this, so far as we know, was the sole denomination. The incuse fractions struck at Metapontion, Sybaris, and other League Cities are wholly unknown at Tarentum. Even when, in the case of the earliest coinage of double relief, fractions began to be struck, they were struck on a different system from that of the other cities. Whilst in the Achæan colonies the monetary unit was divided on the Corinthian system into thirds and sixths, the early Tarentine divisions are by halves and again by fifths, combining thus the Attic drachm and Syracusan litra.[20] It follows that the silver stater or didrachm, as we may appropriately call it here, still remained the medium of exchange so far as these other Italiote cities were concerned. It was only from about 380 B.C. onwards that the Tarentine mint began to issue diobols, identical with those of Hêrakleia, which there is every reason to regard as a federal currency.[21] But these earlier diobols, as already pointed out, do not present the type of Taras on his dolphin, which we are taught by Aristotle to associate with the *nummos*.

The horsemen themselves suggest some interesting enquiries. There can be little doubt that, as pointed out by Raoul Rochette, the type which immediately precedes

---

[20] Cf. Mommsen, *op. cit.* i. 140 *seqq.*
[21] Head, *Historia Numorum*, p. 55.

the present equestrian series, exhibiting the seated figure —whether we are to regard it as itself representing the Tarentine Dêmos or as Taras as its impersonation—owed its origin to the triumph of the popular party at Tarentum, a triumph due, as we learn from Aristotle,[22] to the great slaughter of the Tarentine nobles in a disastrous battle with the neighbouring Iapygians in B.C. 473. Greater difficulty, however, attends the suggestion of Garrucci,[23] that the equestrian type with which we are principally concerned should in turn be regarded as the outcome of a new change of government, which placed the chief authority in the hands of an annual *Stratêgos*. As a matter of fact, it results from the present inquiry that the earliest of the coins presenting the horseman type—struck about the middle of the fifth century B.C.—are altogether devoid of any military characteristics. The youthful rider is seen on these naked and armed only with a whip, and the whole scope of the design is purely agonistic. It is only, as I hope to show, at a distinctly later date, and after fresh alternations of the coins exhibiting the seated Dêmos, that, towards the close of the same century, the more martial type makes its appearance of the horseman with *pilos* on his head and lance in hand, who certainly has a better claim to be regarded as representative of the *Stratêgia*.

Unfortunately, owing to the loss of Aristotle's treatise on the subject, the Tarentine polity remains very obscure, and we know little beyond the fact that it was originally modelled on that of the Spartan mother-city.[24] A Taren-

---

[22] Arist. *Polit.* v. 2, 8; and cf. vi. 3, 5. But see Grote (Ed. 1862, vol. iii. p. 564, note).

[23] *Le Monete dell' Italia Antica.* Pt. ii. p. 124, 125.

[24] The materials bearing on the Tarentine constitutional history have been collected by Lorentz, *De Civitate Tarentinorum.* Lips. 1833.

tine Basileus is mentioned before the Persian wars,[25] and Ephors appear at the Tarentine colony of Hêrakleia. It is also clear that during the time which roughly corresponds to my third Period, when the philosopher-statesman Archytas was exercising a predominant influence on the Tarentine State, his genius did not fail to exercise a modifying effect on the civic constitution. We are told that, contrary to all precedent, his grateful fellow-citizens conferred upon him the annual office of *Stratêgos* seven successive times. Under the guidance of such a man, what Thucydides asserts of Athens under Pericles was no doubt true at Tarentum, and, however nominally a democracy, the government was virtually in the hands of a single eminent citizen. As to the permanent effect, however, of Archytas' rule on the Tarentine Commonwealth we are left in ignorance. The coinage, on the whole, helps us little. The martial type mentioned above is an isolated phenomenon amongst the earlier classes of equestrian coin, and for evidences of preponderating "militarism" in the government we must look to a much later date. It is only from about the time of the Epirote Alexander's expedition that the type of the armed horseman first becomes usual on the Tarentine dies; but when, as I hope to show, at a still later date, towards the close, namely, of the fourth century, the names of magistrates first make their appearance on the coins of this city, there is no reason for supposing that these signatures refer to officials fulfilling the military functions of *Stratêgoi*. The names of known Tarentine *Stratêgoi*, like Agis, whose activity lay within the period when such signatures were rife, are conspicuous by their absence, and on the coins of the Hannibalic

---

[25] Herodotus, iii. 136.

period we look in vain for the well-known names of Nikôn, Philêmenos, and Dêmokratês. It seems, therefore, more probable that the signatures should in each case be referred to the Ephor Epônymos.

The horseman on these Tarentine coins is pre-eminently agonistic, and the cult with which we have to do naturally connects itself with the Heroes and State patrons of the city—with Taras himself or his father Poseidon, with the historic *oekist* Phalanthos, with the Dioskuri as the twin protectors of the Spartan mother-city, with the Amyklæan Hyakinthos. In the youthful rider we may often with great probability recognise Taras himself, and the equestrian contests in which he is engaged may in this case be generally referred to his divine father, from whose prevailing cult Tarentum itself received in later times the epithet of "Neptunian."[26] The maturer figures of the armed horseman may often, with equal propriety, be identified with Phalanthos, for while it is quite possible to suppose that Taras should appear in the same boyish form on the dolphin on one side and on the horse on the other, it is impossible to believe that he could be represented on the same coin both as child and man. Bearing this consideration in mind, we are able, in one instance at least, to determine the fact that the armed horseman on the coin stands for the historic, as opposed to the mythic, founder of

---

[26] *Colonia Neptunia Tarentum.* From the Scholiast on Horace, I. xxvii. 28 (" Neptuno sacri custode **Tarenti**"), we learn that "Phalanthus, Neptune's son," *i.e.* Taras, founded temples at Tarentum to Hercules and Neptune. The cult of Poseidôn at Tarentum was especially connected with Tænaron, and the priests of Poseidôn were in consequence known to the Tarentines as Ταιναρισταί. (Hesychios Lex. s.v. Ταιναριας, and cf. R. Lorentz, *De rebus sacris et artibus veterum Tarentinorum.* Elberfeld, 1836, p. 8.)

Tarentum. On the coin to which I refer, Type C. (Pl. VI. 10) of my Fifth Period, the reverse of which represents Taras himself as a plump child riding on his dolphin, the horseman of the obverse appears as a helmeted figure holding before him a large round shield, the device on which is a dolphin. The dolphin badge is here explained by the confusion which apparently existed in Tarentine folk-lore between the eponymic hero of the original præ-Hellenic city and the leader of the Parthenian colonists, owing to which the old Phœnician myth of the founder landing on his dolphin seems to have been at times transferred from Taras to Phalanthos. Thus Pausanias, in his account of the Anathêmata at Delphi, the work of Onatas of Ægina and Kalynthos, dedicated by the Tarentines out of a fifth of the spoils taken from the Peuketians and Iapygians, after mentioning that there were statues of both footmen and horsemen, and amongst them the Iapygian king Opis lying slain, continues, "And the two who stand over his prostrate form are the hero Taras and Phalanthos of Lacedæmon, and not far off is Phalanthos' dolphin." To account for this latter feature he further relates the tradition that Phalanthos, having been wrecked off the port of Delphi on his way to Italy, consulted the oracle, in accordance with which he was safely conveyed to his destination on a dolphin.[27]

The dolphin was thus a symbol of Phalanthos as well as Taras, and its appearance on the shield of the warrior on the above-mentioned coin may be taken as a clear

---

[27] Pausanias, lib. x. c. 13. "οἱ δὲ αὐτῷ κειμένῳ ἐφεστηκότες ὁ ἥρως Τάρας ἐστὶ καὶ Φάλανθος ὁ ἐκ Λακεδαίμονος καὶ οὐ πόρρω τοῦ Φαλάνθου δελφίς· πρὶν γὰρ δὴ ἐς Ἰταλίαν ἀφικέσθαι [καὶ] ναυαγίᾳ τε ἐν τῷ πελάγει τῷ Κρισσαίῳ τὸν Φάλανθον χρήσασθαι καὶ ὑπὸ δελφῖνος ἐκκομισθῆναί φασιν ἐς τὴν γῆν." (Cf. too Justin, lib. iii. c. 4.)

indication that Phalanthos is there represented. There is every à priori ground for believing that the historic founder of Tarentum should have been commemorated on the Tarentine coinage. The Tarentines, as we know, in return for the patriotic fraud by which the dying Phalanthos had secured the perpetual duration of the city, decreed him divine honours.[28] Judging, indeed, by analogy, we should be inclined to refer to this hero most of the figures of armed horsemen that appear on the present series. It is extremely probable that the interesting type [Pl. II. 5] already referred to of the horseman in peaked pileus and Doric *chiton* is to be regarded as an earlier representation of the leader of the Lacedæmonian colonists. The head-gear worn by the horseman strongly supports this attribution, since one of the principal incidents in the story of Phalanthos connects itself with the conical cap which he wore on his head, and the taking off of which was to be the signal for the rising of the Parthenian conspirators.

The twin figures that appear on some of the Tarentine coins must, of course, be identified with the Dioscuri; on a gold stater, indeed, presenting this device [Pl. V. 9] the inscription ΔΙΟ Ξ ΚΟΡΟΙ is seen in minute letters above the riders. It is highly probable, as I hope to have occasion to point out, that the first appearance of this type contains a direct allusion to the alliance with the Spartan mother city, and is to be referred to the date of Akrotatos' expedition. It is certain that in some of the single riders on the Tarentine didrachms we may also detect at times one or other of the Lacedæmonian twins.

The hippic deities of Tarentum are referred to on an

---

[28] Justin. *Hist.* lib. iii. c. 4.

inscription in which they are associated with those of the
sea, as receiving the thank-offerings dedicated from the
Roman spoils after the naval victory of Krotón in
210 B.C.[29] The best illustration of these equestrian coin-
types has, however, been supplied by the recent discovery
of a vast deposit of votive terra-cotta figures on the site of
a sanctuary of Chthonic divinities within the walls of the
outer city of Tarentum. Many of these terra-cottas, as I
have already pointed out elsewhere,[30] supply the closest
parallels to familiar types of Tarentine horsemen as they
appear on the coins. In some cases we have identical
figures of the Dioscuri, in others a naked warrior in a
peaked-crested helmet is seen seated sideways on a galloping steed [Pl. XI. 12 and 13], holding in his left hand the
large round shield which is so frequent a concomitant of
the equestrian figures on the coins. In another instance a
youthful figure, shield in hand, is seen standing in front
of his stationary horse laying his right hand on its neck,
a scheme which finds its counterpart in a coin of Period
IV. [Pl. IV. 4], where, however, the warrior stands behind
his steed. A still more striking resemblance is to be found
in another characteristic type of these votive terra-cottas, in
which the rider is seen with his knee bent under him, as if
in the act of vaulting from his horse, a design which
reappears on a whole series of Tarentine coins.

---

[29] The inscription in the form given by Carducci, in his Commen-
taries on Aquino (*Delizie Tarantine*, l. i.) p. 111, 112, runs as
follows: "Νικητήριον καθ' ἕκαστον ἐνιαυτὸν Θεοῖς Θαλασσίοις καὶ
τοῖς Ἱππίοις Θεοῖς ἡ Βουλὴ καὶ ὁ Δῆμος τῶν Ταραντίνων διὰ τῆς
προνοίας τοῦ Δημοκράτους Ἐνωμοτάρχου ἐκ τῆς εὐχῆς πολεμικῆς
νεολαίας." Cf. Fiorelli, *Bull. dell' Inst. Arch.* 1841, p. 174.
For this naval victory see Livy, l. xxvi. c. 39.

[30] *Hellenic Journal*, 1886, p. 8, 22, 23. ("Recent Discoveries
of Tarentine Terra-cottas.")

These parallels occurring on a group of objects devoted to a Chthonic cult with which, together with the infernal deities, were associated the deified heroes of Tarentine religion, form a valuable commentary on the coin-types with which we are concerned, and afford additional grounds for supposing that the agonistic exercises performed by the horsemen before us connect themselves with a similar heroic cult. Several of the symbols that appear on some of the earliest of these equestrian types, such as the caduceus, or the bearded Herm, in front of the horse, the *kantharos*, or, somewhat later, the *kylix*, that is seen below, are best explained in this Chthonic connexion. The *kylix* especially, which on a coin of my Third Period (Type E.; Pl. III. 9) appears beneath the type, already described, of the warrior vaulting off his horse—in this case probably the heroized Phalanthos—had at Tarentum a distinctly sepulchral association. From an epigram of the poet Leônidas it appears that it was an usual practice to place a *kylix* above a grave, originally, no doubt, with the idea of receiving libations for the departed.[30] The *kantharos*, on the other hand, is even more intimately associated with the old heroic cult of Tarentum and its mother city. In the votive terra-cottas above referred to it is seen in the hands of the recumbent figure of Aidoneus or the Chthonic Dionysos, who symbolizes on these the heroized departed. Its appearance in the hands of the seated figure on some of the earliest types of the preceding

---

[30] *Leonidæ Tarentini*, c. lxxxvii., where the deceased Maronis, who in her life had been fond of her cups, is made to lament below, not for husband or children, but because the well-known Attic *kylix* laid on her grave ("ἧς ὑπὲρ τάφου γνωστή πρόκειται πᾶσιν Ἀττικὴ κύλιξ") is empty. The practice of placing a drinking vessel over the grave is still common in Eastern Europe.

didrachm series is also very suggestive. Although this figure has with great probability been regarded as an impersonation of the Tarentine Dêmos, it is none the less true that this personification was itself assimilated to the idea of the heroic founder. It is indeed difficult to say where Taras ends and abstract Dêmos begins. There is a striking parallelism between some of the more archaic coins of this type (Pl. I. 7) in which the seated figure holds out a wine-cup as if for oblations, and the old Spartan sepulchral reliefs in which the heroized departed is seen seated in much the same attitude on a similar throne and holding out a *kantharos* in the same manner as the figure on the coin. In one case, at least (Pl. I. 11), the heroic character of the seated figure is deliberately emphasized by the introduction of a tomb or sepulchral altar in front of it, a feature which Raoul Rochette has, perhaps unnecessarily, brought into connexion with the tomb or *hérôon* of the Amyklæan Hyakinthos, a prominent object outside the walls of Tarentum. The same author,[31] after calling attention to the sepulchral associations of the Ionic column as it appears on a whole series of vases and other monuments, adduces strong reasons for believing that the Ionic capital, which

---

[31] *Journal des Savants*, 1833, p. 154. "Je puis affirmer, d'après ma propre expérience, que la colonne ionique représentée sur les vases peints, soit qu'elle y figure isolément, soit qu'elle s'y trouve employée dans la composition d'une édicule, s'y rapporte toujours à une intention funéraire," &c. Avellino, *Adnotationes in Carellii Num. It. Vet. descript.*, prefers to see in this symbol a badge of a magistrate. In the case of some of the equestrian types it certainly occurs at a period when such personal devices were frequent on Tarentine coins (v. *infra*, p. 26). In the case, however, of the earlier "democratic" type on which this symbol also occurs, this explanation is not admissible, since the symbols and attributes on this early class seem solely to connect themselves with the seated impersonation of the Dêmos.

on some of these equestrian coins appears below the figure of the victorious rider, crowning himself in token of victory, must also be taken to indicate the funereal character of the contest commemorated by the type. The same symbol also occurs beneath the feet of the seated figure on a coin belonging to the earlier "Democratic" class, where it stands as the visible emblem of heroization.

As illustrations of the various equestrian games in honour of the state patrons of Tarentum the long didrachm series with which we are concerned has a special value. This ever-changing succession of hippic types gave artistic expression to the passionate love of the turf which was so distinguishing a feature of Tarentine public life. The rider, whether to be interpreted as Taras or not, is often a mere jockey who urges his steed forward to the goal, or crowns or grooms the winner. In some of the later examples we have still more sensational types of the boy rider borne onwards in a headlong gallop, hanging literally to his horse's neck, or reaching forwards the torch of the Lampadêdromia. The type, already referred to, of the *apobates* vaulting from his horse represents what was evidently a familiar exercise of the Tarentine horsemen; and in another instance we trace in the youthful rider leading a second horse a reference to the ἄμφιπποι or *desultores*. Other types, on the other hand, throw a light on exercises of a more military character. We recognise the lancers described by Ælian[32] and Suidas[33] and known as "Tarentines," of which there was more than one variety. They are often represented with three javelins, two of which we are informed they hurled at a distance, while the

---

[32] Ælianus Tacticus, *Statēgēmata*. Ed Robertelli. Ven. 1552, p. 3.
[33] Suidas, *s. v.* Ἱππική.

third was reserved for close quarters;[34] usually, too, they bear a large round shield, from the whiteness or brilliance of which the flower of the Tarentine cavalry were known as Leukaspides. On one of the most spirited of the later didrachm types there occurs an example of another class of Tarentine horsemen, the "Hippakontists," who aimed their darts from afar but did not come to close quarters.[35] It is also by no means improbable that the agonistic type of the ἀμφιππος already referred to throws a light on the evolutions of the Tarentine knights in Philopœmen's following, each of whom, according to Livy,[36] led with him a second horse. There can be little doubt, moreover, that the scheme of the rider with his knee bent under him as if in the act of vaulting from his horse must be taken to illustrate military as well as agonistic manœuvres. At times indeed he appears armed with a spear and round shield, and as if equally prepared for combat on horseback or on foot. The natural sequel to this representation is in fact to be seen on some fragments of a frieze of a good period from the Corinthian temple recently discovered in the old Tarentine Akropolis,[37] where a youthful warrior

---

[34] Ælian, *loc. cit.* "Τινὲς δὲ τῶν Ταραντίνων ἐλαφροῖς δορατίοις χρῶνται· ἅπαξ τε ἢ δὶς προεξακοντίσαντες τὸ λοιπὸν συμπλέκονται τοῖς πολεμίοις ἐγγύθεν ἀπομαχόμενοι." Suidas makes them fight at close quarters with swords or axes, but from the coins we gather that they used a spear or lance.

[35] Suidas, *loc. cit.* "οἱ μὲν μόνον ἀκοντίζουσιν, εἰς δὲ χεῖρας τοῖς πολεμίοις οὐκ ἔρχονται καὶ καλοῦνται ἱππακοντισταί, καὶ ἰδίως Ταραντῖνοι." Cf. Period IX., Type C (Pl. X. 3); Period X. [Pl. X. 12].

[36] *Hist.* lib. xxxv. c. 28. "Quos Tarentinos vocabant equites, binos secum trahentes equos, ad prima signa misit." In this and other passages it is not necessary to infer that the cavalry employed actually came from Tarentum, but that they were exercised and equipped in the Tarentine manner.

[37] *Memorie della r. Accademia dei Lincei*, 1881, tav. ix.; and

with flowing tresses, clad in a chlamys and armed with a spear and round shield, is seen fighting on foot beside his horse.

The appearance of these more martial types among the horsemen no doubt coincides with periods of warlike activity on the part of the Tarentine State. At times too, Taras on his dolphin himself assumes a bellicose attitude, and is depicted dart in hand or rising in a warlike fury on his marine charger, preparing to fit an arrow to his bow. This type recurs more than once in the numismatic annals of Tarentum, but in one instance at least the historic import of the design is fixed from its association with the Pyrrhic elephant.

It is naturally to the reverse type of these coins (as for convenience' sake we may regard it) presenting Taras on his dolphin that we turn for the clearest allusions to the current events of Tarentine story, for here both the attitude and attributes of the principal figure as well as the symbols in the field are brought into direct relation with the personified City. It must of course be borne in mind that in dealing with Greek numismatic art we are rarely able to read off at first sight and without further clue the historic meaning of a design. We have not here to do with the labelled trophies of a Roman medal. Much we can cer-

---

see *Hellenic Journal* (vol. v.), 1884, p. 8, note, where I have endeavoured to combat the theory, that the warrior in question must necessarily be regarded as a barbarian. His free flowing hair and round unornamented shield present, on the contrary, the closest analogy with some of the heroic figures on these equestrian coins. Even if we regard him as one of Tarentum's barbarian neighbours, it must still be remembered that the manœuvres of the Tarentine knights were probably in large measure derived from the horsemanship of the indigenous population, of whom "Messapus equûm domitor" stood out as the eponymic representative in Italian tradition.

tainly never know. Even the altered pose of Taras on his dolphin, his restfulness or his agitation, was pregnant perchance, with the idea of peace or war to those amongst whom each new issue first circulated. Arguing from the known to the unknown we have just grounds for supposing that many of the types and symbols contain a reference to passing events clear enough at least to be intelligible to contemporaries and Greeks. Nor was there ever surely a succession of types better fitted for the exercise of this allusive faculty than the Tarentine series, in which both the obverse and reverse designs seem specially chosen with a view to infinite variation, without prejudice to the general unity of effect. For a space of some two centuries and a half, the Tarentine didrachms, while preserving the essential character of the type unaltered, presented such a succession of changing attitudes and ever new combinations of type, attitudes, and symbols, as is without a parallel in the coinage of any other Hellenic city.

In some cases the references to current history are obvious enough. It is impossible, for instance, to doubt that the elephant which occurs in the exergue of the archer type referred to, connects itself with Pyrrhus' expedition, while the figure of Athênê Alkis that is seen beneath the dolphin on coins of smaller denomination and on the field of the contemporary gold staters is an equally clear allusion to the same episode. The nearer chronological arrangement of the equestrian series, so far as I have been able to arrive at it by the comparative study of recent finds as well as by the morphological succession of the types themselves, has emboldened me to trace direct allusions to other episodes of Tarentine story, and in particular to the Spartan alliance under Archidâmos, and again under Akrotatos, to the expedition of the

Molossian Alexander, and even to the financial assistance rendered to Pyrrhus and the Tarentines by Antiochos I.

In considering the interpretation of the various symbols that appear in association with the eponymic hero of Tarentum in the present series, regard must in the first instance be directed to the period to which they belong. In the earliest classes of equestrian types struck between the approximate dates of 450—350 B.C., as, indeed, on the more archaic types of Tarentine coins, the figure of Taras on his dolphin is in no case associated with a symbol in the field. The marine objects that appear below the dolphin,—the scallop or the purple-shell, the cuttle-fish or the tunny,—may themselves be regarded as an integral part of the type, and as representing, like the curling waves that sometimes replace them, at times the little inner sea of Tarentum, at times the open Ionian waters, on the produce of both of which the life and industries of the city were so largely dependent. The trident and harpoon, the oar or akrostolion in Taras' hands refer to the mythic founder as patron of the Tarentine fisheries and naval power; the arms or wreath evince his tutelary influence over war and games. It is only from about the middle of the fourth century onwards that symbols begin to appear in the field, in some of which, such as the Molossian eagle, as well as in others, like the prow and anchor or the elephant already referred to, that appear below the dolphin, we may trace a more definite allusion to current events. A greater variety is at the same time observable in the symbols or attributes held in Taras's hand; and Eckhel's conjecture [38] that many of these refer

---

[38] *Doctrina Numorum*, I. p. 146. For the Tarentine religious celebrations see especially R. Lorentz, *De rebus sacris et artibus veterum Tarentinorum.* (Elberfeld, 1836.)

to the numerous games and religious celebrations for which the city was famous,[39] must at least be partly true. Taras himself, as I hope to show, is occasionally assimilated in a curious way to the various divinities whose cult he is represented as honouring. At times he assumes not only the trident but the attitude and mantle of his father, Poseidôn; he is seen with Apollo's locks and the flower of Hyakinthos, or is metamorphosed into the infant Dionysos of the Mysteries.

The analogies supplied by the Hêrakleian Tables have led Mazocchi[40] and others to see in a large number of symbols on Tarentine coins an allusion to the Eponymic magistrate of the year. On the Hêrakleian Tables, before the name of the individual ὁριστής or πολιανόμος and after the initials of his tribe or ὄβας, there is inserted the description of his distinguishing badge or symbol, such as a trident, a bunch of grapes, a flower, a caduceus, a tripod, or some similar device.[41] It is obvious that many of these badges present a close correspondence with the symbols that appear on the coins of Tarentum, itself the mother city of Hêrakleia; and the occurrence of certain *types parlants* and of symbols presenting an obvious play

---

[39] Cf. Strabo, vi. c. 4, who says that the Tarentines had more public festivals than there were days of the year.

[40] Mazochii, *Commentt. in aeneas tabulas Heracleenses*, p. 150. Cf. Avellino, *Adnotationes in Carellii Num. It. Vet. descript.* p. 57.

[41] *E.g.* ϹΕ ΤΡΙΓΟΥΣ ΦΙΛΩΝΥΜΟΣ ΞΩΠΥΡΙΣΚΩ. ΓΕ ΚΑΡΥΚΕΙΟΝ ΑΠΟΛΛΩΝΙΟΣ ҺΗΡΑΚΛΗΤΩ. ΑΙ ΠΕΛΤΑΙ ΔΑΞΙΜΟΣ ΓΥΡΡΩ · ΚΝ ΘΡΙΝΑΞ ΦΙΛΩ- ΤΑΣ ΗΣΤΙΕΙΩ. ΜΕ ΕΠΙΣΤΥΛΙΟΝ ҺΗΡΑΚΛΕΙΔΑΣ ΞΩΠΥΡΩ, &c. Mazoch. *Tab. Heracl.* p. 147, *seqq.* At Hêrakleia these badges appear to have descended from father to son; thus Bormiôn, the son of Philôtas, of the tribe Me . . . and Arkas, the son of Philôtas, of the same tribe, both appear with the same symbol of a κιβώτιον or box.

e

on official signatures found on the same piece, shows that many of the symbols that appear during the later periods of the Tarentine coinage must be connected with the names of magistrates.[42] On a piece signed ΛΕΩΝ, for instance, the lion appears beneath the dolphin on the reverse. The name ΟΛΥΜΠΙΣ is associated with the wreath of an *Olympionika*, ΑΠΟΛΛΩΝΙΟΣ with solar emblems, and ΔΑΙΜΑΧΟC attaches the name to a type in which the galloping rider holds forth the torch (ἑαὶς) of the *Lampadēdromia*. Another evidence of the connexion of certain symbols with magistrates' names is to be found by a comparison of didrachms and drachms on which the same names reappear in association with the same symbols but with a different type. The name ΗΙΣΤΙΑΡΧΟΣ is in this way doubly connected with a bunch of grapes, a symbol which also appears on the Hêrakleian Tables. The name ΑΡΙΣΤΙΣ is in the same manner linked with an anchor on coins of both denominations. In another example we find the abbreviated signature ΣΩ, perhaps in this case belonging to a moneyer or engraver rather than a higher official, placed in minute letters between the horns of a *bucranium*, evidently the badge belonging to the name.[43] It is further evident that the symbols referring to magistrates are sometimes placed in the hands of the Eponymic hero. Thus the flower which is associated on drachms with the name of ΗΗΡΑΚΛΗΤΟΣ appears on didrachms with the same signature, sometimes in the field, sometimes in the outstretched hand of Taras.

All the examples referred to of signatures associated

---

[42] See p. 173, *seqq.*
[43] Period IX., Type B. See Raoul Rochette, *Lettre à M. le duc de Luynes sur les Graveurs Grecques,* p. 45 and Pl. IV. 38.

with a personal symbol belong to the later periods of the Tarentine coinage, and to the time when magistrates' names appear at full length upon the dies. It must not, however, be supposed that all the symbols that appear during this epoch are necessarily to be connected with the names of individual officials. On the contrary we have the clearest evidence that in many cases the symbols refer rather to the city itself. The historic import of some of these has been already noticed, and many no doubt refer to the religious festivals of the Tarentines. We find, for example, the signature ΑΝΘ(ΡΩ≶) upon three otherwise identical pieces,[44] coupled with three different symbols—a cornspike, a laurel spray, and a coiling serpent—some or all of which may connect themselves with the Tarentine cult of Dêmêter and Kora, to the importance of which the gold coinage of Tarentum, as well as the recent discoveries of votive deposits, and of the site of a Temple of "the Goddesses," bear sufficient testimony. Connected with this mystic cult was the Tarentine festival of the $\Delta άμεια$ mentioned by Hêsychios.[45]

With regard to the symbols or small objects in the field or exergue of these Tarentine coins, we arrive then at the following general conclusions. On the equestrian types of my first three Periods, as upon the preceding "democratic" issue, and indeed the whole of the earlier coinages of Tarentum, these subsidiary figures must be regarded as an integral part of the type itself. In the case of the horseman they often supply a distinctly Chthonic touch, and indicate the heroic character of the contest in which he is engaged. Seen in conjunction with the figure of Taras

---

[44] Period VII. F 3, 4, 5.
[45] Hêsychios, *Lexicon*, s. v.

on his dolphin, they most frequently must be taken to represent the sea over which he rides in its productive aspects. In the later Periods of the equestrian coinages, on the other hand, the symbols, while still occasionally capable of this simpler interpretation, have for the most part a more transient and individual value. Some, as we have seen, convey distinct historic allusions or have reference to special religious celebrations. Others must certainly be regarded as the personal badges of responsible officials.

As with the symbols, so with the signatures on this didrachm series, a distinction must be drawn in accordance with the time-limits within which they severally fall. In the earliest class of equestrian issues such signatures are either wholly absent or confined to a single letter. In my Second and Third Periods the signatures are still for the most part of single letters, and it is not till after the middle of the fourth century B.C. that monosyllabic signatures become more frequent. Reasons will be adduced in the course of the present inquiry for believing that the whole of this earlier group of abbreviated signatures should be referred to the actual moneyers and engravers of the coins, who seem to have worked in more than one ἀργυροκοπεῖον. In some cases a comparison of several types presenting the same signature affords the clearest evidence that we have to do with the same engraver, not infrequently a true artist, such as, for instance, the engraver who signs "ΚΑΛ;" and it will further be shown that several of the Tarentine engravers worked at the same time for the coinage of other Magna-Græcian cities, notably Hêrakleia and Metapontion. In the case, moreover, of more than one of the early Periods the coins divide themselves into groups representing the variant artistic traditions of different "botteghe," in each of which several ἀργυροκόποι seem to have worked together. It is only towards the close of the Fourth Century that a new class of signatures, written more or less at full length, makes its appearance in the place of honour on the coin, thrusting these more abbreviated forms into a secondary position. These names present a much greater variety but have no connexion with the style of the coin itself, and there is every reason to refer them in each case to the eponymic Magistrate, or Ephor, who gave his name to the year. Hence it appears that during the later periods of Tarentine coinage that immediately precede and follow the date of Pyrrhus' expedition signatures upon the coins are of a more complicated character and include the names both of magistrates and moneyers; the first in a fuller, the second in a more abbreviated form.

PERIOD I.—TRANSITIONAL.

B.C. c. 450.—c. 430.

It is commonly assumed that the Tarentine didrachms presenting the equestrian figure are later in date than the types which bear upon the obverse the seated Dêmos of the city. This, however, is only partially true. That the "horsemen" as a class belong to a later date than the "democratic" series there can be no doubt. It seems equally certain that some of the coins presenting the seated Dêmos are earlier than any of those bearing the equestrian figure; but, on the other hand, there are to be found amongst these equestrian types more than one coin which, whether we judge of it by the standard of style or of epigraphy must be regarded as very little posterior in date to the earliest of the issues exhibiting the seated figure, and as certainly anterior to many of the later coins of that class.

Upon the coins which I have included in the present class the attitude in which Taras appears is little more than a reproduction of the earliest scheme, as it is already seen upon the rare incuse pieces struck by Tarentum as a party to the monetary convention of the Achæan cities and adhered to on the succeeding coinages, presenting on the other side a wheel or hippocamp. On the early equestrian types before us Taras is still seen in a stiff archaic pose, resting his right hand on the dolphin's back and extending his left with open palm, here seen sideways,[46] as on the coins with the wheel and early types with the hippocamp. We find, moreover, the whole design surrounded by a double circle, enclosing a ring of beads or pellets, the immediate descendant of the cable or guilloche border which marks the earliest incuse coinage of Tarentum. This archaic feature is also frequently associated with the wheel and hippocamp classes, but it is only found on some of the earlier types presenting the seated Dêmos. The naive and original rendering of the sea-waves, over which Taras is riding on his marine steed, as seen on the remarkable equestrian piece (Type A, I., Pl. II. 1) is also suggestive of primitive art. The sea is here not merely indicated by a single curling curve or circle, but overspreads the whole lower field of the coin with its tossing billows. Amongst the

---

[46] On the incuse type the palm is sometimes seen fronting the spectator—a more clumsy arrangement.

coins with the "democratic" type the only specimen, so far as I am aware, upon which waves are depicted[47] exhibits the later and less elaborate convention.

The horseman on the obverse of Types A, I. and B is as stiff and inelegant as Taras on the other side, and the steeds themselves betray an even greater degree of rudeness; they have unduly elongated bodies, diminutive heads, and stumpy legs. Compare for a moment these uncouth figures of horse and rider with the perfect mastery of form and luxuriant grace displayed in the treatment of the seated figure on the later didrachms with which that type is associated. Again, the simple archaic scheme of Taras on the equestrian types before us, holding out his open palm as on the earliest of the Tarentine issues, is very different from the more varied design of the same eponymic hero on some of the later "democratic" types, where he appears holding in his hands a shield and lances, a trident, or a wreath, at times with a crested helmet on his head, and, in one or two instances, seated sideways, as if in the act of vaulting off his marine charger. Unless we are to believe that many of the coins of this latter class belong to a considerably later date than these early "horsemen" we may as well cast to the winds every canon of artistic criticism.

The epigraphic evidence supplied by Type B, presenting the remarkable legend TAϷANTINΩN HMI, fully corroborates that derived from the style and design of these coins. The forms of the angular or sub-angular Ϸ and of the N are distinctly earlier than those on many of the types representing the Dêmos, while the character of the legend

---

[47] Carelli (*N. I. V.* Tav. cvii. 75) gives an imperfect representation of this coin without the waves, which, however, are visible on a specimen in my own collection.

itself also indicates an early date. The HMI of the legend has been no doubt rightly explained by Von Sallet [48] as equivalent to EIMI, so that the present is a "speaking coin" akin to the well-known stater reading φαενορ εμι σημα, for φαενορ εἰμὶ σῆμα, or the bronze weight of Gela, inscribed TON ΓΕΛΟΙΟΝ EMI, for τῶν Γελοιων εἰμί. Ἡμί is, in fact, the strong Doric form for εἰμί, and its use in Lacedæmonian Tarentum is thus easily explicable. The appearance of such a dialectic form, as well as the archaic associations of such a legend, must be taken as additional evidence of an early date.

Type A 2, in spite of the better workmanship of the horse, presents on the reverse the same archaic scheme of Taras on his dolphin surrounded by the double-beaded border, and has, therefore, also been included in the present group.

It can hardly be doubted that the first issue of the coins representing the seated Dêmos, or the Eponymic Hero as the impersonation of the Tarentine People, is to be brought into relation with the institution of a democratic form of government at Tarentum, which according to Aristotle took place in the year 473. The appearance of a similar type on the Rhêgian dies is in the same way con-

---

[48] *Zeitschrift für Numismatik*, I. 278, seqq., as against Friedländer (*Wiener Numismatische Zeitschrift*, 1880), who tried to show that HMI=ἡμι ... and betokened the half of a larger monetary unit. But, on the one hand, there is no Tarentine silver unit higher than the didrachm; and on the other, the aspirate form Ϝ is never wanting on Tarentine coins to the very latest period of issue. On some Tarentine terra-cotta roundels of comparatively late date, the legend ϜΗΜΙΩΔΕΛΙΟΝ appears = ϜΗΜΙΩΒΟΛΙΟΝ—another Tarentine Doricism (cf. Prof. P. Gardner, *Hellenic Journal*, iv. 156)—proving that at least a century after the issue of the present coin, ἡμι ... at Tarentum was written with its aspirate.

nected with the revolution by which the citizens of that city recovered their freedom in 466. These Rhêgian coins stand in such close relation to the Tarentine that they supply us with a chronological stand-point for approximately dating some of the democratic types of Tarentum. Upon the earliest Rhêgian pieces of this class, as upon their contemporary Tarentine counterparts [Pl. I. 8], the seated figure is seen surrounded by the olive-wreath, and from the parallel appearance of this significant symbol of Victory as much as from the adoption at Rhêgion of the Tarentine type imaging forth the sovereignty of the People, we may gather that the triumph of the Rhêgian Dêmos was facilitated by the active sympathy of the Tarentines. These Tarentine coins in which the seated figure is seen surrounded by the wreath so closely agree in style with the early Rhêgian coins of the same "democratic" type, that we may confidently assume that they were first issued at the same date, 466 B.C. They form, therefore, a valuable numismatic landmark for fixing a chronological limit to a still earlier class of the same "democratic" type struck at Tarentum, but to which no analogies can be found on the Rhêgian series. This class of coins (Pl. I. 7), in which Dêmos appears under a more archaic aspect, and at times surrounded by the chain or guilloche border in its most primitive form, must have been struck between 474 B.C., the date of the first introduction of this "democratic" type at Tarentum, and 466, when the later class exhibiting the olive-wreath was issued simultaneously at that city and at Rhêgion.

It is, however, with this wreathed series struck from 466 onwards that the early equestrian types before us present the greatest analogy. In both cases, although the guilloche proper, as seen on some of the "democratic" coins of the earliest class, no longer occurs, we find its nearest degeneration, the beaded ring, enclosed between two circles,—a transitional form, which on the later classes of Tarentine coins gives way to a plain ring or to a beaded ring without border. The occasional appearance Ϻ for Ξ on the wreathed "democratic" class implies indeed a certain anteriority, but taking into consideration the generally archaic character of this small group of "horsemen," it would not be safe to bring down their date of issue many years after the first emission of the others. The "wreathed" type itself was at Tarentum of very transient duration, and from its comparative rarity it is probable that its issue was confined to the years immediately succeeding 466. It follows that we shall not be far wrong in assigning to these early equestrian types, which are at least so closely allied to the other that they present the same transitional form of border, the approximate date of 450 B.C.[49] Type A 2, however, as already observed, though presenting certain common characteristics, shows a marked advance in the representation of the horse, and must be referred to a distinctly later date than the others.

I. Type A.

Naked horseman, his right hand resting on the horse's back, holding whip, on galloping horse with elongated body and stumpy legs.

---

[49] I observe that the conclusions that I had independently arrived at regarding the date of the earliest equestrian coins, are generally corroborated by Sambon, in his *Recherches sur les anciennes Monnaies de l'Italie méridionale*, p. 123. He also places the earliest issues of the horseman type not long after the issue of the earlier coins with the seated figure.

Obv.	Rev.
1. Horse to r. Car.[50] cix. 100. Garrucci, T. xcviii. 4. B. M. Cat. 109. [Pl. II. 1. (Bodleian Collection, Oxford).]	TAPA . . . Taras astride on dolphin to r., his r. hand resting on dolphin's back, and his left extended with open palm, seen sideways. Beneath, the sea indicated by a curling mass of waves occupying the whole lower field of the coin. In f. to r., T. Beaded double circle.
2. Horse to l. Car. cix. 100. [Pl. II. 3 (C. W. Oman).]	TA꓿A NTI NΩN. (retrogr.) Taras astride, &c., as No. 1. Scallop shell in place of waves. Beaded double circle.

I. Type B.

Horseman galloping r., as Type A, but with a conical cap on his head.

1. Beneath horse, ☉. Cab. des Médailles. Sambon, *Monn. de la presq. Ital.*, Pl. XIV. 10. [Pl. II. 2. A. J. E.]	TAꝐANTINΩNHMI. Taras astride, &c., to r., resting his r. on dolphin's back and extending his l. with open palm (as before, A 1 and 2). In f. to l., ⊓. Beaded double circle.

I. Type C.

Naked ephēbos on horse walking r.

1. Type described. [Pl. XI. 1. Santangelo Coll.]	NΩNIT NA꓿AT. Taras astride, &c., to r., as before, beneath dolphin, scallop.

PERIOD II.

B.C. c. 420—c. 380.

The comparative rarity of the equestrian types comprised in our First Period affords sufficient indication that their

---

[50] The references are to Carelli, *Numorum Italiæ Veteris Tabulæ*, ccii. (Cavedoni's edition, Leipzig, 1850). Other references are given in the case of rarer varieties, and of types not known to Carelli. Coins in my own cabinet are referred to as "A. J. E."

issue was of short duration. Between these early "horsemen" and the present group there is an obvious "fault" in artistic development, and it is evident that a considerable interval of years separates the two classes, though A 2 of the preceding Period, and A, B, and D 1 of the present, serve partly to bridge over the gap. Whether or not in the first appearance of the equestrian type about the middle of the fifth century B.C., we are to trace the influence of an aristocratic reaction at Tarentum, it is certain that the Tarentine moneyers were not long in reverting to the preceding "democratic" type. It was not indeed till after the revived issues of this class had been again current for some length of time that a fresh revolution took place on the Tarentine dies, the equestrian type now permanently displacing the seated Dêmos.

The "horsemen" of this Second Period with which we have now to deal, still as a rule retain the broad-spread appearance and slightly larger module characteristic of the preceding "democratic" class. The inscription is still occasionally retrograde, in one case taking the form ƧONITNAPAT, and the design is often surrounded by a plain or beaded ring, but the beaded double circle characteristic of Period I. is no longer found. The horseman appears on a stationary as well as a cantering horse, and is sometimes seen at full gallop. It is now, moreover, for the first time that we meet with the remarkable scheme of the rider with his knee bent under him as if in the act of vaulting from his steed. The figure of Taras on his dolphin is still occasionally seen in the archaic attitude resting one hand on the fish's back and with the other extending an open palm: novel versions of the youthful hero, however, now begin to appear. At times he is seen gracefully pointing downwards with his outstretched hand as at some sea creature before him, at which with his other arm he aims a short javelin. The most exquisite version of this scheme is that [Type L 2, Pl. II. 11] associated on its obverse side with the signature ƎΛ in minute letters, which, as I hope to show, there is every reason to identify with the first letters of an artist's name.[51] At times Taras is seen with lance, shield, and helmet, or some other attribute such as an oar or *akrostolion* in his hands, and these latter types—especially that in which he holds on his left arm a lance and large oval shield and extends a crested helmet in his right—show a close affinity to some of the later coins of the previous class, exhibiting on the obverse the seated Dêmos.[52] Another point of resemblance with the "democratic" series is to be found in the scallop shell which is often introduced below the dolphin to symbolize the sea.

Although as a rule the types of this period are broadspread and of large module, traces appear already in Types E 4, H, and K of a more compact style of engraving, which becomes a characteristic feature of a whole series of issues belonging to the succeeding Period III., for the most part associated with the signature Λ, which together with ƎΛ occurs on coins of a similar style of engraving belonging to the close of the present class.

The remarkable type that I have placed at the head of the coins of Period II. [A 1; Pl. II. 5], representing a youthful horseman clad in a loose flowing tunic and wearing a peaked cap, whom I have ventured above to identify with the Tarentine Œkist Phalanthos, throws a valuable light

---

[51] See p. 48. The specimen from which the figure [Pl. II. 11] is taken is unfortunately not very well preserved.

[52] Cf. Car. cvi. 63. Garrucci, xcvii. 32.

on the approximate date of this second period of equestrian issues. This coin, from the broad character of the design as well as the delicate execution of the drapery, has greater affinity to the finest of the types representing the seated Dêmos than any other example of the "horseman" class. Both the horse and rider bear a certain resemblance to two Macedonian types, one of Archelaos I. (B.C. 413—399), and the other of Amyntas III.[53] after his restoration in 381, both of which display a mounted spearman in a flowing tunic or chlamys, and wearing the flat Macedonian *petasos* or *kausia*. A still nearer parallel is, however, supplied by the didrachms exhibiting a similarly attired horseman, though without the cap, struck by the Odrysian king, Seuthes I., in 424 B.C., and bearing on the reverse the well-known legend ΣEYΘA KOMMA.[54]

The horse on the Tarentine piece is somewhat less free in its pose and modelling than those on the Macedonian coins referred to. On the other hand, it displays the closest agreement with that on the Thracian example. Unless, therefore, we are to assume that Thracian and Macedonian art was at this time ahead of the Tarentine, which is in the highest degree improbable, we cannot be far wrong in assigning to the present coin the approximate date of 420 B.C.

One of the latest types of the didrachm class with which we are dealing—and one, moreover, that in some of its varieties supplies a link of transition to the coins of the succeeding Period III.—is that in which a caduceus is seen in front of a stationary horse. These coins have a special value as supplying additional evidence as to the

---

[53] Both coins are reproduced in Gardner, *Types of Greek Coins*, Pl. VII. 4 and 5.

[54] *B. M. Cat.*, Thrace, p. 201.

approximate chronological limits of the present class. In the great hoard of Magna-Græcian coins discovered at Pæstum in 1858, there occurred, besides some earlier Tarentine coins representing the hippocamp and the seated Dêmos, a fair number of pieces belonging to the equestrian class; amongst which, however, only one— namely, of the type of the present Period exhibiting a caduceus in front of the horse—bore a signature of two letters, AΛ.[55]

The absence of any other Tarentine coins presenting more than a single letter in the field is a sure indication that the horsemen discovered in this hoard belonged to the present Period. On the coins of the succeeding Period III., signatures of two and even three letters are not infrequent; but this type exhibiting the caduceus is, with a single exception, the only coin of the present class on which a signature is to be found of more than a single letter. This caducean type, moreover, belongs—at least in one of its varieties—to the end of the period with which we are dealing. It occurs in a broad-spread form which is quite consistent with the prevalent character of the earlier equestrian types of this group, but also in a smaller module, which connects it with the issues of the succeeding Period III.

There seems good reason to regard this coin as the latest of the Tarentine issues represented in the Pæstum hoard; and it follows that if it is possible to determine the date when that hoard was deposited, we shall at the

---

[55] For a summary description of this find see Sambon, *Recherches sur les anciennes Monnaies de l'Italie Méridionale* (Naples, 1863, p. 9). The type is given in Sambon's list of Tarentine Coins, p. 114, No. 47. A similar type is engraved by Carelli, T. cix. 109 and 111, in two modules. In the one case, however, no signature appears; in the other, only A.

same time obtain a clue to the approximate time-limits of the present class of Tarentine didrachms.

In the Pæstum hoard there were found a great quantity of Poseidonian didrachms or diobols, described as "fleur de coin," and belonging to the last issue of that city. The exact date of the capture of Poseidonia by the Lucanians has unfortunately not been preserved; and although the fall of this great Hellenic city must be regarded as one of the landmarks of Greek and Italian history, such is the piecemeal character of ancient annals that it is only by a deductive process that we can arrive at the approximate date of this far-reaching event. From the account preserved by the Tarentine Aristoxenos, a pupil of Aristotle, of the mourning feast in which the Greek inhabitants of what had now become Pæstum revived the memory of the free Hellenic days of Poseidonia, we gather that at the time in which he flourished —from about 336 B.C.[56] onwards—the independence of Poseidonia was already a distant tradition. On the other hand, as early as 390 we find the Lucanians already in possession of Laos, the sister colony of Sybaris, and inflicting under its walls a crushing defeat on the Thurians. As Poseidonia lay nearer the original Lucanian base than Laos, and there is no mention of the Poseidonians in Diodôros' account, we must infer that it, too, was in Lucanian hands at this date; and it was in all probability the fall of these two cities that stirred the Italiote Greeks to form a defensive league against the barbarian invader in 392.[57] Assuming, as we have every reason to do, that the occasion of the deposit of the Pæstum

---

[56] Ol. cxi. Suidas, s.v. Ἀριστόξενος.
[57] Diodôros, xiv. 101. Cf. Grote, c. lxxxiii. (vol. vii. p. 466, ed. Murray, 1862).

hoard is to be found in the Lucanian capture of the city, it follows that the Tarentine coins of the present class, which must be ranked among the most recent contents of the find, were issued during the years immediately preceding 392 B.C.

This conclusion receives corroboration from a small lot of didrachms, evidently part of a hoard, which recently came under my notice at Naples. These consisted of about a dozen coins of Terina,[58] presenting several of the types struck during the period which was cut short by the capture of that city by Dionysios of Syracuse in 388; some coins of Thurii, including two with the signature ΜοΛοΣΣΟΣ; one of Krotôn, with the facing head of Hêra Lakinia and Hêraklês seated on the lion's skin extending a wine cup, the coinage of which, in all probability, immediately preceded the issue of the alliance pieces struck in 390, representing the infant Hêraklês strangling the two serpents.[59] Besides these, there were a few late Kauloniate types, some of which may have been struck shortly before the destruction of the city by Dionysios in 388; a Tarentine coin of the "democratic" type, but one of the latest of its class; and two other Tarentine coins, both of them characteristic specimens of the equestrian group with which we are now dealing. One of these, Type D, 1 [Pl. II. 8] of the present Period, shows on the obverse a horseman cantering, and holding a round shield behind him; while Taras, on the reverse, rides over the sea-waves, holding an oar on his left arm: the other is the type already described, in which the horseman stands before a caduceus; in this case it is signed Λ.

---

[58] Car. clxxvii. 15; clxxviii. 25, 28. *B. M. Cat.* 22; and some others.

[59] See Head, *Historia Numorum*, p. 82.

Everything points to the year 388 as the approximate date of the deposit to which the above coins belonged, and we have here a new indication of the date of the present class of Tarentine coins.

Whether or not some of the later issues of the "democratic" class may have alternated with the earlier issues of this second class of equestrian types it is difficult to determine. One or two of the figures of the seated Dêmos,[60] certainly convey an impression of less primitive design than the warrior in *pilos* and *chiton* placed first among the horsemen of this period. If it was so, the issues of the present class may extend over a somewhat larger space of years than from their numerical representation alone we should be inclined to attribute to them. From the development in style perceptible in some of the later examples it is evident that the mintage of these coins should not be restricted within too narrow chronological limits, and with the evidence of the finds before us we shall not greatly err in assigning to the present numismatic period the approximate dates 420—380 B.C.

II. Type A.

Youthful horseman in flowing tunic and *pilos*, or conical *petasos*, cantering, r., and thrusting downwards with his lance.

Obv.	Rev.
No letter. *B. M. Cat.* App. I. Car. cix. 115. [Pl. II. 5.]	Taras astride, &c., to l., his r. arm raised and his l. resting on dolphin's back. Beneath dolphin, scallop and curling crests of waves in a single curve. In f. to r. ꝗAT.

---

[60] As, for instance, the type, an example of which is engraved by Carelli, cvii. 73.

II. Type B.

Horseman galloping l., on horse of better proportions than Period I. B.

Obv.	Rev.
In f. ⋛A٩AT. [Pl. II. 4. Imhoof-Blumer Coll.]	Taras astride, &c., to r., as before, extending his l. hand; in f. to r. ⊓. Beneath dolphin, a cuttle-fish.

II. Type C.

Naked horseman to l. (sometimes helmeted), his knee bent under him as if vaulting from his cantering horse; his r. holds horse's bridle, and in his l. he holds a round shield, sometimes also a lance behind him.

1. Rider wears crested helmet, and holds lance as well as shield. In f. in front of horse ⋛. *B. M. Cat.* 263. [Pl. II. 6.]	Taras astride, &c., to l., holding behind him a large oval shield and spear, and extending in his r. a crested helmet. Beneath, TAPA⋛.
2. Rider bare-headed. ⋛ below horse. No lance; on shield star of six rays. Plain ring border. *B. M. Cat.* 265. [Pl. II. 7.]	Same, but in f., in front of Taras, ⋛

II. Type D.

Naked horseman cantering l., holding small round shield behind him.

1. No letter. [Pl. II. 8. A. J. E.]	Taras astride, &c., to l., holding oar on l. arm, and with r. pointing downwards. Beneath dolphin, curling crests of waves. In f. to l. ⋛A٩AT. Plain ring border.
2. Same. Santangelo Coll.	Same, but Taras to r. Beneath dolphin TAPA*N* TI*N*Ω[*N*].
3. Same. A. J. E.	Taras astride, &c., to r., pointing downwards with l., and with r. aiming a dart downwards. Plain ring border.

II. Type E.

Naked Ephébos crowning stationary horse to r.

Obv.	Rev.
1. Horse to r. [Pl. II. 9. Santangelo Coll.]	ΤΑΡΑΝΤΙΝΩΝ. Taras astride, &c., to r.; his r. hand resting on dolphin's back; his left extended, with open palm. Scallop below.
2. Same, but caduceus in front of horse. Car. cix. 109.	Same, but no scallop. ΤΑΡΑΣ beneath dolphin.
3. Same. In exergue ΑΛ. Sambon, *Recherches*, &c. p. 114, No. 47. Pæstum find.	Same (?).
4. Same as 1 (rather smaller module). Cf. Car. cix. 111.	Same, but ΤΑΡΑΣ in f. to l. Beneath dolphin, Α.
5. Same. Beneath horse, Λ. Plain ring border. A. J. E.	Taras astride, &c., to r., resting his l. hand on the dolphin's head, and with his right aiming a dart downwards. In f. to l. ΤΑΡΑΣ.
6. Horse to l. (lifting off fore-leg). [Pl. XI. 2. Santangelo Coll.]	Same as 1—4, but Taras extends a distaff.

II. Type F.

Naked Ephébos, bridle arm only visible, seated r. on stationary horse which lifts its off fore-leg.

1. Type described. Car. cix. 102. | Taras astride, &c., to r.; his l. hand resting on dolphin's back; his r. extended, with open palm. Beneath, scallop. Insc. round, ΤΑΡΑΝΤΙΝ.

II. Type G.

Naked Ephébos cantering l., his left hand resting on horse's back behind him.

1. Kantharos beneath horse. Car. cix. 107. | Taras astride, &c., to r.; his l. hand on dolphin's back; r. extended, openpalmed. Beneath, scallop : insc. round, ΣΟΝΙΤΝΑΡΑΤ. In beaded border.

II. Type H.

Naked Ephébos galloping r., with his r. arm thrown back.

Obv.

1. Type described. Λ beneath horse. Plain ring border. Car. cxii. 173.

2. Same. No letter. A. J. E.

Rev.

Taras astride, &c., to l.; his r. arm resting on dolphin's back; his l. extending akrostolion. Beneath, Λ and TAPAϟ. Plain ring border.

Same. No letter.

II. Type K.

Naked Ephébos to l. crowning a stationary horse, and holding in his l. hand behind him a small round shield.

1. Type described. Plain ring border. Not in Car. B. M. Cat. 200.
[Pl. II. 10.]

Taras astride, &c., to r., pointing downwards with l. hand, and with r. aiming a trident. Insc. ϟAᴦAT. Plain ring border.

II. Type L.

Naked Ephébos galloping l., holding reins with both hands.

1. Beneath horse, Λ. Plain ring border. A. J. E.

2. Same. Beneath horse, ƎΛ, in minute characters. Plain ring border.
[Pl. II. 11. A. J. E.]

Taras astride, &c., to l., resting his l. hand on dolphin's back, and with r. extending akrostolion. Beneath dolphin, Λ and TAPAϟ.

Taras astride, &c., to r., pointing downwards with l. hand, and with right aiming downwards with dart. (Cf. Type D 3.) Beneath dolphin, TAPAϟ. Plain ring border.

Period III.—THE AGE OF ARCHYTAS.

B.C. c. 380—345.

The Numismatic Period that now succeeds derives a special interest from the fact that it covers the space of time during which the philosopher-statesman Archytas was exercising predominant influence in his native city. I have included in the present Period all the issues that extend from the conclusion of the preceding class and the approximate date of 380 B.C. to the time when the renewed struggles between Tarentum and its barbarous neighbours assumed a more serious aspect from the appearance on the scene of the still more redoubtable Lucanians. So far, however, as the coins themselves enable us to judge, the period with which we are at present concerned seems to have been largely endowed with the blessings of peace. The horseman appears but rarely with arms in his hand, as is so frequently the case in the succeeding epoch. One of the commonest schemes of Taras on his dolphin that characterizes the present series shows the Eponymic Hero, who may be taken to personify Tarentum itself, in a state of idyllic repose; and in other instances, where he appears in a more active guise aiming a trident or harpoon at a fish below, his activity connects itself with the peaceful industries of his city. These coins and some of the earliest types of Period IV., the theme of which is still the Tarentine fisheries, may well be regarded as a numismatic evidence of the peace and prosperity which the wise government of Archytas had secured to his fellow citizens.

An evidence of the large-minded political activity of Archytas, and of the nearer relations into which the cities of Great Greece were drawn under his influence, is to be further found in a silver coinage of smaller denomination, which about this time issued from the Tarentine mint. Side by side with the litras of the traditional Tarentine system, there now appear obols of Attic standard to serve the purpose of a federal currency. These coins reproduce on their obverse side the head of Pallas, which since the date of the foundation of Thurii had been adopted by several Magna-Græcian cities as a tribute to Athenian influence; while on their reverse they display the fine design of Hêraklês strangling the Nemean lion, the special badge of the Tarentine colony of Hêrakleia, now become the meeting-place of the Federal Council of the Italiote Greeks.

It is somewhat difficult to define in any general terms the artistic features of the great variety of didrachm types of which the generation embraced in the present Period was productive. On the whole, however, it may be said that the horses show a juster proportion and a greater freedom of action than had hitherto been achieved, while in the case of the riders there is greater variety in the time of life represented. Mere boys and jockeys often take the place of the full-grown *Ephéboi* of the earlier groups. The reverse designs of Taras on his dolphin belonging to this Period must be classed amongst the highest products of the Tarentine mint, and demand a more detailed consideration. The inscription is simply TAPA$\text{\textless}$, never retrograde, and the module of the coin has a tendency to become smaller and more compact.

It is further evident that the coinages of this period may be divided, according to their fabric, into two main classes, both alternating with, and on the whole contemporary with, one another, though showing very distinct schools of artistic tradition. In the first of these we are struck with a peculiarly compact style of representation and a tendency to surround the design with a ring or border. In the other class we have a broader and more massive treatment, and the border is apparently quite unknown. Both of these classes, in fact, represent the perpetuation of a dualism in fabric already perceptible in

Period II. In Type E 4, K and L of that Period we already discover the prototypes of the abnormally compact series of figures that appear during the Period with which we are now concerned.

If we examine the coins of the first class, characterized by the compact character of its engraving,[61] we find that, although not so numerous as the other, they show considerable skill in composition, and we seem to acquire distinct evidence of the reaction of individual masterpieces of sculpture and painting on the die-sinker's art. Of singularly sculpturesque aspect is the horseman [Type C, Pl. III. 5] with the bridle-arm in front of his horse's neck, and his head gracefully inclined towards that of his charger —a masterpiece of skilful pose and harmonious balance, which suggests the influence of some familiar relief in marble. It is as it were a detached figure taken from a frieze, and makes us the more regret that so little of the sculpture of the Tarentine temples has been preserved. Not inferior to this in artistic conception, and, indeed, displaying a marked fellow-feeling with it, is the reverse of the same piece, representing Taras, his head bowed forward as before, seated sideways on his marine charger, one arm resting on the dolphin's tail, the other lightly laid upon its forehead, his whole attitude instinct with reverie and repose.

This remarkable coin is signed Λ, assuredly indicating the same artist who signs ƎΛ and Λ during the preceding Period, and the same signature is found on several coins of the present group. The coins with these signatures rank among the best examples of the compact style of engraving described above, and from the correspondence

---

[61] Types A—G inclusive.

alike of signature and of artistic tradition we are justified in concluding that the peculiarities of this class are largely due to the influence of a single engraver. The reverse of the coin signed ƎΛ in minute letters, which I have placed last (Type L, 2) in the series belonging to Period II., is, from an artistic point of view, extremely remarkable. Though the horse on the obverse is still somewhat immature, the exquisite figure of Taras pointing downwards at the sea creature, whatever it may be, at which with his other arm he aims a dart, will not easily find a parallel for playful grace and lightsomeness of touch. In feeling, however, it is curiously in harmony with the beautiful coin signed Λ of the present class, while the obverse designs of other coins with the same signature present an equally close agreement in their type of the galloping horseman. Style, signature, and design alike lead us to refer these works to the same artist whose initial Le.... may find its completion in such well-established Tarentine names as *Leôn* or *Leônidas*.

It is a noteworthy fact that the scheme described above, of Taras seated sideways on the dolphin, resting with one hand on its back, which now first appears and becomes frequent on the Tarentine dies, is almost exclusively confined to the coins of this Period presenting the peculiar compact style of engraving. This differentiation alike of type and style amongst otherwise contemporary issues is a strong indication of the fact suggested by many other phenomena to which I shall have occasion to allude, that there was more than one *atelier* of Tarentine moneyers, and that these different workshops had their peculiar traditions of engraving. Only in this way, moreover, is it possible to account for the distinct dualism in fabric which runs through the coinages of Periods II., III., and IV.

In the scheme above referred to Taras usually appears in perfect repose, and with both hands resting on the dolphin. At times, however, he is seen extending a symbol in his right hand. But there also occurs a more active version of the design, in which Taras, sometimes represented as a youth, sometimes as a bearded man, is seen turning round to aim a trident at a tunny or a cuttle-fish below. Taken together, these latter types present us with the most speaking allusions to a principal branch of the Tarentine industry—the cuttle-fish, like the scallop or the purple-shell, which elsewhere appears in the field, pointing rather to the fisheries of the little inner sea, the present *Mare piccolo*; the tunny, on the other hand, to the open Ionian waters.[62]

These fisher types, again, have for us a special interest as supplying some of the best authenticated examples of engravers' signatures to be found on the Tarentine dies. The remarkable piece (Type F, 3), a reproduction of which, from an unique example in the Santangelo Collection at Naples, is given for the first time on Pl. XI. (Fig. 4), exhibits on the reverse, beneath the design of the youthful Taras spearing a cuttle-fish, and again beneath the horseman on the obverse, the signature ΣΩΚ[63] engraved

---

[62] The best commentary on the Tarentine fisheries, ancient and modern, is to be found in Joannes Juvenis, *De Antiquitate et varia Tarentinorum Fortuna* (Naples, 1589). See cap. ii. *De Tarentinorum Piscatu*. The cuttle-fish, not to speak of the value of its dye, is still a favourite article of food amongst the seafaring population of the Mediterranean, and notably of the modern Tarentines, who catch it especially in March and December.

[63] This is in all probability the same engraver whose signature appears as ΣΩ on a small tessera on a diobol described by Raoul Rochette (*Lettre à M. le duc de Luynes sur les graveurs des Monnaies Grecques*, p. 45, Pl. III., 39), who justly regarded it as an example of an artist's signature. Raoul Rochette being unacquainted with the didrachm described above, sought erro-

on an oblong tablet, which recalls an artistic device adopted by the great Syracusan engravers for disposing of their names on the field of a coin.

In Type G we find the same design in a somewhat variant form, associated with the interesting obverse design already referred to[64] of the youthful ἄμφιππος leading a second horse, which affords at the same time a good example of the compact style of engraving characteristic of the group under discussion. In this case a notable and highly suggestive development occurs in the scheme of the reverse, Taras no longer aiming his trident at the fish with his nearer arm, but bringing round his further arm for the purpose in such a way as to bring the muscles of his breast into strong relief.

On a somewhat later group, again, Type F, 1, of the succeeding Period (IV.), which must be regarded as the sequel of Types F and G of the present class, we find a scheme (Pl. XI. 6) which combines certain features of both its predecessors. In this later development we see this fisherman type brought into connexion with the highly ornate and elaborate design in which the prancing steed is embraced by a boyish figure. There can, however, be little doubt that both designs were engraved by artists of the same school.

From a comparison of the two closely related varieties (Type G, 1 and 3, Pl. III. 7 and 8), it results that the letter

---

neously to identify the signature with that of the engraver who, on a late didrachm of the reduced standard (Pl. X., 2), signs ΣΩ in minute letters between the horns of a bucranium, and also with the Pyrrhic Magistrate ΣΩΣΤΡΑΤΟΣ. The unique diobol above mentioned must be regarded as probably the earliest of those presenting the type of Taras on his dolphin, and which mostly belong to the period after 300 B.C. See p. 10.

[64] See p. 21.

A which in the one case appears in the field must with great probability be taken as the engraver's signature. These two varieties in my own collection have their obverse types struck from the same die; the reverse, however, presents us with a significant alteration. In the one case a small raised tablet appears in the field, such as it is natural, as in the instance above given, to associate with an artist's signature, though no letter can at present be deciphered on it. On the fellow coin this tablet is no longer found, but its exact position in the field is taken by the letter A. On type A, 1, of Period IV., on the other hand, there is no tablet or signature on the reverse, but beneath the figure of the horseman, which may well be from the same hand, appears the signature AP.

But this leads us a step farther. On the present group the initial A is associated with the obverse signatures K and ΦI in conjunction, while in the first instance presenting the tablet in the field, a Ж appears beneath the dolphin. But, as will be shown in considering the coinage of the succeeding Period IV., this conjunction of signatures answers under an abbreviated form to the conjunction of KAΛ, ΦI and API on a group of coins which presents the clearest example of artistic collaboration on the Tarentine dies.[64] The form AP already supplies an intermediate link with the fuller form API, while the signature K, which is also in a special way associated with this exquisite design, undoubtedly belongs to the same engraver, who at a slightly later date attaches his signature to some of the noblest of the Tarentine types, indifferently with the initial K and the fuller form KAΛ.

But no one acquainted with the finest types of the Tarentine colony of Hérakleia can fail to be struck with the evident parallel supplied to the scheme of the hero

---

[64] P. IV. H.

with his head and upper part of his body turned back and his right arm brought round in athletic action, by the noble design of Hêraklês strangling the Nemean lion, as it appears on some of the finest didrachms of that city. It is something more than a mere reminiscence. The representation of the slightly bowed head, the treatment of the hair, the very play of the muscles, though intensified in the Hêrakleian example, present such remarkable points of similarity as must themselves suggest identity of handiwork. A suggestion, derived from a very different design, has been here taken over and applied, with great felicity, to a subject with which it had a less obvious relation.

There can be little doubt that the introduction of this noble design of Hêraklês and the lion at the Tarentine colony was due to the artist whose signature appears as Φ on contemporary coins of Hêrakleia, Thurioi, Terina, and Neapolis, and who, as Mr. Poole has shown,[65] represents the grafting of Athenian art traditions on Italian soil. It may well be that in the case of this noble scheme, which appears about the same time on coins of Mallos in Cilicia (after c. 385 B.C.)[66] and of the Cyprian king Dêmonikos[67] at Kition (c. 374—368 B.C.) we must recognise the influence of a well-known work of statuary analogous to that exercised by the figure on the balustrade of the Temple of Nikê Apteros on the Terinæan engraver, or to the memory sketch of the Theseus of the Parthenon pediment on the coins of Hêrakleia, Krotôn, and Pandosia. On the Mallian coins the hero is represented standing on a

---

[65] *Num. Chron.*, 1883, p. 269, *seqq*.
[66] Imhoof-Blumer, *Annuaire de Numismatique*, vii. p. 109.
[67] J. P. Six, *Num. Chron.*, 1882, p. 91. For the evolution of this design from the earlier archaic scheme of Hêraklês thrusting a sword into the lion's breast, see Furtwängler, *Coll. Sabouroff*, II., Pl. CXLVIII.

distinct basis, a clear intimation that the design is taken from a statue, and M. Six[68] has suggested with great plausibility that the original should be traced to a bronze group of Myrôn.

Fig. 1.

In the Period with which we are now dealing, the work of the artist Φ at Hêrakleia was taken up by two new engravers, one of whom signs ΚΑΛ in the field (Fig. 1), while the name of the other appears either as ΑΡΙΣΤΟΞΕ in minute letters on the exergual line, or on the crest of the helmet on the obverse[69] in the completed form ΑΡΙΣΤΟΞΕΝΟΣ, or again is represented on one or both sides by the simple initial Α. That both of these engravers enjoyed a reputation in their day is evident from the reappearance of the same signatures on contemporary coins of Metapontion,[70] and we have good warrant for believing that both of them worked also for the Tarentine dies.

The Hêrakleian type of the standing Hêraklês, with which they are associated, and the influence of which is felt on the scheme of Taras turning round on his dolphin as it appears on Pl. III. 7-8, was in fact at this very time itself adopted, as already noticed, by the Tarentines for their new coinage of federal diobols. Upon some of the finest of these, moreover, we not only find the initials

---

[68] *Zeitschr. f. Numismatik*, xiv. p. 142, *seqq*.
[69] Imhoof-Blumer, *Berliner Blätter*, v. 33 (T. LIII. 2).
[70] Raoul Rochette, *Graveurs des Monnaies Grecques*, Pl IV., 32--36 ; Garrucci, *op. cit.* ciii. 13—15.

K, Φ, and others of signatures that appear on the contemporary Hêrakleian didrachms which served as their models, but even at times the same symbols, such as a scallop shell, or an owl between the legs of Hêraklês, as it is seen on the noble Hêrakleian piece engraved above (Fig. 1), signed KAΛ. When, then, on the Tarentine didrachms which so evidently betray the work of hands familiar with the Hêrakleian design, we find the signatures K and A answering to the KAΛ and API of somewhat later Tarentine types of the same school, we can hardly avoid the conclusion that we have here to do with the same artists, Kal..... and Aristoxenos, who sign upon the Hêrakleian coins. That the signatures indeed on the Tarentine coins should incline to a more abbreviated form is only what we are led to expect from other analogies. As will be shown later on,[71] the conditions under which engravers signed at Tarentum were different from those of the neighbouring cities. It must, however, be observed that, in the case of the Hêrakleian coins referred to, Aristoxenos combines two systems of signature, signing in minute letters—*en artiste*—on the exergual line of the helmet, but at the same time placing a large A in the field of the obverse as a more official badge,[72] while in other cases he signs simply with his initial letter on either side.[73]

The coins of the second class [74] referred to as belonging to this Period, and the issue of which seems to run parallel with the other, present, as already noticed, a broader and less compact treatment of the design, and, for the same reason, display on the whole a fuller rendering of the horses. Nothing grander of its kind was produced by the

---

[71] See p. 119, *seqq*.   [72] See p. 119.
[73] See *Das Königliche Münzkabinet* (Berlin), Pl. VIII., 723.
[74] Types H—T inclusive.

Tarentine engravers than the massive horse of Type H [Pl. III. 10], standing in front of a bearded Herm. In Type K again [Pl. III. 11, 12, 15] we have another noble steed, which gains in majesty from the contrast with the child rider reaching forward over its huge neck, his long waving tresses streaming to the breeze.

Of the equestrian types of this class of coin that of the horseman vaulting from his horse is the most frequent. On the reverse, in place of the sideways figure which is such a regular concomitant of the parallel group, Taras is almost invariably represented resting his left arm on the dolphin's tail, so as to preserve his balance, while he throws forward his further leg, so that the outline of its foot and shin is seen in front of the fish's head. The persistence of this scheme throughout this group of coins is of importance in its typological relation to the characteristic pose assumed by Taras in a group of coins belonging to the succeeding Periods, where his leg appears thrown still further forward, and at times is visible in its entirety.[75] Both on the obverse and reverse of coins of this group the ring or border now entirely disappears. Taras himself, though sometimes represented with elegance and grace, appears for the most part either as a full-grown ephèbos or as a child of decidedly heavy build. Here again we trace the antecedent stages of a style prevalent in the succeeding epoch.

The natural treatment of the hair is one of the *argutiæ minutiarum*, which on this class of coins, and towards the close of this Period, attained its greatest perfection on the Tarentine dies. Taras on his dolphin or the boy rider bending over his horse's neck are not infrequently depicted with long waving tresses streaming in the wind,

---

[75] An exceptional instance of this scheme is seen in Type A 3 [Pl. III. 3] of the present Period.

displaying even greater freedom and picturesqueness than the somewhat similar style of hair seen on one of the warriors of the frieze from the Akropolis temple of Tarentum.[76] In the case of the horses' manes we find, moreover, a growing elaboration of detail, which in the group with which we are dealing, especially in its latest examples, takes a peculiar form. On these the manes are seen curling up in a regular series of well-defined and wave-like crests—a refinement of which the great Syracusan engravers (who would eagerly have seized on such a detail) were as yet ignorant, and which strongly contrasts with the straight-cropped and more Pheidiac manes of the earlier coins of Tarentum itself. This curled arrangement is found occasionally on sculpture, as, for instance, on a relief at Delphi representing a quadriga; but it seems more appropriate to metal-work, and formed, no doubt, a feature of some of the bronze horses of Tarentine *anathêmata*. This peculiarity in its most exaggerated form may be said to be characteristic of the Tarentine coins of the close of the present Period and of that which immediately succeeds, during which it is at times even more elaborate. It still accompanies the finer horseman types of Period V., but before the time of Pyrrhus it entirely vanishes from the Tarentine dies.

In Types A—G, inclusive, I have grouped together the coins of this Period exhibiting the more compact style of relief.

III. Type A.[77]

Naked youth crowning his stationary horse to r., in plain ring border.

---

[76] *Notizie dei Scavi*, 1881, t. viii. 1.

[77] In this and the succeeding Periods the inscription recording the civic name is generally omitted, and, except in the case of the special variations given, TAPAΣ is to be understood.

Obv.	Rev.
1. Type described. Horse to r. Car. cix. 106.	Taras seated sideways on dolphin, resting r. hand on fish's head, and l. on tail. Beneath sometimes Λ.
2. Same. Beneath horse, Λ. Imhoof-Blumer Coll. [Pl. III. 1.]	Same; but on body of dolphin, H. Beneath, P.
3. Same. Beneath horse, Λ. Car. cxii. 172. B. M. Cat. 128. [Pl. III. 2.]	Same; but Taras astride holding akrostolion. Beneath, Λ.
4. Same. B. M. [Pl. III. 3.]	Same, but Taras holds kantharos, and throws l. leg in front of the dolphin's snout.

III. Type B.

Naked youth galloping to right. The horse of better proportions than Type L. of Period II., from which it can be easily distinguished by the fact that in the present case the horse is invariably to the right, in the other, as invariably to the left.

1. Beneath horse, Λ. Garr. Tav. cxviii. ⊥ for Λ.	Taras astride, &c., holding out akrostolion.
2. Same; but no letter. Car. cix. 113. [Pl. III. 4. A. J. E.]	Same.

III. Type C.

Naked youth on horse to r.; his shield seen sideways behind him; his head inclined toward the horse's, and his bridle-arm in front of the horse's neck. The horse is stationary, but raises its off fore-leg. In plain ring border.

1. Type described. Beneath horse, Λ. [Pl. III. 5. A. J. E.]	Taras seated sideways on the dolphin l., his head slightly inclined forward.
2. Same. Car. cxii. 170.	Same; but P beneath dolphin.

PERIOD III.   59

Obv.   Rev.

3. Same; but Y   Same as 1.
beneath horse.
Santangelo Coll.

III. Type D.

Naked helmeted horseman cantering to l. and holding a small round shield behind him.

1. Λ below horse.   Taras seated sideways on dolphin,
A. J. E.   holding out kantharos. Waves and
                       small fish below, and under fish's
                       tail ⊒.

2. Same.   Taras astride, &c., to l., his further
Santangelo Coll.   leg outlined in front of dolphin's snout,
                       resting his l. hand on fish's back, and
                       his r. holding trident.

III. Type E.

Naked horseman vaulting from cantering horse to l., holding shield behind him.

1. Beneath horse,   Taras to r., his l. foot outlined in
⊥ and kylix, in the   front of dolphin's snout, holding in r.
centre of which is ap- hand dart, and in l. trident on shoulder.
parently a represen-
tation of a helmet.
[Pl. III. 9. Cab.
des Méd. No. 1485.]

III. Type F.

Naked horseman galloping r., raising whip behind him.[78]

1. Beneath horse,   Taras, as a bearded man, seated side-
ΘPA.   ways to r. on dolphin, turning round
Car. cxi. 218.   and aiming trident at cuttle-fish below.
[Pl. III. 6.]   Beneath dolphin, ΘPA.

2. Same.   Taras as before, but represented as a
[Pl. XI. 3. Sant-   beardless youth, and aiming trident at
angelo Coll.]   tunny-fish. No legible inscription be-
                       neath dolphin.

3. Same; but be-   Taras as last, but aiming trident at
neath horse ⋛ΩK   cuttle-fish. Beneath dolphin ⋛ΩK on
on an oblong tablet.   an oblong tablet.
[Pl. XI. 4. Sant-
angelo Coll.]

---

[78] To be distinguished from Type Q, belonging to the second group of this same Period, where the whip is lowered.

III. Type G.

Naked boy (ἀμφιππος) on horse walking l., who holds the bridle of a second horse walking beside the other. He is crowned by a small Victory flying behind. The whole in a plain circle.

Obv.	Rev.
1. In f. to l. K. Beneath horse, Φ Ι. [Pl. III. 8. A. J. E.]	Taras seated sideways on dolphin to l. (cf. A 1), turning round to aim trident at tunny-fish. Below, curling waves. In f. to r. A.
2. Same. Car. cxiv. 214.	Same, but no letter in f., the trident with cross-bar at top.
3. Same. [My own specimen from the same die as No. 1.] B. M. Cat. 185. [Pl. III. 7. A. J. E.]	Same, but beneath dolphin Ͷ, and in field, where on coin No. 1 the letter A appears, a square raised tablet without inscription.
4. Same. Car. cxiv. 213.	Taras astride, &c., to l., his l. hand resting on the dolphin's back, and with his r. extending one-handled vase. In f. to l. K. Below, waves.

In the second group, as displaying a fuller and more broad-spread execution, I have included the following types, the first of which belongs to the very beginning of this Period and has, indeed, some claims to be placed within the limits of Period II.

III. Type H.

Naked youth on stationary horse to r., his r. arm hanging at his side, and the hair of his head bound up in a kind of topknot (*cirrus*), a fashion followed by those who took part in the games.[79]

---

[79] See Avellino's note in Carelli, *N. I. V.* p. 48. Visconti, *Mus. Pio Clementino*, T. V. tab. 36. Suetonius, *In Nerone*, c. 53.

Obv. | Rev.

1. ⊦E beneath horse. In front, bearded ithyphallic Herm, his head bound with a fillet.
Car. cxi. 144.
[Pl. III. 10.]

Taras astride, &c., to l., his body thrown back and its weight supported by his l. arm resting on the dolphin's tail, his right leg thrown forward, so as to be outlined in front of the fish's forehead, holding out in his r. an œnochoë.

2. Same; but beneath horse, HΣ.
B. M. Cat. 105.

Same.

III. Type K.

Naked boy crowning stationary horse to l., which lifts its off fore-leg. The boy has long flowing tresses but the horse's mane is closely cropped.

1. Horse to l.: beneath, a scallop.
B. M. Cat. 139.
[Pl. III. 11.]

Taras as a boy with flowing hair, astride, &c., his l. leg thrown forward, so as to be partly visible in front of dolphin's head. Taras holds kantharos.

2. Same; but no symbol: beneath horse, A P.
A. J. E.
[Pl. III. 12.]

Same; beneath dolphin, X.

3. Same; but Palladium beneath horse.
B. M. Cat. 138.
[Pl. III. 15.]

Same; but no symbol in Taras's hand. Beneath dolphin, P.

III. Type L.

Naked Ephèbos vaulting from horse cantering l.

1. Beneath horse, Λ (or Π).
B. M. Cat. 259: cf. Car. cxiii. 182.

Taras as a fat child astride, &c., holding out a fish downwards;[50] his further leg outlined as above. Beneath dolphin, A.

2. Same.
B. M. Cat. 261.

Same, but beneath P.

3. Beneath horse, ⊦.
B. M. Cat. 258.

Taras as an Ephèbos of solid build astride, &c., his further leg outlined, holding crested Corinthian helmet. Beneath dolphin, | and waves.

---

[50] Poseidôn is represented holding a fish in a similar manner on a fine red-figured amphora (Gerhard, *Trinkschalen und Gefässe*, Taf. xxi.).

Obv.	Rev.
4. Beneath horse, Δ. *B. M. Cat.* 254.	Same; but holding trident, which rests on l. shoulder. Beneath, K and waves.
5. No symbol or letter. A. J. E.	Taras to r. on dolphin, his further leg outlined in front of fish's head, holding trident in l. hand, and with r. hurling short harpoon. Below, ҒA.

III. Type M.

Horseman advancing l. in crested helmet, holding reins in r. hand; shield and spear in l.

1. Beneath horse, Δ. *B. M. Cat.* 193.	Taras holding trident on shoulder (as Type E, 1). Beneath, K and waves.

III. Type N.

Naked helmeted horseman, his back partially visible, and a shield behind him, cantering r.

1. Beneath horse Ғ. [Pl. XI. 5. Cab. des Méd. No. 1448.]	Taras seated sideways, to l., his l. hand resting on dolphin, and with r. holding out a one-handled vase. Beneath, Γ and waves.
2. Same. De Luynes Coll.	Same, but beneath, A and waves.

III. Type O.

Naked boy, his arm hanging at his side, on horse standing r. and lifting its off fore-leg.

1. Beneath horse, ☉. *B. M. Cat.* 106—107.	Taras astride, &c., behind dolphin, sometimes ☉.
2. Beneath horse, Γ. A. J. E.	Taras astride, &c., with open palm; outline of further leg just visible in front of dolphin's head.
3. ☉ under fore-leg; kantharos under horse's body. *B. M. Cat.* 108; cf. Car cix. 108.	Same, but Taras holds kantharos.

III. Type P.

Naked boy, his arm hanging at side, cantering, r.

Obv.	Rev.
1. Ϙ under horse's body. B. M. Cat. 110. [Pl. III. 16.]	Taras astride, &c., with open palm; outline of further leg as above. Behind, sometimes O or ⊙.

III. Type Q.

Naked horseman galloping r., with whip lowered behind him. (Cf. Type F.)

1. Beneath horse, ΔOP. (B.M.Cat. "AOP.") [Pl. III. 13. Imhoof-Blumer Coll.]	Taras, as a child of full proportions, astride, &c., to l., resting his l. hand on the dolphin's back, and throwing forward his l. leg, so that it is outlined in front of the fish's forehead. In his r. he extends a wreath.

III. Type R.

Naked horseman wearing crested helmet on prancing horse to r.

Beneath horse, O [⊙] and *kylix*. Car. cxl. 148.	Taras seated sideways to r. on dolphin, holding trident in l. hand. Plain border.

III. Type S.

Naked Ephêbos cantering l., holding small round shield behind him.

Beneath him, scallop and NI. Car. cxii. 178. B. M. Cat. 202.	Taras astride, &c., to l., his further leg outlined in front of dolphin's forehead, his l. hand resting on fish's back, and with r. extending bunch of grapes.

III. Type T.

Naked horseman vaulting off cantering horse to l., in circle of waves.

Beneath horse, A. B. M. Cat. 252. [Pl. III. 14.]	Taras seated sideways to r. on dolphin holding trident upwards in r. hand, and with l. resting on dolphin's back.

PERIOD IV.—ARCHIDÁMOS AND THE FIRST LUCANIAN WAR.

344—334 B.C.

We have now reached a Period when the evidence derivable from recent finds and other sources enables us to attempt a more exact system of chronology than has been possible in the earlier series. The fourteen years that elapsed between 344 and 330 B.C. embrace some of the most exciting and tragic episodes of Tarentine story. The year 344 was a memorable one in Tarentine annals, for it was at that date that the rich commercial city, hard pressed by its barbarian neighbours, first had recourse to the policy, so momentous in its future developments, of calling in foreign mercenaries and soldiers of fortune to fight its battles. The first summons of the kind was, however, addressed to a quarter which somewhat veiled the real character of the new political departure. The Tarentines, finding themselves unable to cope successfully with their warlike Messapian borderers, who had now begun to receive assistance from the still more powerful Lucanians, turned for help to their Spartan mother-city. Their kinsmen hearkened to their appeal, and the terms of alliance were already concluded in 344, though the actual landing of the Spartan king Archidâmos does not seem to have taken place till shortly before 338.[81] In that year Archidâmos and the greater part of the forces he had brought with him fell in battle under the walls of Manduria, on the same day and hour, Diodoros tells us, as that on which Philip was winning his "dishonest victory"

---

[81] Cf. Diodôros, xvi. 62, 63, and 88.

at Chæroneia. Four years later Tarentum was again reduced to seek a protector in Alexander the Molossian. The arrival of the Epirote prince at Tarentum forms, as I hope to show, one of the most definite landmarks in the numismatic history of this city. It is possible, as will be seen in the succeeding section, to fix certain gold and silver issues of Tarentum as belonging to the date of the expedition of the son of Neoptolemos in 334 B.C., and this fact reacts on the chronology of the present Period, as enabling us to bring down certain types which have the greatest affinity to these " Molossian " pieces, but which still do not present the Epirote badges found on the latter series, to that approximate date.

The policy on which the Tarentines had now definitely embarked of hiring foreign *condottieri* to fight their battles for them entailed a constant drain on the Tarentine treasury, and it was no doubt in a great degree to meet the demands of foreign mercenaries that, during this period, Tarentum began for the first time to issue a gold coinage. The recent discovery, to which we shall have occasion to return,[82] of a hoard of gold Tarentine and Macedonian staters, has thrown a new light on the gold coinage of Tarentum belonging to the Period that succeeds the expedition of the Molossian Alexander. But the types discovered in this hoard are by no means the earliest of the Tarentine gold issues, though in some respects they fit on to them, and we have therefore solid grounds for referring the earliest gold coins of the city to the present Period.

From their style alone there can be little doubt that in the beautiful pieces reproduced in Pl. V. 1 and 2, are to be

---

[82] See p. 97, *seqq.*

k

recognised the earliest gold staters of Tarentum. Both display as their obverse design a noble head of Dêmêtêr or Persephonê-Gaia, with *stephanê* and diaphanous Tarentine veil, the Ταράντιον or Ταραντινίδιον, that seems to have been woven from the gauzy tissue of the Pinna-shell, a form of textile industry still pursued by the inhabitants of modern Taranto. In one instance (Pl. V. 2) this design is accompanied on the reverse by a boy-rider crowning his steed, beneath which is an exquisite and naturalistic representation of a purple-shell or *murex*.[83] In the other case (Pl. V. 1) we find the head of the goddess associated with a reverse, exhibiting the infant Taras raising his hands in suppliant guise to his father Poseidôn, who, seated on his throne, graciously inclines his head towards his little son.[84] This design may, perhaps, be regarded

---

[83] "Τὸ δὲ Ταράντιον ἐξ οὗ διαφανῶς ἡ ὥρα διέλαμπε." Aristænetos, *Ep.* i. 25. Cf. Lorentz, *De Civ. Vet. Tarentinorum*, p. 26, 27. The head itself, the *stephanê* and arrangement of the hair, present a great resemblance to some beautiful terra-cotta heads of Persephonê-Gaia, recently discovered on the site of a temple of that goddess at Taranto (see *Hellenic Journal*, vol. vii. 1886, p. 28, Pl. lxiii.). In some cases there were traces of a veil. I am quite unable to subscribe to the view (*Notizie dei Scavi*, 1886, p. 279), that the head on these coins represents the nymph Satyra. On a fine Metapontine silver coin presenting a similar head (*v. infra*), the name ΔΑΜΑΤΗΡ is attached.

[84] In some cases there appears, as in Plate V. 2, a round shield in the field above; in others a rudder. Beneath the horse is the inscription ΚΥΛΙΚ. It is possible that we may in this case, as probably in the slightly later "Molossian" gold pieces inscribed ΑΠΟΛ, have to do with a magistrate's name; and in that case signatures of this class occur on the gold coinage of Tarentum at a somewhat earlier date than on the silver. (See p. 115.) Fiorelli, *Oss. sopra talune monete rare di Città greche* (Nap. 1843, p. 23), makes the fanciful suggestion that the inscription should be read

as, on the whole, the finest product of Tarentine monetary art. There is still about the majestic attitude of Poseidôn a lingering tradition of the scheme of the seated Dêmos on the earlier didrachm series which, as well as the surpassing beauty of the whole composition, leads us to regard this as the earliest of all the gold types of Tarentum. And if we recall the special character which Poseidôn bore at this city, it will not, perhaps, be considered over bold if we venture to bring this filial appeal of Taras to his father into direct relation with the appeal of Tarentum to its Lacedæmonian fatherland which in 338 found its answer in the landing of King Archidâmos. The Poseidôn worshipped at Tarentum was in fact the Poseidôn of Tænaron, who stood forth as the representative of Laconian maritime power; and so preponderant was this side of the Tarentine cult that the priests of Poseidôn were here called Ταιναρισται.[85] It is further to be observed in this connexion that behind the seated figure of Poseidôn on the present coin is seen the star of one of the Dioskuri, the protecting genii of Lacedæmon. There is certainly a fellow-feeling between this exquisite composition and that of the inscribed Corinthian mirror on which the nymph ΛΕΥΚΑϹ crowns her parent city ΚΟΡΙΝΘΟϹ, personified as Zeus, her mythic sire.[86]

The minute signature K, which appears within Poseidôn's throne on some examples of this fine coin, is of

---

ΚΥΛΙωνος; and that the shell or ΚογΚΥΛΙΟΝ should be regarded as a punning allusion. The murex in the sense of a "whorl-shell," however, may very possibly have been adopted by ΚΥΛΙΚ . . . as a *type parlant*.

[85] Hêsychios, *Lexicon*, s.v. Cf. p. 14.

[86] See especially Prof. P. Gardner, *Hellenic Journal*, ix. 62 ("Countries and Cities in Ancient Art").

great interest in its relation to the same signature on some of the finest silver types of the present Period, at times, as we shall see, taking the more expanded form of ΚΑΛ, in which I have ventured to recognise the first letters of the name of an engraver who was also active at this time in the Tarentine colony of Hêrakleia and in the neighbouring city of Metapontion. These parallels become the more significant when we find the beautiful obverse head of Dêmêtêr, peculiar to these Tarentine gold staters, closely reproduced with the same diaphanous veil, but with a corn-wreath in place of *stephané*, and with the name ΔAMATHP attached, on a fine contemporary didrachm of Metapontion,[87] presenting on its reverse side the signature of the artist ΚΑΛ . . .

If we turn to the didrachm series that, according to our approximate calculation, covered the same period of years as these earliest gold issues of Tarentum, we shall in fact find more than one point in common with the coins that I have ventured to associate with the name of Archidâmos. The picturesque style of art represented on the gold staters by the head of Dêmêtêr, with her luxuriant tresses and transparent veil, or the group of Taras and his father, harmonize well with the prevailing style of the silver coinage.

Period IV. of these equestrian types, with which we are now called on to deal, includes a space of years during which the engraver's art was maintained at the same high level that it had attained towards the conclusion of the preceding Period. In considering some of the noblest types of Period III., attention has already been called to the evidence they supply of the influence of the greater works of sculpture and painting. In the present class,

---

[87] Garrucci, Tav. ciii. 5.

although the sculpturesque element, especially that derived from bronze work, is by no means wanting, it is the limner's art that seems to have exercised the predominant influence. Greater variety in the design is secured by the introduction of new figures, and for pictorial effect Type E (Fig. 2), in which Taras is represented with his chlamys fluttering about him in the wind, while a small Victory flies forward and reaches forth a wreath to crown his brows, is almost unrivalled in the Tarentine series.

Fig. 2.

It is now for the first time that full mobility and freedom of execution is attained in the rendering of the horses. To this and the succeeding Period unquestionably belong the most magnificent and, at the same time, the most animated of the equestrian figures.

As already noticed,[88] the scheme first found in Period III. of Taras sitting sideways on his dolphin and turning round to aim his trident at the fish below, recurs on two rare coins (Types A 1 and F 1) belonging to the beginning of the present group, on which, however, the head of Taras is seen three-quarters facing instead of in profile. The persistent scheme of the preceding Period, in which Taras appears with his further leg thrown forward so that its outer line is just visible in front of the dolphin's forehead, forms a natural morphological link to a similar scheme of Taras as he appears on the present series.[89]

[88] See p. 50. [Pl. III. 6.]   [89] Type C 1 and 2.

The noble transitional scheme seen on the reverse of Type A 2 links this group of coins to another and finer series, which I have placed together under Type H of the present Period (Pl. IV. 9—11). All of these are associated on one or both faces with the signature ΚΑΛ, sometimes in association with ΑΡΙ or ΦΙ, and exhibiting Taras astride on his dolphin steed, with the heel of the further leg drawn back slightly behind the other. In some respects these coins represent the highest development of artistic execution to be found in the whole series of Tarentine issues. They are certainly the most imposing. In the rendering of the Eponymic Hero, here always given as a full-grown Ephêbos, a golden mean is observed between the somewhat heavy proportions of the older canon, as we find it still on some types of the present Period, and the over-attenuation of the style which came into vogue soon after this date. There is a largeness about these noble types of Taras which produce an impression quite disproportionate to the narrow compass of the coins. It is interesting to observe that the scheme of the arms and the upper part of the hero's body is practically identical with that of the fine types signed Α and Κ of the preceding Period, the Hêrakleian origin of which has been suggested above;[90] and this conformity supplies an additional reason for identifying these signatures with the ΑΡΙ and ΚΑΛ of the present series.

The consideration of this beautiful group signed ΚΑΛ leads us to the remarkable piece which I have placed under Type G (Pl. IV. 7), which supplies one of the most convincing examples of an engraver's signature on a Tarentine coin. On the type in question we find the same

---

[90] See p. 52, *seqq.*

signature, ΚΑΛ, associated in minute letters with the highly-finished and elaborate design of the armed horseman received by Victory—an admirable composition, which was imitated, as we shall see, at a somewhat later date, and in a bolder style. The signature itself appears in almost microscopic characters between the horse's hind legs, and again beneath the dolphin on the reverse. In another case we see (L, Pl. IV. 8), the horse and rider received by a standing Ephêbos. Affinity of subject, as well as the signature which at times appears on the reverse, links these to another of the most exquisite types (F, Pl. IV. 5, 6) of the present class, that, namely, on which a boyish figure is seen embracing the prancing steed of a still smaller boy-rider, with a warmth of affection as characteristically Italian in its expression as that of the children clustering round to kiss the legs and arms of the slayer of the Minotaur on the Herculanean fresco. In the present case, as is shown by the flying Victory behind, it is the winner of a race who is thus saluted.

In the case of the two last coins a most remarkable parallel is presented to the two pieces of the preceding Period (Pl. III. 7, 8) that have already on other grounds been referred to the same artistic collaboration as makes itself apparent on the present group. In the former instance we see the signature A alternating on otherwise identical reverses with a small raised tablet. In the present case the signature Κ which appears in the field behind Taras on his dolphin on Type F 3 (Pl. IV. 5), is replaced on the similar reverse of Type F 4 (Pl. IV. 6), by a raised tablet of the same kind, the Κ itself, however, being repeated in this instance in front of Taras. This coincidence must be taken as a further proof of the intimate connexion of the two engravers of this and the preceding Period who sign **A** or **API**, **K** or **KAΛ**. In Type F 5, we find the signature **K** associated with a scallop-shell instead of the tablet, which recalls the fact that on the Hêrakleian coin (Fig. 1, p. 54) already adduced as in all probability the handiwork of an artist who signs as **K** or **KAΛ** on the Tarentine dies, the signature **KAΛ** is seen associated with the same scallop symbol.

These types signed **K** and **KAΛ** must rank, alike for design and execution, amongst the most perfect products of the Tarentine mint, and are, as already suggested, in all probability to be referred to the same artist who, on the gold staters described above, attaches the signature **K** to the beautiful group of Taras and his father Poseidôn. Nor was the activity of this engraver by any means confined to the Tarentine dies. The same signature, as we have already seen, is found at Hêrakleia associated with the fine design of Hêraklês strangling the lion [91]; and at Metapontion it appears on the coin bearing on its obverse the head of Dêmêtêr, with her name **ΔAMATHP** attached;[92] and again on another beautiful piece of the same city, beside the three-quarter face representation of the youthful Dionysos ivy-crowned,[93] a type which has much in common with the three-quarter head of Apollo on a fine

---

[91] *B. M. Cat.*, Heraclea, 28, 29. See p. 54, Fig. 1.

[92] Garrucci, *Monete dell' Italia Antica*, T. ciii. 5. The head of Dêmêtêr, with the diaphanous veil hanging down behind, closely corresponds with that on the Tarentine gold staters of Archidámos and Alexander the Molossian's time. The *stephanê* however, is here replaced by a corn-wreath.

[93] A blundered representation of this almost unique type, with both obverse and reverse inscription wrongly given, is engraved in Garrucci, *op cit.* T. civ. 13. I recently obtained a fine specimen of this piece at Ruvo (Rubi) in Apulia. The obverse legend is **KAΛ** (in Garrucci, "**MOΛ**") the reverse, **ΦIΛO** (Garr. "**Φ**").

silver diobol struck by the Molossian Alexander in Italy.[94] On another Metapontian piece, indeed, the signature ΚΑΛ appears on the reverse of a type exhibiting the oak-crowned head of the Dodonæan Zeus, which must undoubtedly be brought into relation with the landing of the Epirote prince.[95] We have thus an interesting indication that the activity of this engraver continued at least to the approximate date 334 B.C. The fellow-engraver who signs ΑΡΙ is probably, as already pointed out,[96] the artist who, on Hêrakleian and Metapontian pieces contemporary with those cited, reveals the full form of his name, ΑΡΙΣΤΟΞΕΝΟΣ. This Aristoxenos must have been the contemporary of the well-known Tarentine philosopher and musician of that name, the pupil of Aristotle.

The synchronism established by the Metapontian coin already cited, is further borne out by some independent evidence supplied by some Tarentine gold staters and didrachms with "Molossian" types and symbols. The noble obverse types, presenting the same signature, ΚΑΛ [Type II; Pl. IV. 9—11], in which there appears for the first time the well-known scheme of the horseman lancing downwards on his prancing steed — a design of such frequent occurrence on the Tarentine issues of the succeeding age—can in fact be also approximately dated from their affinity to a type struck at the time of the Epirote Alexander's expedition. The scheme as it appears on the present group of coins differs from the later series, on which the same representation occurs, in a particular which is not without its chronological value. The horseman is here seen surrounded by a beaded border, an early characteristic which soon after this time wholly

---

[94] Pl. V. 7.   [95] See p. 82.   [96] See p. 54.

disappears from the Tarentine dies. The same border, however, surrounding the same horseman type, is found on a Tarentine gold stater struck, as I hope to show, at the time of Alexander the Molossian's arrival, and again on the contemporary didrachm series already referred to as presenting the Molossian symbol. The close relation existing between the coins of the present group signed ΚΑΛ and these Molossian types shows that their issue is to be referred to the years immediately preceding 334 B.C.

The reverse of these coins, on which the Eponymic Hero of Tarentum is seen, between the two eight-rayed stars that symbolize the Dioskuri, pensively contemplating a heroic helmet that he holds between his hands, is of a highly suggestive character. The two stars occur again above the riding figures of the Dioskuri on some gold types of the succeeding Period (Pl. V. 10) in which I have ventured to trace a reference to the renewed alliance at that time concluded between Tarentum and its mother-city.

May we in the twin Tyndarid emblem on the present types, as on the gold coin depicting Taras and his father Poseidôn, venture to trace a kindred reference to the earlier alliance with Lacedæmon?

The comparison with the coins struck at Tarentum at the time of the coming of the Molossian Alexander enables us, as we have seen, to refer this beautiful series to the years preceding the date 334 B.C. In 338 B.C. the Spartan King Archidâmos met a hero's death before the rock-hewn trenches of Manduria,[97] and that his fall should have received a numismatic tribute at the hands of the Tarentines will seem the more pro-

---

[97] Diodôros, xvi. 63, "ἐν τινι μάχῃ διαγωνισάμενος λαμπρῶς ἐτελεύτησεν."

bable when taken in connexion with the other honours which, as we learn from historic sources, were paid by them to his memory. Theopompos [98] informs us that the body of the Spartan king was left on the field of the disaster, but that so desirous were the Tarentines of showing him funeral honours that they vainly offered a large sum of money for the recovery of the hero's corpse. For the same reason he alone among the Spartan kings received a monument at Olympia. The attitude in which Taras upon these coins contemplates the casque that he holds between his hands, his head slightly bowed as that of a mourning leave-taker on a monument of the Kerameikos, might itself suggest that in this highly artistic composition we have a graceful allegoric tribute to the death of the Spartan hero.[99] Appearing as it does upon the Tarentine dies at such a time of national disaster and of unsatisfied desire to commemorate the fallen with a worthy monument, this personification of the Tarentine city between the

---

[98] *Ap. Athenæum*, lib. xii. (ed. Schweighauser, iv. 492), "Ἀρχίδαμος ἐν τῷ πολέμῳ ἀποθανὼν οὐδὲ ταφῆς κατηξιώθη, καίτοι Ταραντίνων πολλὰ χρήματα ὑποσχομένων τοῖς πολεμίοις ὑπὲρ τοῦ ἀνελέσθαι αὐτοῦ τὸ σῶμα." From Pausanias, vi. 4, 9 (cf. vi. 18, 7), we learn that the want of a tomb was in some measure supplied by a monument at Olympia.

[99] The type was revived in a somewhat variant form at the date of Pyrrhus's expedition, Taras in this case being, as I hope to show (p. 149), assimilated in pose and *coiffure* to the Apollo on contemporary coins of Antiochos I., and holding in his hand, moreover, a horned helmet of Seleukid type. The reason of this complimentary allusion is to be found in the pecuniary assistance lent by Antiochos to Pyrrhus and the Tarentines; and the helmet, in all probability, is to be interpreted as conveying a respectful tribute to Seleukos Nikâtôr, then recently deceased. If this supposition be correct, we obtain a further warrant for regarding the figure on the present coin as having a memorial character.

two tutelary stars of the Spartan mother-city could hardly be without allusive significance to a hero of whom himself it might be truly said:

"'Αστὴρ πρὶν μὲν ἔλαμπες ἐνὶ ζωοῖσιν ἑῷος
Νῦν δὲ θανὼν λάμπεις ἕσπερος ἐν φθιμένοις."

IV. Type A.

Naked boy rider to r., crowning stationary horse which raises off fore-leg, and crowned himself by flying Victory.

Obv.	Rev.
1. Beneath horse, **AP**. Garr. T. cxviii. 28.	Taras to r. as an Ephêbos, seated sideways on dolphin, and turning round to strike with his trident a tunny fish below. The whole design enclosed in a circle of waves.
2. Beneath horse, ≤ IM. [Pl. IV. 2.]	Taras, as an Ephêbos of somewhat finer proportions to l., on dolphin, his further leg drawn up and visible to the knee. His left hand lightly rests on the fish's back, holding a trident, the lower end of which rests on his ankle. With his r. he extends a kantharos. Beneath dolphin ⊢HP, and curling waves.

IV. Type B.

Naked boy crowning his horse, which stands r., raising its off fore-leg.

Obv.	Rev.
1. Beneath horse, **K** and club. Car. cxii. 163. [Pl. IV. 1.]	Taras to l. riding on dolphin, holding in l. hand a trident and small round shield, and with his r. extending a kantharos. Beneath, Ω and waves. Plain ring border.

IV. Type C.

Naked boy crowning standing horse, as on Type B, but beneath is another naked boy picking a pebble out of the horse's hoof.

PERIOD IV.

Obv.	Rev.
1. In f. to r. Φ. A. J. E.	Taras, as an obese youth astride dolphin, his further leg thrown forward and outlined along fish's head; he holds in his r. hand a kantharos, and in his l. a small round shield and trident. Beneath, E and waves.
2. Same. Car. cxiv. 217.	Same; but no trident. Beneath, Π and waves.
3. Same. [Pl. IV. 3.]	Taras as an obese youth seated sideways on dolphin, holding in r. hand kantharos, and in l. trident and small round shield (as 1 and 2). Beneath, E and waves.
4. Same. Car. cxiv. 218.	Same, but no letter. Beneath dolphin, waves.
5. Same. B. M. Cat. 184.	Same, but Π; beneath dolphin, waves.

IV. Type D.

Naked warrior standing behind his horse r., helmeted, and holding spear and large round shield.

1. In f. to r. Ͱ. Car. cxi. 143. [Pl. IV. 4.]	Taras seated sideways on dolphin to l., holding trident in r. hand, and with l. small round shield. Beneath, A and waves.

IV. Type E.

Horseman in crested helmet, with chlamys flowing behind him, holding shield in his l. hand and a lance, point upwards, in his righ', a prancing horse to r.

1. Beneath horse, ΔAI. Car. cxi. 138. *Mus. Naz. di Napoli.* 1898. [Cf. Garr. T. cxviii. 20. *Obv.* " Δλ." *Rev.* " Λ."] [Pl. XI. 7.]	Taras astride, &c., to l., his chlamys flowing behind him. His l. hand rests on dolphin's back, and his r. holds a trident, while a small Victory flies forward to crown him. Beneath, waves and Ͱ. [See Fig. 2, p. 69.]

IV. Type F.

Naked boy crowned by flying Victory on prancing horse to r., which is embraced by another naked boy. Design in beaded circle.

Obv.	Rev.
1. ⊥ beneath horse. [Pl. XI. 6. Santangelo Coll.]	Taras seated sideways on dolphin to r., turning back to aim his trident at tunny-fish. Beneath, waves. In f. to l., Ϲ, and under Taras's r. arm a square raised tablet.
2. Same; but K beneath horse. Cab. des Méd.	Same: but in f. ⊥.
3. Same; but ⊥. Car. cxi. 150. *B. M. Cat.* 172. [Pl. IV. 5.]	Taras astride, &c. to l., extending one-handled vase. Behind, K.
4. Same. Leake Coll. [Pl. IV. 6.]	Same; but K in front of Taras, and behind, a square raised tablet.
5. Same. Car. cxi. 149.	Same; but scallop in place of tablet.

IV. Type G.

Naked horseman in crested helmet to l., holding in his l. hand behind him two lances and a round shield, on which is a hippocamp. In front, winged Victory, clad in diploïdion, advancing l., turns half round and seizes the rearing steed by the rein and forelock.

Above, TAPAN-TINΩN in minute letters. In f. to r. ͰA. Beneath horse, M and KAΛ in minute letters. Santangelo Coll. Cf. Car. cxii. 167. *B. M. Cat.* 272. [Pl. IV. 7.]	Taras astride, &c., to r., throwing forward l. leg, hurling dart with r., and in his l. holding two spears or lances, while his chlamys, caught on his l. arm, streams in the wind. Beneath, KAΛ in minute letters, and waves.

IV. Type H.

Naked horseman on prancing horse to r., lancing downwards with r. hand; behind, a large round shield and reserve of two lances; the whole within a beaded border.

Obv.

1. In f. to l., ⊢; to r., A. Beneath horse,
KAΛ.
A.
B. M. Cat. 213.
[Pl. IV. 11.]

Rev.

Taras astride on dolphin, holding a crested helmet between his hands, with his head slightly bowed towards it. In f., on either side, an eight-rayed star. Beneath, dolphin ΦI.

2. Same.
B. M. Cat. 210.
[Pl. IV. 10.]

Same. Beneath dolphin, API.

3. Same.
B. M. Cat. 211.

Same. Beneath dolphin, KAΛ.

4. Same. *Nervegna Coll.*

Same. Beneath dolphin, ONA.

5. Same; but in f. to l. A, to r. N. Beneath horse, KAΛ
X.
Car. cxii. 159. B. M. Cat. 212.
[Pl. IV. 9.]

Same: but no stars. Beneath dolphin, KAΛ.

6. Same; in f. to r., N. Beneath horse, KAΛ
N.
Car. cxii. 160.
[Pl. XI. 8. Cab. des Méd.]

Taras astride, &c., to l., his further leg outlined in front of dolphin's head. He holds in his l. hand a small round shield, displaying a hippocamp, and extends his r. to receive a small wreath-bearing Victory. In f. to r., K. Beneath, dolphin, waves, and small tunny-fish.

IV. Type K.

Two Dioskuri cantering, r.

1. Above TAPAN . . . Beneath horse, KAΛ. Microscopic letters. (*Nervegna Coll.*)

Same as H. 6. Taras holds two spears and hippocamp shield. Beneath, KAΛ and waves.

IV. Type L.

Naked male figure standing l., and half turning round to seize forelock and bridle of stationary horse, his l. hand, which is laid on the bridle, holds a wreath. On the horse is a naked boy. The whole in a minutely beaded border.

Obv.	Rev.
1. Above, **TA-PANTINΩN**. In f. to l., ⊢; to r., Δ. Beneath horse, **KAΛ**. Microscopic letters. [Pl. IV. 8, Santangelo Coll.]	Taras as an Ephêbos riding on dolphin to r., his further leg resting on the fish's forehead; he holds out in his l. hand a strung bow and two arrows, and in his r., behind him, another arrow. Beneath, ΦI in microscopic letters.

PERIOD V.—FROM THE MOLOSSIAN ALEXANDER TO THE SPARTAN KLEONYMOS.
334—302 B.C.

The continued progress of the Lucanian, Messapian, and other allied barbarian tribes once more induced the Tarentine in the true spirit of a mediæval Italian Republic to look abroad for the services of some princely *condottiere*. A suitable champion was found in the Epirote King, the Molossian Alexander, son of Neoptolomos, who, through his sister Olympias and his wife Cleopatra, was doubly related to his great namesake of Macedon, and whose ambition was already aroused by his kinsman's growing fame. Blind to the true meaning of his own Dodonæan oracle, which bade him shun Pandosia and the waters of Acherôn,[100] the would-be Alexander of the West set sail for Italy in 334 [101] with fifteen war-ships and numerous transports. The Tarentines, however, were

---

[100] Ἀιακίδη προφύλαξο μολεῖν Ἀχερούσιον ὕδωρ
Πανδοσίαντε ὅτι τοι θάνατος πεπρωμένος ἐστί.

[101] For the chronology of the Molossian Alexander's expedition, cf. Droysen, *Geschichte des Hellenismus*.

not long in recognising in their new ally one who threatened to become their master. The Molossian Prince not only routed their immediate neighbours, the Messapians and Daunians, but carrying his arms to the Tyrrhene shores, had already defeated the allied Lucanians and Samnites in a great battle at Pæstum, and concluded an alliance with Rome against the common foe. He was already too powerful for the jealous Tarentine Republic, and the causes of rupture were not far to seek. Alexander had recovered the Tarentine colony of Hêrakleia, the seat since Archytas's time of the federal council of the Italian Greeks, from the hands of the barbarians, only to retain it under his own dominion, while at the same time he transferred the seat of the Assembly to a site on the territory of the more distant Thurioi.[102] When the Epirote King started on his final campaign against the Bruttians open hostilities seemed about to break out between him and the Tarentines, and the task of observing their movements in Alexander's interest was confided to their Metapontine neighbours. The death of the Molossian in 330 B.C. beneath the walls of the Italian Pandosia, and beside the waters of the Italian Acherôn, brought nothing but a sense of relief to the Tarentines.

The brief but glorious Italian adventure of the Epirote Alexander is of great importance in the history of the Magna-Græcian coinages, for which it supplies more than one landmark. Alexander's arrival at Tarentum is, perhaps indirectly, connected with the first issue by this city shortly after this time, of a class of gold staters pre-

---

[102] Strabo vi. 3. "ὁ γοῦν Ἀλέξανδρος τὴν κοινὴν Ἑλλήνων τῶν ταύτῃ πανήγυριν, ἣν ἔθος ἦν ἐν Ἡρακλείᾳ συντελεῖν τῆς Ταραντίνης, μετάγειν ἐπειρᾶτο εἰς τὴν Θουρίαν κατὰ ἔχθος, ἐκέλευέ τε κατὰ τὸν Ἀκάλανδρον ποταμὸν τειχίζειν τόπον, ὅπου ἔσοιντο αἱ σύνοδοι."

senting the Macedonian types of the youthful head of Hêraklês with a biga on the reverse. These coins continued to be issued in association with other gold types at a considerably later date,[103] but the occurrence on some of them of the Epirote symbols of the thunderbolt and lance-head may incline us to refer the earliest issues to the time of the Molossian's expedition. There is, however, as we shall see, more certain evidence of the connexion of the son of Neoptolemos with the Tarentine gold coinage.

Alexander himself signalized his arrival by striking coins both of gold and silver in his own name. These noble pieces have a distinctly Italo-Greek character, and are generally supposed to have been struck at Tarentum itself. That this is true of some of them need not be disputed, but historical considerations preclude us from supposing that the later of the Molossian's Italian issues were struck at this city.

It is probable that some at least of these were struck at Metapontion, which city, as we have already seen, remained the bulwark of Alexander's power in the South-West at a time when the Tarentines were turning against him. The nearest parallel to the Italian types of the Epirote adventurer is in fact supplied by some fine didrachms of Metapontion, presenting on the obverse the oak-crowned head of the Dodonæan Zeus accompanied by a thunderbolt in the field.[104] On another Metapontine didrachm, evidently belonging to the same time, the head of Zeus is laurel-crowned and accompanied, as upon the

---

[103] See pp. 99, 209.
[104] Car. clii. 54. *Rev.* Corn-spike; *inscr.* **METAPON**, and in f. to r. **KA**.. (on others **KAΛ**).

Syracusan coins of the same approximate date, by the inscription ΕΛΕΥΘΕΡΙΟϚ.[105]

This latter type also suggests comparisons with a class of Locrian didrachms[106] on which, moreover, the treatment of the hair of Zeus presents a striking resemblance to that upon the Molossian coins. What special part may have been played by the Epizephyrian Locrians in Alexander's expedition history fails to record, but the numismatic parallel is by no means confined to the head of Zeus. The thunderbolt that forms the reverse type of the Italian coins of the son of Neoptolemos recurs upon these Locrian pieces alternating with the seated eagle, which in the series struck by the Epirote prince is the almost invariable symbol in the field; there is, moreover, one small Locrian coin which presents the distinctive characteristics of a class of alliance pieces struck at the time of this Molossian connexion.[107] The widening breach between Alexander and the Tarentines, as well as the Western range of his military operations, makes it impossible to suppose that his later issues at all events were struck at Tarentum, and considering that his last campaign was directed against the Bruttians, it is highly probable that at this time he may have had recourse to Locrian moneyers, perhaps even to Syracusan.[108]

---

[105] Gar. cii. 84.
[106] Car. clxxxix. 6—11.
[107] See p. 87. Garr. T. cxii. 20.
[108] The similarity of some Locrian didrachms to Alexander's types inclines me to go a step farther and detect in the well-known Syracusan bronze struck soon after the date of Timoleon's expedition, representing on the obverse the head of Zeus Eleutherios, and on the reverse the thunderbolt and seated eagle, exactly as it appears on the Molossian's coins, a direct tribute to the Western Alexander, the heaven-sent champion of the

That the earliest coins of the Molossian in Italy were struck at Tarentum there can, however, be little doubt. We possess, indeed, direct numismatic evidence that Alexander concluded a monetary convention with the Tarentines, in which the Rubastines [109] and probably other cities joined. There exist some small Tarentine gold pieces only ·3 inch in diameter, and weighing a little over six and a half grains [Pl. V. 5], showing on the obverse side a rayed full-faced head of Hêlios, and on the reverse a thunderbolt with the inscription above and below it— ΑΠΟΛ ΤΑΡΑΝ.[110]

A small silver coin with a similar head of Hêlios was struck at Rubi, in Apulia,[111] and must certainly be regarded as an alliance-piece. But the great interest attaching to the Tarentine type is due to the fact that it in every way resembles certain coins of the Molossian prince struck during the Italian expedition. These coins are of the following types:—

Italiote Greeks against the barbarians, who certainly included Sicily in his far-reaching schemes. The head of Zeus, with the inscription ΕΛΕΥΘΕΡΙΟΣ, on the Metapontine piece already described, strongly corroborates this view.

[109] See Avellino, *Epistola de Argenteo Anecdoto Rubastinorum Numo*, Naples, 1844. The parallelism between the small gold pieces of Tarentum, signed ΑΠΟΛ, and those of Alexander the Molossian, was pointed out by Millingen, *Unedited Coins of Greek Cities and Kings*, p. 11.

[110] See Pl. V. 5; cf. *B. M. Cat.* 30, 31, 32, where the weights are respectively 6·7, 6·5, and 6·6 grs. Garrucci, T. c. 57, 58, one reads ΤΑΡ ΑΠ. This ΑΠΟΛ... must not be confounded with the magistrate who signs ΑΠΟΛ. ΑΠΟΛΛΩΝ in Pyrrhus's time, or the ΑΠΟΛΛΩΝΙΟΣ of Period VIII.

[111] *Rev.* ΡΥ on either side of two crescents; above, ΑΛ; between the crescents, two dots. *B. M. Cat.*, Rub. No. 4; Garrucci, T. xciv 26.

Obv.	Rev.
1 ℕ. Rayed head of Hélios, as above. [Pl. V. 6. B. M.]	ΑΛΕΞ and thunderbolt.
2 Æ. Same. [Pl. V. 7.][112]	ΑΛΕΞΑΝΔΡΟΥ ΝΕ●ΠΤ●Λ above and below thunderbolt.

Here, then, we have monetary evidence of an alliance concluded, about the year 334, between the Tarentines, Rubastines, and the Epirote prince. But the contemporaneity thus established of these small Tarentine gold pieces signed ΑΠΟΛ with the first period of Alexander's Italian sojourn enables us to fix the approximate date of the following gold staters (Pl. V. 3 and 4), on which the same signature appears, associated in the field with the thunderbolt symbol:—

ΤΑΡΑ. Veiled head of Dêmêtêr or Persephoné-Gaia to r., crowned with stephané. Dolphin in field, r. Carelli, T. ciii. 10. [Pl. V. 3, 4.]	Naked horseman, with reserve of round shield and two lances, lancing downwards, on prancing horse. In field, r., thunderbolt; beneath horse, ΑΠΟΛ or ΑΠ.

The exquisite head of the Chthonic goddess, with her diaphanous veil, on the obverse of this coin, is identical in character with the same head on the stater already referred to, which exhibits on the reverse the figures of Taras and his father Poseidôn. Reasons have been adduced for believing that this latter gold stater belongs to the time of Archidâmos' expedition, and may be approximately referred to the year 338, a date which agrees very well with the slightly later issue of the present coin, with the same

---

[112] From the Sim Collection; weight, 17·7 grs.

obverse type, but with a new reverse presenting the thunderbolt symbol in the field—a complimentary allusion [113] to the advent of Dodona's lord in the city of Taras. This symbol, as we have seen, is equally characteristic of the small alliance pieces and of the gold staters of Macedonian type that also make their appearance at Tarentum about this time.

The type of the horseman lancing downwards, as seen on these "Molossian" gold staters, is a familiar feature on a considerable series of Tarentine didrachms. It first appears in the case of the beautiful coins signed ΚΑΛ, already mentioned as representing some of the latest issues of Period IV.; it is only, however, during the present Period that it becomes general, and, indeed, almost universal. In the ensuing series it is less frequent, and about the time of Pyrrhus it disappears entirely from the Tarentine dies. In the case of our gold staters, however, there is an adjunct which reduces the field of comparison to very narrow limits. The whole design is here surrounded by a beaded circle, which has been already noticed as an early characteristic associated with the first silver issues of this lanceman type struck at the close of Period IV. On the later issues of this type it is entirely absent. It occurs, however, on a remarkable group of coins, exhibiting the same design, which I have placed together as Type A of the present Period, and which, from their close affinity to the latest coins struck during Period IV., must be regarded as representing its earliest issue.

---

[113] Compare the elephant symbol which appears below the type of later Tarentine coins, to commemorate the arrival of Pyrrhus.

But the connexion thus established between this didrachm type and the gold stater of Alexander the Molossian's time is borne out by a still more interesting particular. The small group of coins which I have included in Type A are distinguished from all other Tarentine issues by a symbol which might by itself be regarded as sufficient ground for bringing them into relation with the Epirote prince. Each and all of these five coins display in the field a seated eagle with folded wings, a characteristic Molossian device which occurs as the principal type on the coins of the Molossian Commonwealth struck immediately before Alexander's time, and which he himself perpetuated on his bronze Epirote coinage. As a symbol it admirably personified the settled and indwelling divinity of the Dodonæan oak—that Zeus Naïos, "the abider,"[114] whose oracle the Molossian had so fatally misread. Alexander, however, was not unmindful of his national emblem in his trans-Adriatic enterprise, and the seated eagle appears beside the thunderbolt in the field of most of his Italian silver pieces. That it was used, moreover, by his Italian allies as a federal badge appears from a small Locrian silver piece,[115] which, from its analogy with the other small alliance pieces already described, must be placed in the same category. Its obverse type, a thunderbolt, with ΛΟΚ above and two annulets below,

---

[114] It is impossible not to believe that this was the underlying idea of the epithet ναῖος, as applied to the Dodonæan Zeus in early times. Homer, Il. ii. 233, harps on the aspect of Zeus as the "dweller," and of his ὑποφῆται, " dwelling " round him. The scholiast's explanation of ναῖος as " flowing," or " watery," was certainly not the Homeric sense. Settled dwelling is the root idea of all tree-divinities. The god is first the tree itself; afterwards the tree is the god's abiding seat.

[115] Garrucci, T. cxii. 20.

closely copies the pieces struck in the names of the Tarentines, Rubastines, and Alexander himself; but on the other side, in place of the rayed head of the Sun, we find in this case the seated Molossian eagle. There can be little remaining doubt that this same symbol occupying the field of these Tarentine didrachms points to the same connexion, and we may therefore fix the date of their issue during the years (334—331 inclusive) that intervened between Alexander's landing and his final rupture with Tarentum, which seems to have taken place shortly before his death in 330.

V. Type A.

Time of ALEXANDER THE MOLOSSIAN, 334—330 B.C.

Naked horseman lancing downwards, &c., to r., within beaded circle. On the reverse, a seated eagle.

Obv.	Rev.
1. In f. to r. ΑR. Beneath horse ΦΙ. [Pl. VI. 1. A. J. E.]	Taras, of corpulent proportions, astride, &c., to l., his farther leg outlined in front of dolphin's head. His l. hand is lightly laid on the fish's back, and holds a trident; in his r. he holds out a one-handled vase. Beneath, large curling crests of waves. In f. to r., seated eagle with folded wings.
2. Same; but ΑR to l. (ΦΙ beneath horse, as before.) Car. cxiv. 215.	Taras as a plump child, a flower-like top-knot rising from his forehead, astride to l., laying his r. hand on dolphin's head, and holding in his l., which is raised to his side, a distaff, with spirally twisted wool. Beneath, ΦΙ and curling waves. In f. to l., seated eagle with folded wings.
3. Same. A. J. E.	Taras, a plump child, as before, but of larger dimensions. In f. to l., ΦΙΛΙΣ; to r., seated eagle. Beneath, large curling waves.

PERIOD V.   89

Obv.	Rev.
4. Same. A. J. E.	Same; but child Taras not so large; eagle to l.; and ΦΙ and smaller waves below.
5. Same. Car. cxiv. 216. B. M. Cat. 235. [Pl. VI. 2.]	Same; but ΦΙΛΙΣ in f. to l., and eagle to r. Beneath, waves as before.
6. Same; but ΣΙΜ beneath horse. Car. cxiii. 192. B. M. Cat. 233.	Same as No. 4.
7. Same as No. 6. Car. cxiii. 193. [Pl. VI. 3.]	Same; but eagle in f. to l.; ΦΙ and large curling waves below.
8. Same: but beneath horse, ΣΙ. [Pl. VI. 4.]	Same; but no waves.

The coins of this "Molossian" type are characterized by the appearance on the Tarentine dies of a peculiar and well-marked representation of Taras as a decidedly fleshy child, holding in the left hand a distaff wound round with wool. The rounded obese figure, as seen on the earliest coins of this class—in some cases even verging on caricature—fits on morphologically to the somewhat stumpy and heavy though maturer form of the Eponymic hero as he appears on some of the most characteristic types of the two preceding Periods.

The motive for the intrusion of this somewhat ungainly type into the Tarentine series was, perhaps, supplied by a certain aspect of local religious cult, on which a new light has been recently thrown by the discovery of large deposits of votive terra-cotta figures, in tombs and upon the site of temples formerly contained within the walls of

Tarentum. In the tombs have been found a class of abnormally fat childish figures, some of which, as, for instance, a winged genius crowned with ivy-leaves and berries, have a distinct Bacchic connexion. And the curious phase in Tarentine art-fashion attested by these figures seems, in fact, to have been associated with a deeply-rooted Tarentine cult of the Chthonic Dionysos, his consort Persephonê-Kora, and their mystic progeny, the infant Iacchos, the plastic representations of whom have been found by the thousand on the site of a local sanctuary.[116] In the manifold representations of the Eponymic founder on the Tarentine coinage, it is usual to find him endowed, not only with the attributes, but also with the attitude and aspect of various divinities. Not only does he bear the trident of his father Poseidôn, but at times he brandishes it in a distinctly Poseidôn-like fashion. Not only do we see him with the tripod or the laurel spray, the arrows of the Python-slayer or the Hyacinthian flower, but at times he wears Apollo's locks and imitates his pose.[117] The kantharos of Dionysos is of frequent occurrence, and it is found, though at a slightly later date, in the hand of the strange infantile type of Taras with which we are dealing,[118] in which case it singularly recalls the mystic cup stretched forth by the infant Iacchos on the votive Tarentine terra-cottas. A still more unfailing accompaniment, however, of this impersonation of Taras is the distaff wound round with wool, which, again, suggests an interesting comparison with a figure of the infant Dionysos of the Mysteries as it occurs on an

---

[116] *Hell. Journal*, 1886—8.
[117] See p. 149.
[118] Cf. VL F 1, reading on obv. **NIKOΔAMOΣ**; rev. **ΣOP**.

Apulian krater.[119] On this vase, which, if not actually of Tarentine work, at least belongs to the Tarentine school of ceramic art, the mystic offspring of Kora is seen depicted as a plump child, and holding in his right hand what is described as a thyrsos, but which, with its spirally-twisted top, is hardly to be distinguished from the distaff on the coins. He is represented in a squatting attitude, half-raising himself on one knee, and with the other drawn up under him, while he props himself up on his left arm. Above him is inscribed the name Dionysos, and to the left appears the head of Persephonê-Kora, accompanied by the first four letters of her mystic Samothracian name Axiokersa. Both the figure on the vase and Taras in his peculiar infantile impersonation have their hair bound up into a kind of top-knot above the forehead—a feature seemingly confined to this distaff-holding type. In the case of a small Tarentine gold coin,[120] the parallel to the figure on the vase is even closer. There the infant Taras is represented in an almost identical attitude, half raising himself on one knee and with the other bent under him, and holding the distaff in his right hand. The head on the obverse of this small gold type is probably that of Persephonê.

These comparisons lead us to the conclusion that the

---

[119] *Archæologische Zeitung*, 1850, Taf. xvi., described by Gerhard, p. 161, *seqq*.

[120] Pl. V, 13 (B.M.); cf. Carelli, T. cii. 8; Garrucci, *Monete dell' Italia Antica*, T. c. 63. The left arm of Taras in this representation, though held downwards, does not, as in the case of the figure on the vase, rest on the ground; nor could it, since a small dolphin below indicates the sea. In Taras's left hand is seen a circular object, perhaps a wreath, towards which the child directs his gaze. The infant Dionysos on the vase looks to the right towards the figure of his mother Axiokersa.

plump infantile representation of Taras which at this time makes its first appearance in the Tarentine dies, is to be regarded as approximating to that of the mystic child Iacchos, and marks the influence of a prevalent Chthonic cult on that of the Eponymic founder. The type was revived more than once on later periods of the Tarentine coinage, but these revivals are easily distinguished from their prototypes of the present class, which, besides their earlier fabric, are in almost all cases associated with the signature ΦΙΛΙΣ or its abbreviations.

In Type B, Nos. 1—5 inclusive, I have collected a series of coins which both from their type and their signature ΦΙ, ΦΙΛΙ, stand in immediate relation to the Molossian group. On these coins, however, the beaded border and the eagle symbol are no longer found. The child Taras too is rendered with less exaggerated corpulence, and after successive modifications is transformed into a youth of elegant proportions, the somewhat slimmer successor of the noble Ephêbos who appears on the coins signed ΚΑΛ at the close of the preceding Period IV. This type now again begins to predominate.

That these coins in fact belong to the period of Tarentine history that succeeded the fall of the Molossian Alexander in 330, is fully corroborated by the evidence of an interesting find of Tarentine and Campanian and other coins that I saw at Naples in 1884. The find itself was discovered in Samnium, to the west of Benevento, and for convenience I shall refer to it as the Beneventan Find. It contained besides about two hundred Campanian pieces of Neapolis, Hyrina, and Nola, some coins of Velia, and a few of Metapontion and Tarentum, and—especially valuable as an indication of date—a certain number of Romano-Campanian pieces, some of the type representing the bearded head of Mars with the horse's head on the reverse, and others fresh from the mint bearing on their obverse the youthful head of Hercules and the wolf and twins on their reverse. A brief account of the specimens belonging to this find that I was able to secure will be found under Appendix A.

Of the Romano-Campanian coins, those with the bearded head of Mars, both from their style and the condition in which they were found in this find, are obviously the earlier. Mommsen [121] is of opinion that the issue of the coins reading **ROMANO** is to be referred to the earliest period of the Roman occupation of Capua, and therefore begins shortly after the year 338 B.C. On the other hand, coins of slightly reduced weight also reading **ROMANO** began in all probability to be struck before 300. It therefore appears that the date of the deposition of the Beneventan hoard, which contained no coins of the latter class, must lie between these two years. At the same time, the comparatively used condition of the coins presenting the bearded head of Mars brings down the issue of the other type with the head of Hercules, several specimens of which occurred in this hoard, absolutely *fleur de coin*, to the latest limits of this first period of the Romano-Campanian coinages. Bearing in mind the similarity of the obverse type on this latter coin to the head of Hêraklês on some Syracusan bronze pieces struck under Agathoklês, we shall not therefore be far wrong in fixing the approximate date of 310 B.C. for the deposit of this Beneventan *tesoretto*.

The Tarentine coins found in this hoard comprised a

---

[121] *Op. cit.*, ed. Blacas, I. p. 262. Cf. Babelon, *Monn. de la Rep. Romaine*, I. p. 10.

somewhat used specimen of Type C of Period IV., and several specimens of Type B of the present Period [122] in good preservation, and one or two of them in brilliant condition, thus affording additional evidence that the didrachms of this type belong to the decades which succeeded the expedition of the son of Neoptolemos. Perhaps the most remarkable feature of this hoard is the fact that although discovered in Samnium, where at a later period the "Campano-Tarentine" coins were current, no Tarentine coins of the Campanian standard were found, the coins of Neapolis and other Campanian cities being here on the contrary associated with the ordinary full weight didrachms of Tarentum. I shall have occasion to return to this important negative phenomenon.

The approximate determination of the date of the didrachm issues represented in Type A and the earlier coins of Type B, the first as belonging to the time of the Molossian Alexander's expedition, and the second as struck, for the most part, during the ensuing decades, supplies a chronological standpoint for a whole series of more or less related types, several of which form a continuation of Type B. The horseman lancing downwards is still the usual obverse type generally associated with the signature ΣA, while the prevalent scheme of Taras on the reverse is that of a somewhat slim Ephêbos astride on his dolphin— a revival of the beautiful design associated in Period IV. with the signature ΚΑΛ. The earlier coins of Type B represent in fact a return by a gradual transition from the infantine type of Taras to this nobler form, which was already coming into vogue when the Benevento hoard was deposited.

---

[122] V. B 2, 3, and 5.

The scheme of Taras on his dolphin as he appears on Type A 1 [Pl. VI. 1] is the natural morphological outgrowth of a common type of the two preceding Periods, in which the outer line of his farther leg is seen behind the fish's forehead. The present development of this scheme is characteristic of a small group (Types D, E, and G) of coins belonging to the present Period, and taken in connexion with the above-mentioned example (A 1), in which it is associated with the eagle symbol of the Molossian prince, must be regarded as a valuable evidence as to the approximate date of the series on which it occurs. In this scheme Taras is seen with his outer leg no longer merely outlined, but thrown slightly in front of the dolphin's snout, while his left hand is lightly poised on the fish's back behind him, holding at the same time a symbol, such as a reed, a palm-branch, or a trident, the end of which rests on his slightly drawn-back nearer ankle, thus imparting to the whole design a peculiar rhythm and equipoise. The same scheme occurs on some gold half-staters [123] associated with the signatures ⊢H and ⋜A, and the head of two female divinities, which, both on the grounds of signature and design, must be referred to the present Period.

Of the coins of this Period presenting this particular

---

[123] (1.) Car. ciii. 8; *B. M. Cat.* 10. *Obv.* "Head of Hêrê," wearing stephanê and necklace; behind, E; border of dots; *ins.* TAPANTINΩN. *Rev.* Taras in attitude described above, holding dolphin and trident; beneath, ⊢H. (2.) *B. M. Cat.* 17. *Obv.* Same; but no letter. *Rev.* Same; but thunderbolt in f. (3.) Car. civ. 20; *B. M. Cat.* 19, 20. "Head of Aphrodite?" (perhaps the nymph Satyra) wearing earrings and necklace, the hair bound by two cords; behind neck, ⋜A. *Rev.* Taras, as before, but wearing chlamys and receiving wreath bearing Nikê; below, ⊢H and waves.

scheme, Type D [Pl. VI. 9] is remarkable for several reasons. This coin is distinguished from all other Tarentine types of this class by the fact that both the rider on the obverse and Taras on the reverse have their right hand raised as if to greet some welcome arrival. On the obverse of this coin a naked youth on a caracolling horse is seen raising his hand above the horse's head with open palm; on the reverse Taras with his right leg thrown forward, in the attitude which characterizes this group of coins, extends his right hand, while in his left he holds a palm-branch with a fillet attached to it. In the field to the right, where on the parallel piece, Type A 1, is the seated Molossian eagle, there is here seen a crested Corinthian helmet, and below in conspicuous letters is the inscription ΣΥΜ. The whole design of this exceptional piece seems to contain an allusion to the advent of some friendly personage.

The inscription ΣΥΜ on the reverse does not occur on any other types of Tarentine coins or with other associations of signature, and in that respect is unique among the types of this or the succeeding Period of the Tarentine coinage. It is possible that it stands for the personal name ΣΥΜΜΑΧΟΣ, which is found moreover on the Hêrakleian tables. On the other hand, the exceptional character of its appearance, as well as the remarkable type with which it is associated, makes it worth while to consider at least the possibility that we have here a written expression of alliance. The absence of any Epirote symbol forbids us to refer this type to Alexander the Molossian's time. It might, on the other hand, with some plausibility be brought into relation with the part played by the Tarentines in the great coalition formed by the exiled Syracusans and their allies against Agathoklês. The Spartan Akrotatos, whose services had been enlisted for this Sicilian enterprise, landed at Tarentum in 315 B.C., and the hope of liberating Syracuse as well as the example of the mother-city, induced the citizens to join the expedition with twenty ships.[124] The gross misconduct of Akrotatos, however, frustrated the plans of the allies, and in the ensuing year (314 B.C.) the Tarentines withdrew their ships from Sicilian waters.

The landing of the Spartan prince on the Italian shore may well have had a semblance in the minds of those who invited him to the earlier landing of Timoleôn at the call of Syracuse and the Sicilian Greeks, and it is hardly necessary to recall the fact that on the occasion of Timoleôn's Sicilian expedition alliance coins were struck with the inscription ΣYMMAXIKON.[125] The shortened form ΣYM, moreover, would find a precedent in the ΣYN of earlier series of coins commemorative of the Theban alliance struck by Knidos, Ephesos, Samos, and Rhodes after the battle of Knidos in 394 B.C.[126]

It is probably to the date of this expedition that we must also refer the deposit of an interesting hoard of gold staters found at Taranto in 1883. The hoard consisted of ninety-two gold pieces, including eighty staters of Philip of Macedon, and five, somewhat worn, of his son Alexander, together with seven coins of Tarentum itself.[127] Of the

---

[124] Diodoros, lib. xix. 70 " πλευσας (ὁ 'Ακρότατος) εἰς Τάραντα καὶ παρακαλέσας τὸν δῆμον συνελευθεροῦν Συρακοσίους ἔπεισε ψηφίσασθαι ναυσὶν εἴκοσι βοηθεῖν."

[125] Head, *Coinage of Syracuse*, p. 89. *B. M. Cat.* Sicily, p. 83. Cf. Gardner, *Types of Greek Coins*, p. 82.

[126] Waddington, *Mélanges Numismatiques*, Pt. ii. p. 7—19.

[127] For a summary account of this find see Professor Luigi Viola's report, *Notizie dei Scavi*, 1886, p. 279. The condition of the coins is thus described: " Di esse 7 erano stateri di

Tarentine coins, all of which were in fine preservation and *fleur de coin*, three were of the types [Pl. V. 9 and 10] representing on the obverse the veiled head of Dêmêtêr, and on the reverse the Dioskuri, and four of the type already referred to with the youthful head of Hêraklês and Taras driving a biga [Pl. V. 11]. The other coins presenting the type of the Dioskuri include two main varieties, in the one case [Pl. V. 9] with the inscription ΔΙΟΣΚΟΡΟΙ in minute letters above the riding figures; in the other case [Pl. V. 10], the twin, eight-rayed stars.[128]

This type of the Dioskuri fits on in many ways to a somewhat later gold type, presenting, in place of the divine twins, a single horseman [Pl. V. 14]. The inscription ΣΟΡ, with which these later staters are sometimes associated,[129] appears as a characteristic signature on the didrachm types belonging to the latest full-weight issues—in other words, to the issues of my sixth Period, which immediately precedes Pyrrhus' expedition. The head of Dêmêtêr on the coins presenting the Dioskuri is, however, decidedly superior to the same head as it appears on these later staters, while, on the other hand, the inscription ΣΑ, which generally appears beneath the horses on these coins, is also, in the same position beneath the horse, the regular

---

Taranto tutti benissimo conservati, fior di conio; 80 di Filippo di Macedonia, e 5 di Alessandro suo figlio; dei Filippi nessun fior di conio, ma una metà ben conservati; gli Alessandri erano alquanto sciupati."

[128] These Tarentine gold types are of great interest from the fact that they were imitated by the Gaulish moneyers of the Amiens district (cf. Rigollot, *Revue Numismatique*, 1838, p. 218, and Pl. VIII. 1; Anatole de Barthélemy, *Rev. Num.* 1883, p. 8, and Pl. II. 1 and 2).

[129] Pl. XI. 9, De Luynes collection. Cf. Garrucci, T. c. 51.

concomitant of a whole series of didrachm types struck from Alexander the Molossian's time to the conclusion of the present Period. The signature KOИ[130] beneath the head of Dêmêtêr on these gold staters affords even more conclusive evidence that they should be referred to the present Period, for it appears with the same reversed И beneath Taras on his dolphin on Type E [Pl. VI. 11], exhibiting a scheme which must be regarded as one of the most characteristic of the present group. This latter type has the strongest resemblance to that already referred to, bearing the inscription ΣYM, and both may confidently be referred to the same date.

The Tarentine staters of Macedonian types found in this hoard displaying on the obverse the head of the youthful Hêraklês and the biga on their reverse, as well as the abundance of Macedonian gold coins, may be justly regarded as directly or indirectly a result of the Molossian Alexander's expedition. On the other hand, the fact that the coins of Alexander the Great contained in this deposit were somewhat worn inclines us to bring down its date some years after that event. The absence of the Tarentine gold coins reading AΓOΛ, which were unquestionably struck at the

---

[130] This is the right reading. See Pl. V. 9 (from the Luynes collection in the Cabinet des Médailles, Paris). I have also verified the signature on a fine example of this coin in the cabinet of Signor Nervegna at Brindisi. (See too *K. Münzkabinet* (Berlin), No. 710; Millingen, *Unedited Coins of Greek Cities and Kings*, where, however, it is printed KON. Carelli, *I. V. N.* Tav. ciii. 12.) The readings AKON (*Notizie dei Scavi*, 1886, p. 180) and ΛIKOM (Garrucci, *Monete*, &c. T. c. 54) are due to the misinterpretation of the two chevron-like folds of the veil as seen behind the bust. For AY under the head of Dêmêtêr (*Not. dei Scavi, loc. cit.*) read ΛY. This signature ΛY is again an indication of a comparatively late date, as it occurs on some silver types of my sixth Period.

time of the Epirote Alexander's arrival, and of the still earlier gold types struck in Archidâmos' time, must also be taken as an argument for referring the withdrawal of the present hoard from circulation to a somewhat later date, which may be approximately stated as 315 B.C.[131]

This being the case, we can have little difficulty in recognising in the beautiful type representing the Dioskuri another instance of a design commemorative of an alliance between Tarentum and its mother-city. In the earlier stater, on which Taras is seen appealing to his father Poseidôn, I have already ventured to trace a reference to the earlier appeal which found its answer in the arrival of the Spartan King Archidâmos. In the present case the appearance of the two Lacedæmonian twins on these Tarentine gold coins may be taken to convey as clear a reference to the renewed brotherhood in arms entered into with the Spartan Prince Akrotatos, the glorious scope of which was the liberation of Syracuse from the hands of the oppressor.

In Type L of the preceding Period (Pl. IV. 8) we have the earliest representation of Taras riding on his dolphin in a warlike fury and preparing to fit an arrow to his bow. It is possible that the first introduction of this warlike type, which seems in a principal degree to refer to naval enterprise, was occasioned by the arrival of the Molossian Alexander. This highly bellicose design

---

[131] The absence of the later gold types exhibiting the single horseman seems to me a fatal objection to bringing down the deposit of this hoard to the last years of the fourth century or the beginning of the third, as suggested by Professor Viola (*loc. cit.*). The style of the head of Déméter, and the abundance of coins of Philip of Macedon, some well preserved, weigh in favour of a somewhat earlier date.

was, in fact, reproduced in an inferior style and with the elephant symbol below it at the time of Pyrrhus's expedition (Pl. VIII. 1, 4, 5), a circumstance which may give us a retrospective warrant for tracing a historical reference in its earlier appearances. In Type B 16 to 18 [Pl. VI. 12] of the present Period, the same design is repeated, though the workmanship of these coins lacks the minute excellence of Type L of the close of the preceding Period, and inclines to place these didrachms amongst the latest of the present class. In these instances we shall not be far wrong in connecting the appearance of this warlike type with the arrival of the Spartan Kleonymos in 302, and the successful military demonstration by which, for a while at least, the Lucanians and their allies were overawed.

V. Type B.

Horseman lancing downwards, &c., as before, sometimes helmeted. No border.

Obv.	Rev.
1. Beneath horse, ≼A. *B. M. Cat.* 228. A. J. E.	Taras astride, &c., to r., as a child, holding in l. hand spirally wound distaff, and extending a small dolphin in his r. Beneath, ΦΙ and curling crests of waves. [ΤΑΡΑ≼ in microscopic characters.] In f. to r., ivy-like leaf.
2. Same. *Car.* cxiii. 188.	Taras astride and holding distaff as before, but holding out in r. hand a small uncertain object. A flower-like tuft rises over his forehead. Beneath dolphin, prow of vessel.
3. Same; but horseman helmeted. Beneath horse, ΦΙΛΙ. [Pl. VI. 5. A. J. E.]	Same as No. 1.

Obv.	Rev.
4. Same (from same die as No. 3; A. J. E.) Car. cxiv. 203.	Taras, as before. In f. to l., ΦΙ; to r. convolvulus-like leaf. Waves below.
5. Same as Nos. 3 and 4. Beneath horse, ΔΑΙ. Car. cx. 3.	Taras as an Ephêbos of elegant form, astride, &c., to l., holding in l. hand a shield on which is a hippocamp, and in r. a trident, which rests on his r. shoulder. In f. to l. ΦΙ. Beneath, a purple-shell.
6. Same. B. M. Cat. [Pl. VI. 6.]	Same; but in f. to l. ΦΗ, instead of ΦΙ.[132]
7. Sam. Mus. Naz. di Napoli.	Same; but in f. to l. ΗΗ.
8. Same; but beneath horse, ΔΑ.. [ΔΑΙ]. Mus. Naz. di Napoli, No. 1891 ["ΛΑ"].	Same; but beneath the purple-shell, Ε.
9. Same but beneath horse, ΗΗΡΑ. De Luynes Coll.	Taras as an Ephêbos, astride, &c., to l., holding on his l. arm a plain round shield and two lances, and with outstretched r. hand receiving small flying Victory, who holds forth wreath to crown him. Beneath dolphin, ΦΙ.
10. Same; but beneath horse, ΣΑ. Car. cxii. 9.	Same as No. 1.
11. Same. Car. cxiii. 189.	Taras astride, &c., to l., holding out kantharos with r. hand, and with l. resting on dolphin's back and holding trident. In f. to l. Æ. Beneath, small dolphin.

---

[132] This rare variety, a specimen of which exists in the British Museum, is in every way identical with the common type, No. 5, presenting the signature ΦΙ; and the ΦΗ in this case must be regarded as the alternative orthographical equivalent of the first syllable of ΦΙΛΙΣ ...

Obv.	Rev.
12. Same. B. M. Cat. 232.	Same; but in f to l. K.
13. Same. B. M. Cat. 221.	Same; but in f. to l. {A {K.
14. Same. Mus. Naz. di Napoli, 1916.	Same; but ⋛ Ω and dot.
15. Same. B. M. Cat. 229. [Pl. VI. 7.]	Same; but in f. to l. {Ω {⋛.
16. Same. B. M. Cat. 222.	Same; but in f. to l. {A {P.
17. Same. B. M. Cat. 223.	Taras as an Ephébos to r., his left foot raised so that it rests on the dolphin's forehead, extending in his l. hand a strung bow and two arrows, while in his r. he holds a third. Beneath, ⊢HP.
18. Same. Car. cxiii. 186. [Pl. VI. 12.]	Same. Beneath, ⊢ HP HP.
19. Same. B. M. Cat. 225.	Same; but beneath, ⊢ HP R.
20. Same; but beneath horse, API. Above and in f. to l. and r. respectively, EΓA. A. J. E.	Taras astride, &c., to l., holding oar in l. hand, and with r. extending kantharos. In f. to l. KΛ.
21. Same; ⊥ in f. to r. Beneath horse, API. Car. cx. 134.	Same; but KΛ in f. to l. Taras more straddling. Beneath, EΓA.

Obv.	Rev.
22. Same; but A in f. to r. A. J. E.	Same; but A or Λ in f. to l. No inscription beneath dolphin.

V. Type C.

Phalanthos in crested helmet, on cantering horse to l., and covering himself with a large round shield on which is a dolphin.

1. In f. to l. A. Beneath horse, KAΛ. Cf. *B. M. Cat.* 271.	Taras, of infantine Dionysiac type. astride, &c., to l., holding distaff in l. hand and his r. resting on dolphin's head. In f. to l. ΣOI. In f. to r. trident.
2. Above, ⊥. In f. to r. Λ; in f. to l. Λ. Beneath horse, ΑΓΗ. Berlin Cabinet. [Pl. VI. 10. Cabinet des Médailles.]	Same.

V. Type D.

Naked boy on prancing horse to r., holding up his l. hand with open palm, as if in the act of salutation.

1. Beneath horse, ΣA. Car. cxiii. 190. [Pl. VI. 9.]	Taras as a youth of somewhat corpulent build, astride, &c., to l., further leg thrown forward, extending his r. hand with open palm, and holding in his l. a palm-branch, which rests on his heel. From the palm hangs a fillet or lemniskos, and in the field below is a Corinthian helmet. Beneath, ΣΥΜ.

V. Type E.

Naked boy, crowning himself on stationary horse, which raises its nearer fore-leg.

1. Beneath horse, ΣA, and capital of Ionic column. Car. cxiii. 185. [Pl. VI. 11.]	Taras as a youth of corpulent build, astride, &c., to l., his further leg thrown forward (as D), and holding out in his r. a water-snake. Beneath, ΚΟИ.

V. Type F.

Naked boy crowning stationary horse to r. (as E).

Obv.	Rev.
1. Beneath horse, ΑΡΗ.[133] *B. M. Cat.* 140. [Pl. VI. 8.]	Taras astride, &c., to l., holding trident in l. hand, and with r. extending kantharos; in f. to r. Φ.
2. Same; but beneath horse, owl flying. Santangelo Coll.	Taras astride to l. holding out one-handled cup. Beneath dolphin, ⊢H.

V. Type G.

Naked youth on cantering horse, holding out a whip behind him.

1. No letter visible. Santangelo Coll. A. J. E.	Taras, of somewhat heavy build, with disproportionately small head, astride, &c., to l., his further leg thrust out in front of the fish's forehead. In f. to r. caduceus: beneath dolphin, ⊢H.

ARTISTS', ENGRAVERS' AND MAGISTRATES' SIGNATURES.

In considering the coins of this Period we are once more brought face to face with the question : How far the signatures on these Tarentine coins represent the names of the actual engravers of the dies?

In treating of some of the earlier Tarentine coins I have

---

[133] This signature (cf. C 2) recurs on the fine Metapontine tetradrachms struck about this period.

already partly answered this question by anticipation. The occurrence on a didrachm of Period III. of two raised rectangular tablets containing the initial letters ≶ΩK, has supplied us with an example of an artist's signature of the most typical kind on a Tarentine coin. In Periods II. and III. attention has been called to a series of coins of great artistic excellence and displaying certain common features both of style and composition, all of which are marked by the signature Λ or ƎΛ, and which taken together, afford strong presumption that we have here to deal with an engraver of no ordinary power. In Periods III. and IV. again we find the same evidence of common handiwork in the beautiful group of coins signed K and KAΛ, sometimes in microscopic characters, and in those signed A and APl. In Types H 1 and L 1 of Period IV. we find, moreover, one or both these signatures associated with that of another artist who signs ΦI, in the last instance in microscopic characters.

It is with the signature ΦI, which, as we have seen, appears in association with two other well-authenticated engravers' signatures on some of the finest types of the Archidamian epoch, that we are at present more specially concerned, from its recurrence, at times in a more amplified form, throughout one of the most characteristic groups of coins belonging to the Period before us. A comparative study of the coins included in Types A and B 1—5, enables us in fact to arrive at the important conclusion that on one or both sides we have here too to do with the handiwork of the same engraver who signs himself ΦI, ΦIΛI, or ΦIΛI≶.

It is to this engraver that the first appearance on the Tarentine series of the peculiar and infantine version of Taras must be ascribed; but it becomes evident that he

was by no means tied down to this representation, the
introduction of which was due to considerations religious
rather than artistic. We find, in fact, a perfect chain of
transitional types, all with the same signature, and marked
with the same minute character of engraving by which
the fat earlier type of the child Taras is metamorphosed
under our eyes into an Ephêbos of slender and elegant
build, such as he figures on a whole series of coins belonging to the succeeding classes. On the other hand, we
find ΦΙ (in association with ΚΑΛ on the obverse) executing
the noble design already referred to, and in which I have
ventured to trace an allusion to the fall of Archidâmos,
where Taras is seen holding a heroic helmet between two
stars, while in Pl. IV. 8, as already observed,[134] this signature reappears in the same association, attached to a
coin which amongst all the Tarentine pieces is characterized by the microscopic minuteness of its engraving.

The technique of these coins as seen in their various
developments points to some interesting conclusions. We
have here all the characteristics of an engraver who,
having accustomed himself to working on hard materials,
has afterwards taken to one of a less intractable nature.
In other words, we have here, as in the well-known instance of Phrygillos,[135] the case of a gem engraver who
has been employed as a die-sinker. Two of the natural

---

[134] See p. 100.
[135] Those who have consistently held to the opinion, first
expressed by Raoul Rochette, that the gem with the figure of
Eros, signed Phrygillos, belongs to the same date as the Syracusan coins with the same signature, and that it must in all
probability be referred to the same engraver, will find new support as against Von Sallet and others in Furtwängler's recently
published dissertation on signed gems (*Jahrbuch d. k. deutschen
Arch. Inst.* 1888, p. 197).

consequences of such a change in material are visible on several coins of the above group, one artistic and one mechanical. We are struck, very notably on Type B 3, 4 (Pl. VI. 5), by an exaggerated depth in the line engraving which in spite of the great minuteness of detail affects the design with a certain harshness. It further appears as if this over-incision of the engraving gave the metal a tendency to stick to the die and somewhat blur the impression. This over-incision and its consequences are well illustrated by the reverses of some of the Syracusan tetradrachms signed EYΘ [136]; but a still more remarkable parallel is supplied by the Naxian didrachms of the engraver Proklês. In other respects the work of this Tarentine die-sinker Philis... suggests a hand accustomed to intaglio on gems. The engraving itself is often of microscopic minuteness, and we are occasionally struck by a certain preposterous perverseness in the exercise of this Lilliputian faculty, the personal signature being writ large, while that of the Tarentine City shrinks to almost invisible dimensions. It looks like the satisfaction taken by an artist who, accustomed himself to sign in full though as inconspicuously as possible, found the expression of his skill in minute lettering hampered by the contemporary custom of the Tarentine mint, which obliged him to attach to his handiwork an abbreviated but manifest signature, as an official rather than an æsthetic guarantee. Nor could he, as in the case of Philistiôn on the Velian coins, gratify his taste by combining his full signature with the design on one side and signing large with the first letters of his name on the reverse. The character

---

[136] Cf. the coins with the signature in Rudolf Weil, *Die Künstlerinschriften der Sicilischen Münzen*, T. 1, Nos. 6 and 8.

of the Tarentine types, the entire absence of such facilities as that supplied by the helmeted head on the Velian pieces, or even of an exergual line capable, as at Thurioi, of being used as a label, precluded all such expedients. As it is, many of the signatures of Philis . . . on this Tarentine series, in spite of the variations mentioned above, are abnormally minute, and notably so on the remarkable type (Pl. IV. 8) mentioned above, which is of truly gem-like execution.

It will be seen, however, from a survey of the above types, that it is not only the microscopic character of many of the works with these signatures that reveals a skilled engraver. Amongst their number are to be found types which for composition and design rank amongst the most admirable productions of the Tarentine mint, and abundantly show that we have here to deal with an artist of no mean power. The archer type of Taras (Pl. IV. 8) on the last piece transcends alike in spirit and harmonious proportions all other representations of this warlike class. The noble figure of Taras contemplating the heroic helmet between the two rayed stars that stand for the twin patrons of Tarentum and its mother-city (Pl. IV. 10, 11), has already been referred to as one of the finest of the Tarentine silver types; while for naturalistic beauty of design B 5 and 6 of the above list, showing Taras, trident on shoulder, with the hippocamp shield, and, beneath his dolphin steed, the spiral buccinum shell, are certainly unrivalled in this long series (Pl. VI. 6).

In this case again the interesting question arises : Was the activity of this artistic die-sinker, who signs ΦI, ΦIΛI and ΦIΛIΣ on these Tarentine coins, confined to this city? Judging by the analogy of signatures that occur on other more or less contemporary Tarentine types—at times even in conjunction with that of Philis. . .—there is every probability that it was not. The signatures ΚΑΛ, ΑΡΙ, ΔΑΙ, ϟΙΜ, ΑΓΗ, ΗΗ, and others, the four first of which are found on the Tarentine coins in conjunction with ΦΙ, reappear among the very limited number of signatures found about the same date on the coins of Hêrakleia, Metapontion and Thurioi. The signature ΦΙ itself occurs on coins of the two former of these cities, and though in these cases it may, occasionally at least, be an abbreviation for the name of another artist who also signs ΦΙΛΟ or ΦΙΛΩ, there are, as we have seen, strong *a priori* grounds for suspecting the collaboration of Philis . . . When on a small Terinæan piece of late fabric [137] we find the inscription ΦΙΛΙϟΤΙ (ΦΙΛΙϟⱢΙ), we seem to be led a step farther towards the completion of our artist's name; the more so if, as seems by no means improbable, this coin may be referred to the brief period of restored independence which from about 334 B.C. onwards Terina owed to the intervention of the Molossian Alexander. A remarkable

---

[137] Garrucci, cxvii. 17; Carelli, clxxx. 17, 18. The lateness of these coins is shown by the resemblance, if Garrucci's representations can be trusted, of the head and coiffure on the obverse to that of other small Terinæan silver pieces, as well as some of bronze, bearing upon them the Brettian crab, and therefore later than the date of the Brettian conquest of 356. Mr. R. S. Poole, indeed, *Num. Chron.* 1883, 273, *Athenian Coin Engravers in Italy*, brings a small coin of the same class reading ΦΙΛΙϟ, into possible connexion with the signature Φ, on a fine series of Terinæan, Pandosian, Hêrakleian, Thurian, and Velian coins, which he inclines tentatively to refer to an earlier Philistiôn, the grandfather of the later Velian engraver, in accordance with the Greek fashion of giving a name in alternate generations. The figure, however, on the cippus on these coins reading ΦΙΛΙϟⱢΙ, shows certain points of resemblance to the Eirênê on the Locrian didrachms, struck, according to Mr. Head (*Historia Numorum*, p. 86), circ. B.C. 344—332.

didrachm,[138] presenting on one side Taras on his dolphin preparing to discharge an arrow from his bow—a design allied to that which first appears on the Tarentine dies with the signature ΦI—and on the other side the Terinæan Nikê holding a wreath, must in all probability be brought into relation with this historic episode, and brings Tarentum into a special connexion with Terina. And in view of this chain of evidence, it is impossible to avoid the suggestion that the full name of our Philis ... is to be read ΦIΛI Ξ-TIΩN, and that he is in fact one and the same with the engraver who has left his signature in full on some of the coins of Velia. On the grounds of style alone, especially in the case of an artist whose activity covers a considerable period of years, and who, in harmony with the influences of his time, has passed through more than one "manner," it is difficult indeed in such minute work as die-sinking to establish satisfactory criteria. Even in the case of the great Syracusan engravers of a better age, the most careful critic must be often at a loss in the endeavour to lay down definite canons of distinction. With regard to date, however, no valid reason can be urged against the proposed identification, and in the present case a careful analysis of the types themselves will be found to supply some valuable indications of common handiwork in other designs with these signatures which make their appearance at Velia and Tarentum.

The period of years during which Philis ... seems to have worked for the Tarentine coinage, from shortly before the date of the Molossian Alexander's expedition onwards, certainly squares very well with the approximate

---

[138] *Berliner Blätter*, III. p. 9, and T. xxix. 3.

date of the Velian coins bearing Philistiôn's signature. More than this, there are certain features on the Velian works of Philistiôn which unmistakably betray a close familiarity with designs in vogue in three at least of the cities of the Ionian shore—Hêrakleia, Metapontion, and Tarentum itself—already referred to as used to employ the same engravers. Thus we find this engraver for the first time introducing on the Velian series a Corinthian form of helmet, which about the same date makes its first appearance on the coins of Hêrakleia and Metapontion, where during the last quarter of the fourth century B.C. it becomes quite usual. At Velia, on the other hand, this deviation from the usual Athenian type of Pallas' headpiece is confined to Philistiôn's work, which combines in a remarkable way motives supplied by the contemporary coinage of Hêrakleia and Metapontion. So far as the general outline of the head and helmet is concerned, the crest and the arrangement of the hair, Philistiôn's Velian Pallas is almost a reproduction of the contemporary didrachm type of Hêrakleia. In the ornamental design, however, with which the upper part of the helmet is decorated, the quadriga, with horses at full gallop, we see a close adaptation of the same device in the same position as it appears on the helmet of Leukippos on the fine tetradrachms of Metapontion.[139]

But the parallel goes a step farther. The peculiar method adopted by Philistiôn for attaching his signature

---

[139] On some of the didrachms of Metapontion, with the head of Leukippos, the signature ΦΙ appears associated with the triquetra symbol. The same symbol appears on coins of Velia dividing the same letters, in this case in all probability the signature of Philistiôn.

to the helmet on the Velian coins, the utilization, namely, for this purpose of the curved line at the base of the crest, is borrowed from the practice of the artist Aristoxenos (*ex hypothesi* the master or associate of the artist ΦΙ . . . on Tarentine coins),[140] who on the fine didrachms of Hêrakleia[141] of a slightly earlier date, first invented this device. Amongst all Greek coin engravers this mode of signature is confined to Aristoxenos and Philistiôn.

More than this, in the noblest of all Philistiôn's Velian types, that, namely, upon which the wounded lion is depicted seizing in its jaws the lethal shaft, the artist has introduced between the first two letters of his name, wherewith on this side of the coin he contents himself, a figure of the two Dioscuri, which is no less suggestive of Tarentine types. In other instances there appears on the the neck pieces of the helmet, signed in this case ΦΙΛΙΞ-ΤΙΩΝ, a rider on a stationary horse which lifts up one of its forelegs, a design literally reproduced from some contemporary Tarentine coins.

These are minute coincidences, but taken together they afford a substantial link of evidence, the more so when it is remembered that each and all of these features are absolutely confined on the Velian series to Philistiôn's handiwork. Comparing in a less general fashion the work of the Velian engraver with that of the Tarentine Philis . . . we distinguish in them both a certain fondness for naturalistic representations, which amongst the contemporary engravers of the respective cities seems peculiar to these two. The elegantly finished ivy-leaf (Pl. VI. 5), of which every vein is delicately indicated, and the pretty twisted shell (Pl. VI. 6) introduced

---

[140] See p. 54, &c.   [141] Garrucci, Tav. ci. 34.

in another work of the Tarentine artist, beneath the dolphin, find their appropriate parallels in the lifelike figure of the locust or the graceful vine-spray [142] with which Philistiôn at times divides his signature. Both engravers, considering the general practice of the age in which they work, show a remarkable tendency to adhere to the more archaic practice of surrounding the type with a beaded circle. One still more suggestive point of resemblance remains to be pointed out. Upon the Tarentine series there are several types in which the curling crests of the sea waves are introduced beneath the figure of Taras on his dolphin. This device, though on the series as a whole of only occasional occurrence, becomes an almost universal characteristic of the group of coins signed ΦIΛI<, ΦIΛI, and ΦI. On the types of the other Greek cities at this time existing in Southern Italy, it is altogether absent, till on the Velian coinage this purely Tarentine feature is suddenly introduced by Philistiôn, and that, as far as can be seen, without any inherent appropriateness and simply from the force of decorative habit, beneath the figure of his wounded lion.

On several of the Tarentine coins of the present group, which I would tentatively attribute to the same Philistiôn who worked for the Velian mint, we find his signature associated on the other side with that of an artist who signs < A. This signature is for the most part confined to Class V., but it also is found on some types belonging to the succeeding class. In all cases, however, it is

---

[142] Perhaps a reminiscence of the exquisite vine-spray associated on a Velian coin of earlier date with the signature Φ, according to Mr. Poole's felicitous suggestion (*loc. cit.*), the work of an earlier Philistiôn.

associated with equestrian types.[143] This artist, it will be seen, specialized in the portrayal of horses, and some of the noblest steeds in the Tarentine series are of his workmanship. The same specialization is observable on the work of another contemporary engraver who signs himself ⋚IM., and it is noteworthy that, as at Tarentum, this signature is exclusively associated with the horse type, so at Thurioi, where it reappears, it is only found in connexion with the reverse design of the butting bull. The powers of Philistiôn, if we may venture so to complete his name, were of wider range, for his signature is associated with some of the most spirited representations of the lancer on his prancing steed, as well as with the most varied types of Taras on his dolphin.

It would appear, from what has been already said, that during the Period with which we are concerned and those that precede it, the signatures on the Tarentine coins, with the possible exception of the gold coins signed **KYΛIK** and **AΓOΛ**,[144] are those of the actual die-sinkers rather than of civic magistrates. Either we have well-marked groups which, on the ground of internal evidence alone, we are justified in referring to the same engraver, or we find the same signatures recurring on coins of the same period belonging to other Magna-Græcian cities—as, for instance, **KAΛ**, **ΔAI**, **⋚IM**, &c. In the succeeding Period (VI.), which, as we shall see, embraces the last of the full-weight didrachm series, a remarkable change takes place. For the first time full-

---

[143] On the gold coinage the signature of ⋚A is associated with the beautiful type representing the Dioskuri. It is also found with the head of a nymph (Carelli, civ. 4), an exception to his usual practice.

[144] See p. 66, *note*.

length signatures appear which have no relation to the workmanship of the coins, and which there is every reason to refer to civic magistrates of Tarentum. And when these appear they naturally take the post of honour beneath the principal type, thrusting aside the signature of the actual engraver of the coin into a secondary position in the field. This process is well illustrated by the case of the artist ≶A . . ., who prolonged his activity through the early part of the period of full-length signatures. This engraver still continues to associate his name, as before, with purely equestrian types, but instead of signing, according to his wont, beneath the body of the horse, he now resigns this front place to succeeding magistrates, and contents himself with a position in the field above. The same revolution is well illustrated by the case of another engraver who first begins to work on the Tarentine dies shortly before the reduction of the standard. This engraver, who signs EY (often retrograde), and whose productions, owing to their exaggerated relief, stand out so clearly amongst contemporary types, that it is possible to pick them out without first searching for the authentication of the signature, invariably follows the same rule as ≶A . . . ., placing the first letters of his name in the field and leaving the space below the horse for the full name of the magistrate.

It is true that the conspicuous lettering of these signatures clashes with the received ideas as to the custom amongst the best engravers of ancient dies. Even Raoul Rochette, who, following out the argument derived from the appearance of the same signatures on coins of different Magna-Græcian cities, was inclined to admit the claims of a wider class of engravers, was afterwards prevailed upon to draw back from some of the logical consequences of his own method.[145] Undoubtedly amongst the monetary artists of the best period the highly refined device prevailed of inscribing the name in almost microscopic letters, and of hiding away the signature in some part of the design, — beneath the neck, in a fold of the sphendonê, on a plate of the helmet, or even the exergual line. But even in the case of cities where, from the largeness or the general character of the design this plan was feasible, it was by no means invariably followed. At Syracuse itself the signatures of Eumenos, of the engraver who signs EYΘ, of Phrygillos, of Evænetos, are often conspicuous enough. What was comparatively easy of achievement on the noble pentekontalitra, or even on tetradrachms, was not so feasible on coins of lesser module. At Thurioi, where on some of the tetradrachms, and in imitation, it would seem, of Syracusan practice, IΣToPoΣ signs on the exergual line beneath the bull, in letters which vie in minuteness with the analogous signatures of Kimôn or Evænetos, it was found advisable in the case of the didrachms to follow a less ambitious plan. Either the exergual line was widened into a regular base, on which, for example, the legend MoΛoΣ-ΣoΣ[146] is often visible enough, or when the exergual

---

[145] Compare his *Lettre à M. le duc de Luynes sur les Graveurs des Monnaies Grecques* (Paris, 1831), which certainly contains some rash assertions, with his more cautious *Lettre à M. Schorn, Supplément au Catalogue des Artistes de l'Antiquité grecque et romaine* (Paris, 1845).

[146] The Thurian didrachms signed MoΛoΣΣoΣ, belong to two distinct types. In the first of these, characterized by a large head of Pallas on the obverse, the signature is much finer; in the other case it is at least a third in diameter larger and associated in the obverse with an exceptionally small head of the goddess.

line was left we find the name sprawling across it in a most ungraceful fashion, as in the signature AMΦ.., supplied by a hoard of coins recently found near Oria. Yet the very failure of these attempts to follow the practice of the masters of the art has a special value as showing that the signatures of both IΣTOPOΣ, and AMΦ... belong to the same general category, and cannot be separated by any definite line of demarcation. The Thurian pieces, indeed, enable us to carry the chain of connexion a step farther. To avoid the sprawling effect of such signatures as the last it only remained to complete the transition already partially effected in the last instance, and to transfer the name to the interspace between the bull's legs immediately above the exergual line, as is done in the case of ΛIBYΣ, ΦPY, EYΘY, and other signatures.

In the case of Velia, again, though Philistiôn on the obverse of his coins follows the classical practice of inserting his signature at full length and in small letters beneath the crest of Pallas's helmet, it is impossible to doubt that the abbreviated but conspicuous signature ΦI found in the field on the reverse of the same pieces, and associated with a design of far greater merit than the head on the obverse side, is that of the same engraver.[147] The same remark holds good of the engraver APIΣTOΞENOΣ at Hêrakleia. In some cases he signs in minute letters both on the exergual line of the reverse and on the Pallas' helmet of the obverse. In other cases, on the other hand, while still continuing the miniature signature on the

---

[147] This is further shown by the parallel instance of the other known Velian engraver Kleudôros, who signs his name in full on the helmet on the obverse, and repeats the first two letters of his signature in monogram on the reverse.

reverse, he contents himself with a large A beside the helmet on the other side.[148] On one of his Metapontine pieces he combines both systems, signing with a large capital A in the field, beneath which, in small characters, are contained the second two syllables of his name. The Hêrakleian artist, again, who signs EYΦP in minute letters on the exergual line, varies the practice by placing a conspicuous EY in the field above it between the legs of the struggling Hêraklês. We see from these and other examples that in the Italian parts of Magna-Græcia as well as in Sicily, the same engraver follows both practices, sometimes, too, on the same coin.

But on the silver pieces of Tarentum, with which we are more specially concerned, there was little opportunity for the exercise of the artistic refinement of interweaving the signature with the design. In one instance, indeed, a didrachm of larger module and of the earlier kind, exhibiting the seated Dêmos of Tarentum, a small E is seen on the back of the dolphin on the reverse,[149] which, judging by contemporary analogies,[150] we have every right to refer to the name of the engraver. On a

---

[148] On the coin with the name of Aristoxenos on the base of the crest of the helmet, A also appears in the field in the same position; it looks as if, in this case, Aristoxenos had attached his signature in two capacities:—as an artist and as a responsible mint official.

[149] Von Sallet, *Die Künstlerinschriften auf Griechischen Münzen*, p. 15, 43. Even Von Sallet inclines to regard this as the initial of an artist's name. Otherwise he pronounces against all Tarentine claims to artists' signatures. "Auf allen anderen Münzen von Tarent finden sich keine irgendwie sicheren Künstlernamen."

[150] Cf. the EYAI on the small dolphin in front of the nymph's head, on a tetradrachm by Evænetos, and the more conspicuous KIMΩN on the dolphin of a decadrachm.

later didrachm, also, an Η appears in the same position.[151] But these are altogether exceptional instances, and it must be acknowledged that as an artistic device the expedient in this case was not felicitous. The facilities for "hide and seek" offered by the didrachm types of neighbouring cities, such as the convenient section of the neck afforded by the heads on Metapontian coins, or the vacant plates on Athena's helmet at Hêrakleia or Thurioi, were altogether wanting in the Tarentine coins with which we are dealing. Even an exergual line was not usually to be found on the Tarentine didrachms. Frankness was thus inevitable.

There is, moreover, another side of the question which does not seem to have been sufficiently considered by those who have approached the subject from the standpoint of pure art criticism. It seems sometimes to be assumed that the actual engravers only signed in their artistic capacity. Modern specializations of calling which separate the die-sinker's art-work from that of those who actually strike the coins, and both again perhaps from that of the responsible mint official, must not be allowed to pervert our judgment. The whole character of the signatures on these Tarentine pieces shows that the engravers signed as those responsible for the weight and metal as well as the execution of the individual piece that bore their mark. This is in perfect keeping with mediæval analogies, and fits in with what we know of the system in vogue at Antioch in Antiochos Epiphanês' day,[152] and

---

[151] *Zeitschrift für Numismatik*, II. 1. Owing to the kindness of Dr. Imhoof-Blumer I am enabled to represent an example of this coin on Pl. III. 1.

[152] The story of King Antiochus, going about the city as a private person and visiting the workshops of the moneyers

apparently in other Asiatic Greek cities where the coinage was in the hands of private individuals, who, like Dêmêtrios the Ephesian, seem to have united the callings of moneyer and silversmith or jeweller. The appearance of more than one die-sinker's name on the same coin is easily accounted for by the existence of Συνεργασίαι or companies of moneyers and gold or silversmiths, of which we have epigraphic evidence,[153] or even of smaller partnerships in business. The appearance of more than one signature on the same side of a coin may occasionally afford an illustration of a practice not unknown in the allied craft of gem-engraving, and of which an instance may be cited in the celebrated cameos inscribed ΑΛΦΗΟC CYN ΑΡΕΘΩΝΙ where ΕΠΟΙΟΥΝ is obviously understood.[154] Such a collaboration, so familiar in the greater works of ancient art, enabled either artist to contribute his special faculties towards the production of a composition. On the whole, however, it is safer to suppose that in most cases the presence of more than one signature on the same die indicates the joint responsibility of several *maestri* working in the same *bottega*. It is further to be observed that in these cases one of the signatures occurs at greater length than the others—an indication that this more

---

(ἀργυροκοπεῖα) and goldsmiths is given by Athenæos (Lib. 10) on the authority of the 26th book of Polybios : "Μάλιστα δὲ πρὸς τοῖς ἀργυροκοπείοις εὑρίσκετο καὶ χρυσοχόοις, εὑρεσιλογῶν καὶ φιλοτεχνῶν πρὸς τοὺς τορευτὰς καὶ τοὺς ἄλλους τεχνίτας." The conjunction here with the *Toreuta* is significant.

[153] C. I. G. 3154. (Cf. Lenormant, *La Monnaie dans l'Antiquité*, iii. 251). ΣΥΝΕΡΓΑΣΙΑ ΤΩΝ ΑΡΓΥΡΟΚΟΠΩΝ ΚΑΙ ΧΡΥΣΟΧΟΩΝ.

[154] See Raoul Rochette, *Lettre à M. Schorn : Supplément du Catalogue des Artistes de l'Antiquité grecque et romaine* (Paris, 1845) p. 113, as against Koehler's view, that the inscription refers to a joint dedication of the work.

emphatic signature belongs to the actual engraver of the die. Thus we find the artists who sign ΚΑΛ, ΦΙ, and ΑΡΙ grouped together in a series of coins of Period IV., all presumably from the same *atelier*, but on coins where ΦΙ occupies the principal place on a die we find signatures of the others in the abbreviated forms of Κ or Ρ. This practice must be distinguished from that of the later Tarentine coinages, where, as I hope to show, the principal, and generally full-length signature, is that of a magistrate, and has no visible relation to the style of the engraving.

The private character of the moneyers' industry explains how it is that the same signatures appear on the coins of different cities, it being natural that an Ἀργυροκόπος who had earned a reputation as a good engraver, should at times obtain employment even from remote quarters. But where a system of this kind prevailed and the coinage of the State, instead of issuing as at Athens from a central mint, was entrusted to private enterprise, it became the more necessary that the individual pieces should receive the guarantee of the moneyer or firm of moneyers, who had made themselves responsible for their sterling weight and standard, as well as their artistic excellence. A coiner, who was also his own die-sinker, signed in both qualities. It was open to him in some cases, if he was a great artist, to lay stress on that side of his character and sign upon a coin as he might upon a gem. But local custom, or the accident of the type he had to deal with, was not always favourable to the adoption of such a practice. In cities where private moneyers supplied the public needs, it may well have been required by law that the signature that authenticated the coin and fixed the responsibility of the individual should be made clearly manifest. So at Velia we find both Philistiôn and Kleudôros, although on one side of the coin they follow the purely artistic tradition, signing conspicuously enough on the other side with the first letters of their names, and in a style which recalls the contemporary Tarentine practice. At Tarentum itself, whether owing to special regulations on the part of the State or to natural causes inherent in the type, this seems to have been the only form of signature current, if we except some microscopic signatures of ΚΑΛ and ΦΙ. It is a form which emphasizes the official responsibility of the moneyer in all his capacities. But it covers his artistic qualifications; it does not exclude the possibility of his having achieved fame in other fields as an engraver, and where we find, as in the case of Kal . ... of Ari . . . or of Phi . . . a signature associated with excellent work, we have as much right to place him in the rank of artistic engravers as if he had hidden his name in some part of the design.

No one doubts that the small and concealed signatures of an earlier period, such as those represented by the great Sicilian works of the close of the fifth and beginning of the fourth century, have a purely artistic value. They belong to a time when, whether owing to the monetary system then in vogue or to other causes, it was not thought necessary for moneyers as such to attach their sign manual. When we find a signature of this kind we have a right to exclaim, "It is an engraver's signature, and therefore an artist's." But, as we see from the Tarentine series, a practice grew up during the fourth century of engravers initialling every single piece. At times, as in the case of the Velian coins referred to, they continue or revive the older practice of interweaving their name full-length, or in an abbreviated form, with some part of the design. But even in such a case as this they usually repeat their signature in its more official form on the other side of the same coin. At times, as at Thurioi, we are able to trace a regular transition from signatures of the old artistic character to the regulation stamp. But to seize on this difference of type as a proof that the later signatures are not those of the engravers of the dies is to mistake the point at issue. The truth is, that during the later period with which we are specially concerned, it is not the lack of engravers' signatures that should cause perplexity, but their abundance. There are some who, from the noble style of their designs, the gem-like finish of their work, and the fact that they were employed by different cities, evidently enjoyed an artistic reputation in their own day although they may not have signed in the older artistic fashion. There are others, such as the die-sinker who signs **EY** at Tarentum, who, by the evidence of their own work, have no claim to rank as artists. But to take the last-named example as a crucial test, the very grossness of the features that characterize the coins signed **EY** proclaims identity of handiwork. The magistrates' names that occur beneath the horses on this group of coins continually vary, but the signature in the field and the style of engraving go hand in hand; they come in and they depart together. It is an engraver's signature, but not an artist's.

PERIOD VI.—FROM KLEONYMOS TO PYRRHUS.
302—281 B.C.

In the coinage of Period VI. I have included all the full-weight didrachms that exhibit signatures at full length, together with one or two other types which, from their close connexion with the others or their approximation to some of the earlier issues of reduced standard, must be regarded as belonging to the present class. It must, however, be borne in mind that though considerations of convenience have led me to group together the coins with the full-length signatures in the present class, it is probable that a few of these, such as Type B, for instance, come chronologically within the limits of the preceding Period. The present Period extends to the time when the weight of the Tarentine didrachm which, from the date of the first coinage of this city, had been maintained at about 123—120 grains, was reduced to about 100 grains. Of the date and circumstances of this reduction of the standard in which other Magna-Græcian cities participated, there will be occasion to say more in treating of the first coinage of the didrachms of lighter weight. Here it may be sufficient to mention that there are cogent reasons for connecting the reduction of the Tarentine silver standard with the coming of Pyrrhus. Assuming then that the issues of the preceding Period V. reach down to the approximate date of 302 B.C., we have left for the duration of the present class a space of somewhat over twenty years.

It is a remarkable, and at first sight, enigmatic fact, that while, as I hope to show, the reduction of the didrachm weight did not take place till the time of Pyrrhus, a class of drachms makes its appearance during the present Period, the standard of which corresponds to that of the reduced didrachms. These are the pieces presenting on one side the helmeted head of Pallas, and on the other the owl on the spray, and the average weight of which is rather under than over 50 grains.[155] That the early drachms of this type belong, in fact, to the present Period appears not only from their style, but from the inscription ΙΟΡ which they universally bear, and which is peculiar to the didrachms of Period VI. These early drachms present the following principal varieties:—

Obv.	Rev.
1. Head of Pallas to l., in crested helmet, on which is Scylla hurling a rock.	Owl with closed wings to l., seated on olive spray. In f. to l. **TAP** to r. $\begin{smallmatrix}P\\O\\H\end{smallmatrix}$ or $\begin{smallmatrix}H\\O\\P\end{smallmatrix}$
2. Same.	Same, but club in f. to r. and insc. ΙΟΡ.

A still more cogent proof of priority in date of these drachms to the others of the same class, the inscriptions on which correspond with those of didrachms of the reduced weight, may be drawn from the evidence of a recent Calabrian find, the analysis of which will be found under Appendix B. In this find, which included all the earliest didrachm issues of the reduced weight, the drachms found belonged exclusively to the later class presenting magistrates' names of the Pyrrhic epoch. The negative evidence supplied by the Calabrian find receives, moreover, a strong corroboration from the contents of another hoard of Tarentine and other Magna-Græcian coins found between Oria and Manduria in 1884. Some two hundred coins belonging to this hoard, which, for convenience, may be referred to as the Oria find, passed through my hands, and, although owing to the fact that they had unfortunately been partly mixed with

---

[155] There is a solitary instance (Carelli, *Descr.*, No. 405) of a coin of this type weighing as much as 56 grs. (3·64 grammes).

other specimens I have in this case avoided attempting a detailed analysis of the deposit, it has yet been possible to draw some broad conclusions from its composition. The Tarentine didrachms belonged, for the most part, to the present and the preceding Period [156]; they were all of full weight, and there is every reason to suppose that the hoard was deposited between 300 and 281 B.C. Numerous specimens of Types E, F, and G of the present Period occurred *fleur de coin*, and with them, some in equally fresh condition, were associated drachms of the type described above exhibiting the signature ΙΟΡ.

It is probable that the Tarentine drachms with these Athenian types were originally struck not for internal circulation so much as a part of the federal currency of the Italiote League, and it is noteworthy that a considerable proportion of the diobols belonging to this same federal series, presenting on one side the head of Pallas and on the other Hêraklês strangling the lion, which, to judge from their fabric, belong to the same approximate date as these early drachms, were struck on the same reduced standard. The weight of this class of diobol, sixteen grains and under, corresponds, in fact, to the third of the drachms with the inscription ΙΟΡ. It is always possible that the didrachm standard was reduced in some

---

[156] In this hoard there also occurred didrachms of Metapontion, Hêrakleia, Thurioi, and Krotôn, all of full weight. The best preserved of these were the coins of Hêrakleia with the inscription ΑΘΑ (*B. M. Cat.* 33), and the Metapontine coins with the head of Leukippos, and also those with the head of Persephonê wearing a barley wreath, and with the inscription ΑΘΑ, ΛΥ, ΛΑ, &c. (*B. M. Cat.* 106, 108, 110, &c.), were fairly, but not so brilliantly, preserved. Two somewhat worn specimens of the very scarce Metapontine tetradrachms were also found.

of the neighbouring Magna-Græcian cities, and notably at Hêrakleia, at a somewhat earlier date than at Tarentum.

Meanwhile, as the silver staters of this city show, the Tarentines, for their own purposes, still continued to adhere to their time-honoured system, and it further appears that in the litras of the present Period, which represented the traditional small currency of the citizens themselves, the old standard was equally preserved. The didrachm, for instance, Type G, of the present Period, on the reverse of which Taras, holding a bunch of grapes, is seen associated with the signature AΓA, obviously corresponds to the litra of the full weight of twelve grains[157], on which the bunch of grapes appears as a symbol between the letters AΓ. The doe looking back,[158] the spear heal[159] and the hippocamp[160] which occur on other litræ and hemilitra of full weight, are also symbols otherwise solely associated with didrachms of the present Period.

Amongst the familiar schemes that continue to appear on the didrachms of this Period are the lancer on his prancing horse, and the rider holding a round shield behind him in the act of vaulting off his horse. The fine type of Nikê receiving the victorious horseman is also revived, probably at the very beginning of this Period, as in some cases it occurs without the full-length signature below ΛΥΚΙΑΝΟΣ, with which on other specimens it is associated. The general effect of these later versions is bold and grandiose, but the details, such as the horse's mane, are careless and unfinished, the folds of the drapery

---

[157] *B. M. Cat.* 406, wt. 12 grs.; Car. *Descr.* 637, 638, 11 grs. and 11·4 grs.

[158] In my collection, wt. 10¾ grs.

[159] *B. M. Cat.* 407, wt. 12·5 grs.

[160] Car. *Descr.* 678 litra 11 grs.; 677 hemilitron 5·9 grs.

have lost their skilful undulations, and we have no longer here the minute and elaborately beautiful work that characterizes the masterpiece of the artist ΚΑΛ . . . in the prototype of Period IV. The reverse of this coin is remarkable for the energetic scheme of Taras rising to his full height with one knee on the dolphin's back [161], a new departure in design led up to, perhaps, by the bowman of the preceding class, who places his foot on the dolphin's head. On the greater number of the coins of the present Period Taras is represented astride on his marine charger as in the prevalent scheme of Period V.

With regard to the appearance for the first time of full-length signatures on the coins of this Period, it has already been pointed out that in these signatures we have to deal with the names of magistrates rather than engravers. These names, of which we now obtain a considerable list, find no analogies in the signatures on the coins of other Magna-Græcian cities. For such analogies we have still to refer to the shorter signatures, such as ΣA, ΣI, and Ᵽ, which continue throughout a part of this Period, though they are now relegated to a secondary position on the coin. In the case of ΕΥ, as already remarked, we see the secondary signature in every case associated with designs in an abnormally bold relief, and unmistakeably proclaiming the handiwork of the same, by no means admirable, engraver. But this very group of coins, the identical authorship of which is thus attested by the initials ΕΥ in the field, presents us with a varied list of full-length signatures, such as ΑΝΘΡΩΣ, ΑΡΙΣΤΙΑΣ, ΝΙΚΟΔΑΜΟΣ, ΝΙΚΩΝ,

---

[161] The Ε which is seen upon his shield recalls the ΕΙC that appears upon the shield of the armed horseman on a coin of the Pyrrhic Period VII.

NIKΩTTAΣ and ΦIΛΩN. These latter names, therefore, can have nothing to do with the actual die-sinker.

A good example of the same kind occurs in another well-marked group of coins characterized by sharply-cut figures and a peculiar lengthening and attenuation both of the mounted warriors and of their steeds. All the coins of this group are marked in the field by the initials ΣI, but the full-length names beneath the horses vary as on the coins signed EY. There can be little doubt, moreover, that in this case the reverse figures of Taras, which present the same characteristics as the equestrian types on the obverse, were the work of the same engraver, and that the ΛY, which occurs on the reverse of a coin of this group, refers not to the engraver, but to the magistrate ΛYKΩN, who, alternately with ΔEINOKPATHΣ, signs in full on the obverse of coins of the same group, bearing the initials ΣI in the field. No one, I think, who has minutely studied the technique of Type C, No. 3, will doubt the correctness of the conclusion, that both sides are by the same engraver.

From the recurrence of the same signature ΣOP—so typical of the silver coinage of this Period—on some gold staters,[162] presenting on the obverse a head of Dêmêtêr in a somewhat later style than appears on the pieces exhibiting the two Dioskuri and in all probability commemorative of the Spartan alliance of 315 B.C.[163], we may refer this gold issue to the same date as the present class of didrachms. The reverse type of these staters, a boy rider crowning a stationary horse which lifts up his off fore-leg, now again becomes common on the silver issues,

---

[162] Pl. XI. 9, Santangelo Coll.; Garrucci, Tav. c. 51.
[163] See p. 98, *seqq.*

where the youthful rider often assumes such an androgynous appearance that the figure has been described as that of a girl.

It is perhaps to the latter part of the present Period that we may also refer the earliest issues of a peculiar class of Tarentine didrachms which are based on the Campanian standard, and attain a maximum weight of about 116 grains, instead of the normal Tarentine weight of 122. Upon these coins, the constant obverse type of which is the boy rider crowning a stationary horse, the type of Taras on his dolphin is replaced by a female head displaying points of affinity with the Parthenopê or Dia Hêbê on the coins of Neapolis [164]; but in this case no doubt portraying the nymph Satyra, the mother of Taras, whose head alternates with that of Taras himself on some of the earlier Tarentine silver pieces. The view that these coins were intended for circulation outside the Tarentine territory[165], in the Samnian and Apulian[166] districts dominated by the Campanian system, is strongly corroborated by the fact that among numerous finds of Tarentine coins, including large hoards as well as isolated specimens, made at Taranto itself or in its neighbourhood that have come under my own observation, not a single specimen belonging to this class has come to light.

That the first issue of these Campano-Tarentine coins took place at a comparatively late period, is shown by

---

[164] A good example of this resemblance is seen on the coin reproduced in Pl. VII. 13. For another fine Campano-Tarentine type see Pl. XI. 10.

[165] See Head, *Historia Numorum*, p. 48.

[166] The same type and standard were adopted at Teate in Apulia. See Sambon, *Monnaies de la Presqu'île Italique*, p. 218 (Pl. XV. 7); Garrucci, Tav. xcii. 1—3; Head, *op. cit.* p. 41.

their significant absence from the Beneventan hoard, buried, as we have seen, about 310 B.C., where, if anywhere, this class of coin would have come to light had it been already in existence, and in which Tarentine didrachms of the ordinary type were associated with Campanian silver pieces. Moreover, it is only some of the earliest and best-executed of the class that can with any probability be referred to so early a date as even the close of the present Period. Strong reasons will be given in a subsequent section,[167] for believing that as a matter of fact, much as it may conflict with the prevailing notions of numismatists, the great bulk of this peculiar issue must be referred to the post-Pyrrhic epoch of the Tarentine coinage.

VI. Type A.

Naked boy of androgynous aspect crowning standing horse to r., which sometimes lifts its off fore-leg. The boy's hair is bound up in a krobylos behind.

Obv.	Rev.
1. In f. to l., ϟA. Beneath horse, ΑΡΕΘΩΝ. Car. cix. 8. [Pl. VII. 1.]	Taras as an Ephêbos astride, &c., to l., holding out in r. hand a tripod. Beneath, ΓΑϟ.
2. ⱶ in f. to l. Beneath horse, ϟΩΚΡΑΤΗϟ. Not in Car. B. M. Cat., 141. [Pl. VII. 2. A. J. E.]	Same, but holding olive-branch Beneath, ΙΟΡ.
3. In f. to l., ϟA. Beneath horse, ΦΙΛΙΑΡΧΟϟ Car. cxiii. 2. [Pl. VII. 3.]	Same, but holding bunch of grapes. Beneath, ΑΓΑ.

---

[167] See p. 170, *seqq.*

Obv.	Rev.
4. In f. to l., **AΓΩ**. Beneath horse, **KPATINOϚ**. Car. cxi. 4.	Same, but holding kantharos. Beneath, **ΙOP**.
5. In f. to l., **A**. Beneath horse, **ϚΩKPATHϚ** Car. cxii. 18.	Taras astride, &c., to l., holding in l. hand a distaff, and extending Victory on r. In f. to r., **K**.

VI. Type B.

Nikè to l. seizing forelock of prancing horse, much as Per. IV., Type L, but her left arm, with which in the other instance she seizes the bridle, is here behind the horse's neck. The horseman has helmet and javelin as before, but the small round shield on his l. arm is plain. The inscription **TAPANTINΩN** is also wanting.

1. Beneath horse, **ΛYKIANOϚ**. Car. cxi. 9.	Taras rising on dolphin to l., on which he kneels with his l. leg; his r. hand is extended, and in his l. are two javelins and a small round shield, upon which appears the letter **E**. Beneath, waves. In f. to l., **ΙOP**.
2. Same, but no inscription. [Pl. VII. 4, B. M.]	Same.

VI. Type C.

Naked horseman cantering l., holding behind him small round shield, and sometimes two javelins.

1. In f. to l., **ΦΙ-ΛΩN**. Beneath horse's fore-legs, **EY**. Cf. Car. cxiii. 10. [Pl. VII. 5.]	Taras astride, &c., to l., holding out small Victory, who extends a wreath towards his head. Beneath, waves.
2. Same, but **EY** in f. to r., and beneath horse, **NΩΛΙΦ**. Car. cxiii. 11.	Same, but with left leg thrown forward.

Obv.	Rev.
8. Same, but E in f. to r., and beneath horse, ΦΙΛΟΚΛΗΣ. Cf. Car. cxiii. 6. [Pl. VII. 6.]	Taras astride, &c., holding out wreath. Beneath, ΛΥ.

VI. Type D.

Naked horseman on prancing horse to r., lancing downwards. Behind, large round shield and reserve of two javelins.

1. Beneath horse, ΑΝΘΡΩΣ. Car. cix. 3. [Pl. VII. 7.]	Taras astride, &c., to l., holding out kantharos in r. hand. In f. to r., anchor; in f. to l. ΕΥ. Beneath dolphin's tail, ΑΡ.
2. In f. to L, ΣΙ. Beneath horse, ΔΕΙ- ΝΟΚΡΑΤΗΣ. Car. cx. 5. [Pl. VII. 8.]	Taras astride, &c., to l., holding dolphin.
3. In f. to l., ΣΙ. Beneath horse, ΛΥ- ΚΩΝ. Car. cxi. 12.	Same as No. 2.
4. In f. to l., ΘΕ. Beneath horse, ΑΛΕ- ΞΑΝ. Car. *Descr.* 132. Cf. Sambon, *op. cit.*, p. 117.	Taras astride, &c., to l.; in his l. hand holding a club which rests against his arm, and with his r. extending kantharos.

VI. Type E.

Naked horseman to l., vaulting off prancing horse. The horseman holds a small round shield on his l. arm, and sometimes a javelin. In No. 1 he is helmeted.

1. In f. to r., ΕΥ. Beneath horse, ΝΙ- ΚΩΤΤΑΣ. Cf. Car. cx. 18. [Pl. VII. 9.]	Taras, &c., to r., throwing forward l. leg. He hurls a small javelin with his r. hand, and in his l. holds a javelin which rests on his shoulder. In f. to l., ΤΟΡ. Beneath dolphin, a hippocamp.

Obv.	Rev.
2. In f. to r., **EY**. Beneath horse, **NIKΩN**. Car. cxi. 20. [Pl. VII. 10.]	Taras astride, &c., to l., holding out corn-spike. In f. to l., **API**. Beneath dolphin, a spear-head.

VI. Type F.

Naked horseman galloping r.

1. In f. ? Beneath horse, **NIKOΔAMOS**. Car. cxii. 175. [Pl. VII. 11. Berlin Cab.]	Taras as child astride, &c., to l., holding distaff in l. hand and with r. extending kantharos. Beneath, a doe looking back and **ΣOP**.
2. In f., **EY**. Beneath horse, **APIS-TIAS**. B. M. Cat. 120. [Pl. VII. 12.]	Same type, but Taras holds out a bunch of grapes. Beneath dolphin, **KΛH** or **KAN**.

VI. Type G.

Naked horseman helmeted to l., on stationary horse raising its off fore-leg. He holds behind him a round shield seen sideways.

In f. to l., **YƷ**. Beneath horse, **NIKOΔAMOS**. (Cf. B. M. Cat. 198 "**Ξ**" "**NIKA..?**") [Pl. VII. 13. A. J. E.]	Taras as a child (Dionysiac type) to l., with a tuft above his forehead, holding distaff in l. hand, and extending in r. a bunch of grapes. In f. to r., a cock. Beneath, **AΓA**.

VI. Type H.

Naked horseman on prancing horse to r.

In f. to r. **E[Y]**. Beneath horse, **EYAP XIΔA[S]**. [Pl. XI. 11. Santangelo Coll.].	Taras as a child astride, &c., to l., as preceding, but with r. hand extending lighted torch.

PERIOD VII.—THE PYRRHIC HEGEMONY.

B.C. 281—272.

Before considering the probable date of the reduction of the didrachm standard at Tarentum, we may briefly glance at the political circumstances of the Tarentines and their neighbours during the period that intervenes between the expedition of the Molossian Alexander and that of Pyrrhus. So far as Tarentum was concerned the local hostilities with the Lucanians and their allies continued, and the citizens, like the other Italiote Greeks, had much to fear from the growing power of Agathoklês of Syracuse. On two successive occasions we find them once more relying on the arms of the princely Condottieri of their Spartan mother-city. The Sicilian expedition under Akrotatos ended as we have seen in failure, but before long the continual onslaught of the Lucanians led the Tarentines to call in the services of his brother Kleonymos, who arrived with his mercenaries about the year 302. The military preparations now made so impressed the Lucanians that they concluded a peace, apparently without waiting the issue of a combat. Kleonymos, however, proved himself even more oppressive than his predecessor. He treated his allies as if they were slaves. On Metapontion refusing allegiance he succeeded in obtaining possession of the city by treachery and carried off six hundred talents of silver and two hundred noble virgins for his harem. The Tarentines eagerly seized the opportunity of Kleonymos' absence in Corcyra to throw off his hateful yoke, but the tyranny of the Syracusan seemed only the more imminent. By the conquest of Corcyra, Agathoklês had already secured a commanding position in the

Tarentine seas, and he had further engaged to supply the barbarian neighbours of the Tarentines, the Peuketians and Iapygians, with piratical vessels wherewith to plunder the shipping of the wealthy Republic, stipulating himself for a share in the loot.[168] In 299 by the capture of Krotôn he obtained a secure footing on the South Italian shore. But Tarentum was to enjoy a reprieve. Agathoklês was called off by Brettian and Punic wars and in 288 met with a violent end.

Meanwhile a more formidable foe was approaching the very gates of Tarentum. So long as the struggle between Rome and the Samnites had seemed doubtful the Tarentines could afford the part of lookers-on. But with the defeat of the Samnites the most formidable obstacle to the progress of the Roman arms towards the Ionian Sea was removed, and in 292 the great rival of Tarentum for Italian hegemony founded the military colony of Venusia, only two marches distant from Tarentum itself. Thurioi had concluded an alliance with Rome and the same was imposed on the Lucanians. In 284 the breach of this treaty, due to the Lucanian chieftain Stenius Statilius attacking Thurioi, brought about a state of hostilities which was in fact the beginning of the struggle between Rome and Tarentum. Thurioi now received a Roman garrison and the *casus belli* was supplied by the Romans formally breaking the treaty (when concluded we are not told) according to which their navigation was confined to the

---

[168] Diod. xxi. 4. In the fragmentary form in which this notice appears, the name of Tarentum does not occur. But the expression ὁμόρους, as applied to the Iapygians and Peuketians, can only refer to Tarentum. It has certainly no reference to Krotôn, the capture of which is mentioned in the preceding paragraph.

West of the Lakinian promontory. The sinking of the Roman squadron which had appeared within actual sight of their city by the infuriated Tarentines was the beginning of hostilities, rapidly followed by the capture of Thurioi and the surrender of its Roman garrison. The Thurians were punished by the triumphant Tarentines " because, although they were Hellenes they had thrown themselves on the protection of the Romans and not of their kinsmen." The die was cast. The overtures of the Romans, then anxious to gain time, for a peaceful settlement were rejected, and in 282 the Tarentines and their allies called to their assistance the greatest soldier of the age, Pyrrhus of Epirus.

It is to the date of Pyrrhus' expedition that I venture to refer the reduction of the Tarentine didrachm weight. It has been already shown in the preceding section that federal drachmæ answering to a silver stater of reduced weight had been already struck by the Tarentines during Period VI., side by side with didrachms and litras of the full traditional standard, and the inference has been drawn from this, that the weight of the silver stater in other Italiote cities had already been reduced before Pyrrhus' time. It is to be observed, on the other hand, that at Metapontion, taken by the Lucanians shortly before 300 B.C., and at Krotôn, sacked by Agathoklês in 299, no didrachms or silver staters of reduced weight are forthcoming, and it is therefore probable that at Hêrakleia and Thurioi the reduction did not take place till after that date. The issue of the reduced federal drachms at Tarentum during a considerable part of Period VI. may, on the other hand, be taken as an indication that some at least of the League cities of the Ionian shore had reduced their standard at least not long after the date of the capture of Metapontion and Krotôn. Tarentum, however, as has been shown, still held on for a while to its traditional metric arrangements, so far at least as its internal currency was concerned.

The dual monetary system, however, thus introduced could not have been satisfactory in its practical working, and the reduction of the didrachm and litra standard at Tarentum itself in conformity with that of its federal drachmæ and diobols was not long delayed. That the Tarentine didrachms struck at the time of Pyrrhus' Italian campaigns were already of the lighter standard is evident from the occurrence, on some of the earliest didrachms of the reduced weight, of the elephant symbol which we have every historic reason for connecting with the Epirote King. A minuter examination of the evidence at our disposal reveals the fact that the reduction of the didrachm weight at Tarentum from c. 123—120 to c. 102—99 grains took place shortly after Pyrrhus' arrival, and must on every ground be connected with that event.

Besides the didrachms of reduced weight showing on their reverse the elephant symbol we find other certain evidence of Pyrrhus' influence on the Tarentine mint. There exists in the Berlin Cabinet a gold stater [169] presenting on the obverse the laureate head of Zeus to the right, and on the reverse an eagle with unfolded wings, seated to the left on a thunderbolt, in front of which is a figure of Pallas Promachos, precisely as she appears on the well-known coins struck by Pyrrhus himself in

---

[169] By the kindness of the Director, Herr von Sallet, I am enabled to give a representation of this coin, Pl. V. 17. (Cf. Friedländer und Sallet, *Das kœnigliche Münzkabinet*, No. 512, p. 147.)

Syracuse.[170] The main types themselves, the head of Zeus and the eagle on the bolt, are characteristically Epirote, and we are thus enabled to refer with confidence a series of gold Tarentine staters of the same class as the above, but with varying symbols, to the time of Pyrrhus' expedition or the immediately succeeding Period. That this class of Tarentine gold coins is, in fact, posterior in date to the types presenting the veiled head of Dêmêtêr, and at least to the earlier of those with the youthful Hêraklês coifed in the lion's skin, is evident, not only from their style, but from their absence from the Tarentine gold-find of Alexander the Great's time, already described.[171]

The following may be taken as a summary of the other Tarentine staters of this Pyrrhic type, showing the symbols and signatures with which they are associated.

Obv.	Rev.
2. Head of Zeus to l.; NK behind. Car. ciii. 1. 133·08 grs., 9·62 grammes.	Eagle to l., owl in front, ΣΩΚ behind.
3. Same. B. M. Cat. 1. 131·3 grs., 8·5 grammes.	Eagle to r. In front, two stars above two amphoræ. Beneath thunderbolt, NIKAP.

---

[170] Cf. Head, *Coins of Syracuse* (*Num. Chron.*, 1874, p. 56). The goddess represented is probably Athena Alkis, the tutelary goddess of the royal Macedonian city of Pella, Alexander the Great's birthplace. The type, as Mr. Head has pointed out, was adopted as a symbol of sovereignty over Macedon, and first appears on the coins struck by Ptolemy I. for the young Alexander Ægos, the son and rightful heir of Alexander the Great.

[171] See p. 97, and *Notizie dei Scavi*, 1886, 279. The gold types with the youthful head of Hêraklês seem to have gone on, however, to a very late period, and this type was apparently revived in Hannibal's time (see p. 209).

Obv.	Rev.

4. Same.
B. M. Cat. 3. 132·3 grs. 8·57 grammes.

Same; but **NIKAP** behind eagle.

5. Same.
B. M. Cat. 2. 131·7 grs., 8·52 grammes.

Same; **ΦΙ** above; beneath, thunderbolt …?

6. Head to r., **NK** behind.
Car. ciii. 2. 133·4 grs., 8·65 grammes.

Eagle to l.; in front **Ʀ**.

7. Same; (hair somewhat differently treated). **NK** behind.
Car. ciii. 4.

Same; in front, **Ʀ**; above, **Σ**.

8. Same; but **K** behind.
Car. ciii. 6.

Eagle to r.; in front, **ΑΠΟΛ**, and helmet with cheek pieces.

From the identity of the signatures, as well as of the reverse type, we are further entitled to regard the following quarter staters as belonging to the same group.

1. Head of Apollo laureate, r. In front, **NK**.
Car. civ. 22. Wt. 33·27 grs., 2·156 grammes.
 [Pl. V. 15.]

Eagle on thunderbolt as before; in front, **Ʀ** and spear-head. Beneath, **ΙΑ**.

2. Same.
Car. civ. 21.

Same; but in front **ΦΙ**, and two stars above two amphoras.

3. Same; no insc.
Car. civ. 23. Wt. 33·27 grs., 2·156 grammes.

Same; no symbol or insc.

These Pyrrhic gold types of Tarentum supply us with some valuable data for fixing the contemporaneity of certain silver types of the same city. Amongst the symbols that appear on the above gold series one of the most interesting and characteristic is the spear-head which is seen in front of the eagle and bolt on the quarter-stater (No. 1) associated with the signatures Ƨ and ΙΑ. The spear-head badge, which the Æakid princes took in virtue, it would seem, of some traditional connexion with the Ætolian Meleagros[172], and which the Molossian Alexander had already placed on his Italian coinage, became at a later period a recognised type of the autonomous Epirote mints. Although Pyrrhus himself does not seem to have placed this symbol on coins struck by him in his own name, the appearance of the spear-head on a Tarentine piece, coupled with a type and signature that place it among the Pyrrhic issues of the city, must be taken as an evident allusion to the Epirote hero. On the quarter-stater referred to this symbol is seen associated with the monogram Ƨ, which obviously belongs to the same magistrate or moneyer who on a stater of the same series signs ƧΙ for ΑΡΙ. When, then, we find the same symbol of a

---

[172] So, for example, we find (Arrian, *Anab.* l. 24) that conversely the father of Meleagros, a distinguished general of Alexander the Great, bore the typically Æakid name of Neoptolemos. The Illyrian, like the Epirote princes, claimed Æakid descent, and it was no doubt owing to this connexion that the Illyrian Monounios placed the spear-head symbol in association with the jawbone of the Calydonian boar on his Dyrrhachian staters. Meleagros was said to have dedicated the spear, with which he slew the monster, to Apollo, in the temple at Sikyôn, where Pausanias (ii. 7) describes it. The spear-head as a symbol of the Epirote king, recalls a line of the Tarentine Leónidas' epigram on Pyrrhus (c. xxiv. 4): "Αἰχμηταὶ καὶ νῦν καὶ πάρος Αἰακίδαι."

spear-head occurring on a silver didrachm (VI., E 2, Pl. VII. 10)[173] in association with the signature ΑΡΙ we are justified in concluding that both pieces belong to the same approximate date.

Judging from its style, this didrachm with the spear-head symbol is one of the latest of the full-weight issues. But the close relationship thus established between one of the latest of the full-weight didrachms and a quarter gold stater of Pyrrhic type has a very important bearing on the chronology of the Tarentine silver coinage. It certainly tends to show that some at least of the full-weight issues were struck as late as 282 B.C., when the Tarentines concluded their bargain with the Epirote king. We find, moreover, on another Pyrrhic gold stater of the type presenting on the reverse the eagle on the thunderbolt the signature ΣΩΚ, apparently only an abbreviated form of the ΣΩΚΡΑΤΗΣ which occurs on two other types of the same Period VI. (A 2 and 5), in one case also associated with the monogram ℞. The signature ΣΩΚ, on the other hand, does not answer to any name that appears on the ensuing didrachm series of reduced weight.[174]

The conclusion to which we are led by these coincidences, that the issue of the silver didrachms of full weight

---

[173] The lance-head also occurs as a symbol on a litra (*B. M. Cat.* 407), which from its weight, 12·5 grs., must have been struck previous to the reduction of the silver standard, and which bears the signature ΑΓ, an indication that it belongs to Period V.

[174] The name ΣΩΚΑΝΝΑΣ, another possible completion of the abbreviated form ΣΩΚ, only occurs at a time which places it out of the range of comparison with the Pyrrhic gold-pieces (see Period X.). The earlier ΣΩΚ of Period III. is also one of the field of comparison.

continued, in fact, at Tarentum to the date of Pyrrhus' expedition, involves, as its logical consequence, the further deduction that it was directly or indirectly to the Epirote king that the reduction of the weight of the silver stater in this city was actually owing. The occurrence of the elephant symbol on some of the earliest of the reduced weight issues shows that the change of weight must have taken place soon after Pyrrhus' arrival; and that the reduction of the Tarentine silver standard should have been effected at a time when the mint was practically under Pyrrhus' control, fits in well with the monetary revolution subsequently carried out by him at Syracuse in his own name.[175]

That the reduction of the Tarentine silver standard in fact took place during the time when the Epirote king was exercising a dominant influence over the city receives additional corroboration from a comparison of two remarkable Tarentine silver litras, both stamped with Pyrrhic symbols. The first of these (Pl. V. 16) presents on the obverse the usual scallop, and on the reverse, below the dolphin, a figure of Pallas Promachos as she appears on the coins of Pyrrhus, and the signature Δ. The weight of a specimen of this coin in my own cabinet is, as nearly as possible, 12 grains (0·76 gramme),[176] and exactly corresponds to the

---

[175] There is, however, no evident relation between Pyrrhus' Sicilian pieces of c. 90 grs. and the reduced didrachms of Tarentum, &c., weighing c. 100 grs. It is clear, indeed, that as the new Pyrrhic currency dominated the Brettian country and the whole of South-Western Italy, an official tariff, making these the equivalent of the reduced didrachms of the Italiote cities, would have had favourable results for the royal exchequer.

[176] The weights of three coins, of the same type and symbol, given by Carelli, are 11·396, 11·09, and 10·298 grains, exactly agreeing with that of the litræ with the signature ΑΓ and the

full didrachm weight of about 120 grains.[177] This is the normal weight of the litra down to the conclusion of Period VI., as is shown by correspondences of symbol and signature with those of didrachms belonging to that Period.[178] But, as appears from another interesting piece, of which there is a specimen in the British Museum,[179] the litræ of reduced weight began already to be struck during the period of Pyrrhus' domination. On this litra (Pl. V. 18) the significant symbol of an elephant replaces the figure of Athênê Alkis beneath the dolphin, and the weight, 8·7 grs., brings it well within the margin of the inferior standard—9½ grs. being about the normal weight of silver litras that can be shown to correspond to the didrachms of the reduced weight.[180] We are left to infer that the reduction of the silver standard at Tarentum took place between the issues of these two litræ, and we may further conclude that of the two Pyrrhic badges on the Tarentine coinage the figure of Pallas Promachos precedes that of the elephant.

The fact which we may now, therefore, regard as esta-

---

bunch of grapes belonging to Period VI. The weights of two specimens of these latter, as determined by Carelli, are 11·396 and 11·09 grains.

[177] Carelli (cxvii. 297) has engraved what is obviously the same piece, but the figure of the goddess has been wrongly rendered, and resembles rather a figure of Mars. Its weight is 0·74 gramme (cf. Mommsen, *op. cit.* I. 294), which is almost identical with that of my example.

[178] See p. 128.

[179] *B. M. Cat.* 402. Carelli gives the coin (cxvii. 319), but not the weight.

[180] The average weight of the litræ of the great Taranto hoard belonging to this late Period is c. 9½ grs. (See Appendix C.) The litræ in *B. M. Cat.*, 393—4, with the signatures ↑ and ꓤ, which occur on a very late didrachm with the magistrate's name ΑΡΙΣΤΙΠΠΟΣ, weigh 9 grs.

blished, that the last issues of the full-weight didrachms were struck as late as 282 B.C., may possibly throw a new light on one of the latest of these types. This is the piece [VI. D 1] presenting on the obverse the name of the magistrate ΑΝΘΡΩΣ (whose name in an abbreviated form recurs on two early coins of the reduced weight), and on the reverse the symbol of an anchor, accompanied with the signatures ΕΥ ΑΡ, which recalls the combination ΕΥ ΑΡΙ on the Pyrrhic type presenting the spear-head. But there is a good analogy for supposing that the anchor, like the spear-head itself, the figures of Pallas Promachos or of the elephant on the contemporary pieces, has an historic significance. On a late Tarentine obol [181] there appears as the reverse type an anchor coupled with a laurel wreath or spray, evidently intended as a trophy, which Fiorelli has brought into relation with the maritime victory gained by the Tarentines under Dêmokratês over the Roman fleet off Krotôn during the period of the Hannibalic occupation.[182] This victory was

---

[181] Described by Fiorelli, *Medaglie incerte di Taranto*, in Bull. dell' Inst. Arch., 1841, p. 174. Fiorelli has unfortunately not given the weight of the piece, but from the kantharos, surrounded by three pellets, which forms the obverse type, it may be assumed to have been an obol or sixth of a drachm (cf. Mommsen, *op. cit.* p. 146). Garrucci (c. 25) gives another similar coin, but with five pellets on the obverse and four on the reverse, but omits, as usual, to give the weight. The number of pellets five, four, and three, or even one on these small Tarentine pieces presenting the kantharos, has no visible relation to the weight (cf. *B. M. Cat.* 432—447.) The weights fall into two classes, one of slightly under 10 grains, answering to the sixth of a drachm of full weight; the other of c. 8 grs., standing in the same relation to the reduced drachm of c. 50 grs. In one case only the abnormally low weight of 5·7 occurs. (Cf. too Mommsen, *op. cit.* p. 297.)

[182] Livy, lib. xxvi. c. 39.

commemorated in an inscription found on the Tarentine site recording the erection of a trophy "to the marine and hippic gods" out of the spoils of the captured vessels. Whether Fiorelli be right or wrong in assigning this occasion for the issue of the small silver type that he describes, its occurrence certainly seems to show that the anchor on a Tarentine coin [183] was regarded as a symbol of naval victory, and although on the didrachm that we are at present considering it is not coupled with a laurel spray, its appearance on a piece struck about the time of Pyrrhus' expedition must be regarded as highly significant. We recall the memorable occasion of the first open hostilities with Rome, the sinking or capture of the Roman galleys which, in open violation of the treaty that limited their right of navigation to the Lakinian promontory, had appeared in Tarentine waters in full sight of the citizens then celebrating the Dionysia in the theatre.

It further appears that besides the coins with such indubitably Pyrrhic symbols as the elephant, the eagle on the bolt, or Athênê Alkis, additional references to the arrival of the Epirote king are to be traced on some of the earliest didrachms of the reduced weight series.

These appear on a curiously parallel series of coins signed ΑΡΙΣ and ΠΟΛΥ, both associated with signa-

---

[183] The anchor also occurs on a didrachm of reduced weight, coupled with the signature of ΑΡΙΣΤΙΣ, and on a drachm, apparently of the same magistrate, but signed ΑΡΙCΤΙC; it serves as a perch for the owl. It further appears on a litra (wt. 0·52 gramme), Car. cxvii. 312. It is probable that the piece described by Fiorelli fits on to this series. If so, it may contain an allusion to some naval action unrecorded by history, and the date of which would be between the Pyrrhic and Hannibalic periods.

tures belonging to coins with the well-known Pyrrhic badge,[184] and the first of the two apparently identical with the magistrate who, under the abbreviated form AP or the fuller ΑΡΙΣΤΙΠ, attaches his signature to pieces that present the elephant symbol. There are two coins, Type A, 2—4 [Pl. VIII. 2, 3] signed ΠΟΛΥ on the reverse, in both of which Taras is seen holding out his hand to receive a small Victory, who reaches forth a wreath to crown his head. On one of these the Epirote symbol of the thunderbolt, adopted on their Italian coinage both by Pyrrhus and his predecessor, the Molossian Alexander, appears in the field, while on the other, below the dolphin, in the place occupied by the elephant on contemporary pieces, is seen the prow of a galley, characterized by a projecting beak and a high curving akrostolion ($\chi\eta\nu i\sigma\kappa o\varsigma$), which itself curiously resembles a raised proboscis. The alternation of the thunderbolt and the prow of the war vessel on these twin coins may be aptly regarded as covering an allusion to the arrival of Pyrrhus' fleet at Tarentum.

Two other types [C 2, 3], one signed ΠΟΛΥ (Pl. VIII. 6), the other ΑΡΙΣ, but which in other respects are identical, afford, however, some still more suggestive materials for comparison. Upon the reverse of these Taras is represented seated sideways on his dolphin, to the left, resting his left hand on its back, and holding out with his right a helmet of remarkable shape, having ear-pieces, and in front a projecting horn. In the field on either side are two stars, and the coin thus shows a certain analogy with

---

[184] Thus we find the parallel groups ΙΩ ΝΕΥΜΗ—ΑΡΙΣ, two stars; ΙΩ ΝΕΥΜΗ—ΠΟΛΥ, two stars; and ΙΩ ΝΕΥΜΗ—ΑΡ, elephant. (See *infra*.)

the noble type already described, and in which I have ventured to trace an allusion to the fall of Archidâmos. In the present case, however, not only is the style very much inferior to the other, but the attitude in which Taras is represented is wholly new on the Tarentine dies. The attitude in which the Eponymic hero here appears is in fact nothing less than a direct reproduction of that in which Apollo is made to appear on some well-known types struck by the Diadochi in Syria and Macedonia, the only difference being that here the figure holds a helmet in place of a bow or arrow. The style is the same, and we have the same somewhat attenuated proportions of limbs and body. Nor is the reproduction by any means confined to the attitude and style of the figure. By an extraordinary departure from the received manner of depicting the Eponymic hero, Taras is here represented with hair knotted behind and falling over his shoulders in curling tresses, exactly as Apollo's hair is treated on the coins of Alexander's successors, from which the scheme of the figure itself was taken.

The earliest example of this type seems to be the Apollo on a bronze piece of Seleukos Nikâtor [185] (312—280 B.C.), which itself is an adaptation of an almost similar type that appears on a silver double stater of the Cypriote King Nikoklês of Paphos [186] (310—305 B.C.). On the silver as well as the bronze coins of Nikâtor's son Antiochos I. (293—261), this design becomes usual, and it is common on the coins of his successors to the middle

---

[185] *B. M. Cat., Seleucidæ*, Pl. II. 5, and cf. Prof. Gardner's remarks, p. xv.

[186] Mionnet, *Suppl.* vii. 310. The only difference in the scheme is that the hand holding the bow rests on the r. leg instead of being raised.

of the third century. On these Seleukid coins Apollo is seen seated on the omphalos and holding a bow and one or more arrows. On some Macedonian coins of Antigonos Gonatas [187] Apollo again appears in the same attitude, but seated on the prow of a vessel, the occasion of the adoption of this type being in Dr. Imhoof-Blumer's opinion [188] the victory gained by Gonatas over the Egyptian fleet off Cos in 265 B.C. This being admitted, it is impossible to regard this Macedonian coin as the prototype of our two Tarentine pieces, and we are reduced to look to a Syrian source. The coin signed ΠΟΛΥ and that signed ΑΡΙΣ present an obverse type identical both in its design and its double signature ΙΩ ΝΕΥΜΗ, with another piece bearing upon its reverse the elephant symbol, and we have therefore the strongest grounds for assigning them to the date of Pyrrhus's expedition. It follows therefore that it is to the coins of Antiochos I. of Syria that we must look for the model from which the Tarentine engraver drew his novel scheme of Taras.

But this conclusion is borne out by another remarkable feature in the design. Comparing one example with another, the head-piece in Taras's hands is seen to have a distinct horn in front, and to be in fact the counterpart of the horned Asiatic helmet adopted in somewhat variant forms by Seleukos Nikâtor, and which

---

[187] Accepting the view that these coins are to be referred to Gonatas rather than Dôsôn.

[188] *Monnaies Grecques*, p. 128. For myself I cannot refrain from expressing a suspicion that the coins of Antigonos Gonatas, with this naval type, were struck at an earlier date in his reign. Already in 280 we find him aiding Pyrrhus with his ships. He had inherited his naval power from his father Dêmétrios Poliorkêtês, and there seems no good reason why he should not have alluded to it on his earliest coinage.

seems from its reappearance in a more exaggerated style on later coins[189] to have been used as a sort of badge by the Seleukid kings. A helmet of the same kind appears on some of the Pyrrhic gold staters struck at Tarentum[190] as a symbol beside the eagle on the bolt; a type which as we have seen is otherwise associated with the Macedonian device of Athênê Alkis. Held in the hands of Taras as assimilated to the Apollo of Antiochos I.'s monetary cult, it enhances the definiteness of the allusion, and conveys an obvious compliment to the son of the recently deceased "Conqueror" of the East, who died the year before Pyrrhus's expedition. Nor, if we consider the circumstances of Pyrrhus's Italian enterprise, is the occasion of this numismatic tribute far to seek. The royal contemporaries of the Epirote Prince, however great their mutual rivalries, had at least the common interest of seeing the greatest warrior of the age embarked in Western adventures which took him far away from their own dominions. Accordingly, as Justin informs us, Ptolemy Keraunos supplied five thousand foot soldiers, four thousand horsemen, and fifty elephants, and Antigonos ships for the transport of the expeditionary

---

[189] *E.g.* Antiochos VI. and Tryphôn, *B. M. Cat.*, *Seleucidæ*, Pl. xix. 7, xx. 1—3. As a symbol in the field it occurs on coins of Antigonos Gonatas, associated with the type of Athênê Alkis.

[190] *B. M. Cat.*, 4, with the signature ΑΓΟΛ (see p. 141, No. 8). Carelli (ciii. 6) wrongly represents it as a Phrygian cap. The signature ΑΓΟΛ on these Pyrrhic staters is not to be confounded with the ΑΓΟΛ on the earlier types of Alexander the Molossian's time. It is to be identified rather with the magistrate who signs ΑΓΟΛ, and in the fuller form ΑΓΟΛΛΩ-ΝΙΟΣ on some of the earliest didrachms of reduced weight. The form ΑΓΟΛ is found on these in close association with the signature ΠΟΛΥ.

force. Antiochos, "who was better provided with wealth than soldiers, supplied a sum of money," which if it was at all the equivalent of these other subsidies must have been of considerable amount. We have here at least a very substantial reason for the influence of Antiochos' tetradrachm types on the Tarentine dies, and for the compliment that they seem to convey to the son of Seleukos.

The internal evidence supplied by a series of types, symbols, and signatures, thus enables us to group together a series of didrachms of the reduced weight which may with confidence be ascribed to the time of the Pyrrhic hegemony at Tarentum. In this earliest class of reduced weight coins may be reasonably included (1) those with a known Pyrrhic badge; (2) those intimately connected with the above in signature and device, as, for instance, the coins already alluded to with the signatures ΙΩ ΝΕΥΜΗ, ΠΟΛΥ, ΙΩ ΝΕΥΜΗ ΑΡΙ, ΑΠΟΛ ΠΟΛΥ, and several varieties with ΓΥ in the field; (3) a few coins presenting the greatest resemblance to the latest full-weight types of Period VI., or with the same collocation of names, as in the case of the reduced weight didrachm reading ΣΙ ΛΥΚΩΝ.

Happily, however, in endeavouring to determine the Tarentine silver issues of the Pyrrhic Period, we are no longer restricted to the internal evidence to be deduced from the connexity of types and signatures. It was not till after I had arrived at the results explained in the preceding pages, that I had an opportunity of inspecting a recent find of Tarentine coins, which throws a welcome light on the coinage of this Period, and at the same time affords a strong retrospective corroboration of the general conclusions already elaborated.

The hoard in question, of which all I cou'd learn was that it came from Calabria, and was discovered towards the end of 1887, must in its original form have been of considerable bulk. Whilst re ently at Naples I was enabled to inspect and describe between four and five hundred pieces belonging to it that had not yet been dispersed, but many had already found their way into the Paris and London markets. A succinct account of the coins that I saw together will be found under Appendix B. They were for the most part in brilliant condition, and with a single exception—the coin reading ΔΕΙΝΟ-ΚΡΑΤΗΣ belonging to the last Period of the full-weight issues—all were of the reduced standard. The great interest attaching to this find is due to the fact that it includes the whole of the earliest group of the reduced weight coinages, and at the same time apparently coincides with the Period of the Pyrrhic hegemony.

Of seventeen varieties which on grounds of internal evidence I had already before the discovery of this find ventured to attribute to the Pyrrhic Period,[191] no less than fifteen were represented in the present deposit by well-preserved specimens. Together with these were seven fresh varieties which must certainly be regarded as more or less contemporary with the others. From the absence on these, however, of the more definite Pyrrhic indications, as well as from the greater abundance and singularly brilliant condition of most of them, it is reasonable to suppose that they belong to the later years of the Epirote connexion, when Pyrrhus had himself recrossed the Adriatic. There can indeed be little doubt that the occa-

---

[191] Type A 1—5; B 1; C, 1—7; D 1; E 1—2.

sion of the Calabrian deposit is to be sought in the circumstances which attended the Roman occupation of Tarentum in 272. The fact, however, that a few coins of the present hoard presenting the signatures NK ΦΙΛΟΚΡΑ seem rather to attach themselves to a succeeding post-Pyrrhic group makes it probable that the actual deposit did not occur till a short time after the Roman entry into Tarentum. These few pieces in all probability represent the first issue of the new régime, and I have accordingly included them among the types of the First Period of the Roman alliance.[192]

The most abundant types represented in this hoard were those associated with the signature ΑΠΟΛΛΩ, to be identified with the later ΑΠΟΛΛΩΝΙΟΣ, and ΑΝΘ or ΑΝ, which recalls the ΑΝΘΡΩΣ of the last full-weight issue. With the Tarentine didrachms were a certain number of drachms, also of the reduced weight, bearing the signatures ΣΩΣ-ΔΙΟ, ΣΩ-ΔΙ, ΑΠ-ΔΙ, and of ΝΕΥΜΗΝΙΟΣ in association with ΠΟΛΥ and ΑΡΙ, and it is evident, as much from a comparison with the didrachm signatures of this Period as from their occurrence in the present find, that these drachms must also be ascribed to the time of Pyrrhus. The only non-Tarentine coins contained in the hoard were some late types of Hêrakleia and Thurioi, which from their fresh condition must be held to be contemporary with the most recent Tarentine issues of the deposit. The coins of Hêrakleia in particular with ΦΙΛΟ in the field representing Hêraklês standing, and another type with a thunderbolt in the field, in which the same hero is seen sacrificing over

---

[192] VIII. A 5; C 2 and 3.

an altar, were *fleur de coin*, and must have been struck very shortly before the withdrawal of the hoard from circulation.

The contents of the Calabrian find show that the period of the Pyrrhic connexion at Tarentum was a time of prolific mintage. It is evident indeed that Tarentum was called on to defray a large part of the expenses of Pyrrhus's Italian enterprise, and the moneyers seem to have been kept exceptionally active by the constant exactions of the Epirote ally. The fine state of preservation in which the whole of the twenty-nine didrachm types contained in this hoard were discovered, itself affords unmistakeable evidence that the reduced-weight issues could not have been current many years at the date when this hoard was withdrawn from circulation. Even were there not such strong historical probabilities as to the actual occasion of this deposit it would not be safe to bring it down more than ten years after the date of the first issue of the didrachms of the reduced weight. It is noteworthy that the single specimen of a didrachm of full weight found in the hoard was itself in fine condition.

The occurrence of the signatures EY, ΘI, or ΣΩΓY, on Pyrrhic types of the Calabrian hoard has enabled me to add to the series some other excessively rare types (H, K, and L), one of which presents these signatures combined. On the reverse of two of these is seen a revival of the interesting design of Taras contemplating a heroic helmet, to which attention has been sufficiently called under Period IV., while the obverse of K and L (Pl. XI. 12, 13) shows us the horseman in a new attitude, seated sideways on his horse—a design repeated on some votive terra-cottas from the site of a Chthonic sanctuary at Tarentum, to which attention has already been called. Another very rare piece, M 1 (Pl. VIII. 14) equally absent from the Calabrian hoard, in which a boy jockey is seen at full gallop holding out behind him the torch of the *lampadedromia*, must also be included in the same series, from its similarity both in design and signatures with type L 1 (Pl. VIII. 13). In the one case the name of the monetary magistrate appears as ϜΗΡΑ, in the other as ϜΗΡΑΚΛΗΙ, which is probably an abbreviation of the official who signs in full as ϜΗΡΑΚΛΗΤΟΣ during the succeeding Period. We shall have occasion to return to the interesting agonistic type with which this name is connected.

From its parallelism with the type of the armed horseman with the radiate shield, I have also added to the present class a remarkable piece, F 6 (Pl. VIII. 12); a specimen of which exists in the Bodleian Collection, exhibiting upon the shield the three letters ΕΙC. This inscription is doubtless an amplification of the single Ε borne by Taras on his shield upon two coins of Period VI. (B 1—2). It would, however, be overbold were we by the light of later numismatics to attempt to explain the inscription as referring to an ΑΓΩΝ ΕΙCΕΛΑCΤΙΚΟC, which in this case might, of course, be brought into relation with a triumphal entry of the Epirote king.

VII. Type A.

Naked horseman (sometimes helmeted) on prancing horse to r., lancing downwards, and with round shield and reserve of two lances behind him.

Obv.	Rev.
1. In f. to l., ΓΥ; beneath horse, ΑΡΙ ΣΤΙ Γ Car. cx. 127. [Pl. VIII. 1.]	Taras riding in warlike fury on his dolphin (revival of Pl. IV. 8 and Pl. VI. 12), preparing to fit an arrow to his bow. Beneath, ΔΙ and elephant.
2. Same; in f. to l., ΓΥ. Beneath horse, ΣΩΣΤΡΑΤΟΣ. [Pl. VIII. 2.]	Taras astride, &c., to l., holding cornucopiæ in l. hand, and with r. receiving small Victory, who holds forth a wreath to crown his brow. In f. to l., ΠΟΛΥ; to r., thunderbolt.
3. Same; in f. to l., ΕΥ. Beneath horse, ΣΩΣΤΡΑΤΟΣ. Car. cxiii. 198.	Same.
4. Same; (helmeted). In f. to l., ΕΥ. Beneath horse, ΦΙΝΤΥΛΟΣ. Cf. Car. cxiv. 212. [" ΕΥ ΦΙΝΤΙΑΣ —ΛΥ."] [Pl. VIII. 3.]	Same; but holding in l. hand trident. In f. to l., ΠΟΛΥ. Below dolphin, prow of vessel.
5. Same; in f. to l., ΘΕ. Beneath horse, ΑΛΕΞ. Car. cx. 117.	Taras, astride, &c., to l., holding trident in l. hand, and with r. extending wreath. In f. to r., ΣΙ; beneath dolphin, star.
6. Same; but to r. small Victory flies forward extending wreath. In f. to l., ΣΙ. Beneath horse, ΛΥΚΩΝ.[193] Cf Car. cxii. 169. [" ΕΥ ΛΥΚΩΝ."]	Same; but extending kantharos. In f. to r. ΓΥ or ΥΊ.

---

[193] The two signatures ΣΙ, ΛΥΚΩΝ, are associated on one of the latest full-weight didrachms of a slightly different type, VI. D 8.

VII. Type B.

Naked boy on horse walking l., which is received and crowned by a standing male figure (revival of Pl. IV. 8).

Obv.	Rev.
1. In f. to r., ΓΥ. Beneath horse, API ⋛TI Γ Car. cx. 126. [Pl. VIII. 4.]	Taras riding on dolphin as A 1, with bow and arrow. Beneath, elephant, and sometimes ΔΙ.

VII. Type C.

Naked boy-rider crowning stationary horse (generally to r., and lifting up fore-leg).

1. In f. to l., ΙΩ. Beneath horse, NEY MH B. M. Cat. 147. [Pl. VIII. 5.]	Taras riding on dolphin, with bow and arrow as before. Beneath dolphin, Ʀ, and elephant.
2. Same.	Taras seated sideways on dolphin to l., holding out a horned helmet. On either side a twelve-rayed star. In f. to r., ΑΡΙ⋛.
3. Same. Car. cxii. 174. [Pl. VIII. 6.]	Same; but in f. to r., ΠΟΛΥ.
4.[194] Same; but in f. to l., Ʀ. Beneath horse, ΔΑΜΟΚΡΙ.	Taras astride, &c., holding in l. hand trident and small round shield, on which is a hippocamp, and extending with r. a cornucopiæ.

[194] For the signature Ʀ, and a very similar obv. and rev. type, see Type E. For rev. see also Type D. In both cases the type is associated with the characteristically Pyrrhic signature ΓΥ.

Obv.	Rev.
5. Horse to r. In f. to l., **EY**. Beneath horse, in minute letters, **ΑΠΟΛΛΩ** and two amphoras. [Pl. VIII. 7.]	Taras astride, &c., to l., holding trident in l. hand, and with r. extending kantharos. In f. to r., ⊙I.
6. Same. Car. cx. 119.	Same; but in f. to r. **B**, to l. ⊙I.
7. Same; but in f. to l., ⊢I. Beneath horse, **ΑΠΟΛΛΩ**, and two amphoras.	Same; but in f. to r., ⊙I.
8. Same; horse to l. In f. to r., ⊢I. Beneath horse, **ΙΩΠΥ**, and small squatting figure holding horn. [Pl. VIII. 8.]	Taras astride, &c., to l., holding distaff in l. hand, and with r. receiving small wreath-bearing Victory. In f. to l., ✷.

VII. Type D.

Two Dioskuri with flowing mantles, cantering l. (Revival of IV. K).

1. In f. above, ✪. Beneath horse, ⋛**ΑΛΩ-ΝΟ**⋛. [Pl. VIII. 9.] Car. cxiii. 184.	Taras astride, &c., to l., holding behind him two lances and a small round shield with hippocamp device, while with r. hand he receives small wreath-bearing Victory. In f. to l., **ΓΥ**. Taras has a tænia round his head; beneath, waves.

VII. Type E.

Single Dioskuros with flowing chlamys l., holding out wreath to crown his horse's head. The horse paces r.

1. In f. to l., ⱰR. Beneath horse, ⋛**ΑΛΩ-ΝΟ**⋛ (?). [Pl. VIII. 10.]	Same as D 1; and with same legend **ΓΥ** in f. to l.

Obv.	Rev.
2. Same; no letters in f. Signature beneath horse uncertain.	Taras astride, &c., to l., in a Poseidonian attitude,[195] with back half turned to the spectator, hurling trident with r. hand, and with chlamys hanging from his l. arm. In f. to l., ΓΥ.

VII. Type F.

Helmeted warrior on horse, cantering l., wearing crested helmet, and holding before him a large round shield, on which is the eight-rayed star; in the case of No. 6, the letters ЄIC.

1. In f. to r., ΙΩ. Beneath horse, ⊢Ι ΑΓΟΛΛΩ	Taras, of plump Dionysiac type, astride, &c., l., holding distaff, and with r. hand extending bunch of grapes. In f. to r., ΑΝ⊙ or ΑΝ.
2. Same; but beneath horse, ΑΓΟΛΛΩ	Same.
3. Same.	Same; but in f. to r., spray of laurel.
4. Same. Calabrian find. [Pl. VIII. 11.]	Same; but in f. to r. coiled serpent raising its head.
5. Same. Car. cx. 120.	Same; but in f. corn-spike.
6. Same; ЄIC on shield. In f. to r., ΙΩ. No inscription visible beneath horse. [Pl. VIII. 12. Bodleian Coll. Wt. 100 grs.]	Same; in f. to r., ΑΝ⊙. No symbol.

---

[195] The upper part of this figure of Taras presents an unmistakeable resemblance to that of his father Poseidôn, as he appears on the tetradrachms of Dêmêtrios Poliorkêtês (306—283), the father of Antigonos Gonatas. Here again, as in the case of the copies of the Seleukid Apollo, we may detect a complimentary allusion to the assistance rendered by the Diadochi to Pyrrhus and Tarentum. This type of Taras was repeated on Tarentine coins of a later period.

VII. Type G.

Naked boy-rider crowning himself on horse standing l., and lifting up off fore-leg.

Obv.
1. In f. to l., ΤΩ. Beneath horse, ΤΑ-ΛΟ and capital of Ionic column.
Car. cxi. 145.

Rev.
Taras, holding distaff, and with r. hand extending akrostolion. In f. to r., ΑΝΘ or ΑΝ.

VII. Type H.

Naked youth, cantering l.

1. In f. to r., ΕΥ. Beneath horse, ΤΩΠΥ.
B. M. Cat.

Taras astride, &c., to l., holding palm bound with lemniskos, and with r. hand extending kantharos. In f. to r., a crested Corinthian helmet. In f. to l., ΘΙ. (Revival of V. D.).

VII. Type K.

Naked youth, with both legs extended together, seated sideways on horse cantering l.

1. In f. to r. Τ. Beneath horse, ΤΩΓΥ.
[Pl. XI. 12. Santangelo Coll.]

Same as H, l., but no lemniskos and no insc. ΘΙ.

2. Same.
[Pl. XI. 13. Cab. des Médailles, No. 1480.]

Taras astride, &c., to l., holding distaff in l. hand, and with r. receiving wreath-bearing Victory. In f. to r. fillet and uncertain object.

VII. Type L.

Naked youth, cantering r., and holding out torch behind him.

1. Beneath horse, ΗΡΑ.
[Pl. VIII. 13. Calabrian find.]

Taras astride, &c., holding in l. hand two lances, and with r. aiming a dart. A chlamys flows from his l. arm. In f. to l. ✕, below dolphin Τ and diota.

VII. Type M.

Naked boy-jockey galloping r., and holding torch behind him.

Obv.	Rev.
1. Beneath horse, ΗΡΑΚΛΗΙ. Car. cxi. 151. B. M. Cat. [Pl. VIII. 14.]	Same as K 1. Same monogram and symbol; but Ⱥ in place of Ɪ.

Amongst drachms belonging to the Pyrrhic Period may be specified the following:—

1. Head of Pallas r., with Scylla on helmet. Calabrian find. Car. cxv. 234.	Owl, seated sideways to r., on olive branch, with closed wings. In f. to l., NEYMHNIOƧ; to r., API. [Cf. VII. C 1 and 2. IΩ NEYMH, Ⱥ, elephant; and APIƧ, two stars.]
2. Same. Car. cxv. 233.	Same type. In f. to l., NEYMHNIOƧ; to r. ΠΟΛΥ. [Cf. VII. C 3. IΩ NEYMH, 2 stars.]
3. Same. Cab. des Médailles.	Same. [ƧΩ]ƧΤΡΑΤΟƧ; to r. ΠΟΛΥ. In f. EY. [Cf. VII. A 3 EY ƧΩƧΤΡΑΤΟƧ—ΠΟΛΥ.]
4. Same; but on flap of helmet, Ɪ. B. M. Cat. 312.	Same; in f. to l., ƗΑΛΟ; to r., ΑΝ. [Cf. VII. G 1, ƗΩ ƗΑΛΟ ΑΝ, or ΑΝΘ.]
5. Same; Ɪ on flap of helmet. A. J. E. Calabrian find.	Same; but owl to l. In f. to r., ΤΑΡΑƧ. In f. to l., Ꙟ; beneath owl, Ⱥ. [Cf. VII. F. ƗΩ ΑΠΟΛΛΩ ΑΝΘ.]
6. Head of Pallas in Scylla helmet to l., with hair flowing down behind. Beneath, sometimes, EY. Calabrian find. B. M. Cat. 317—321. Car. cxv. 222.	Owl seated on thunderbolt, with opening wings, the further only partly visible. In f. above, ΤΑΡΑΝΤΙΝΩΝ. In f. to r., Ω or Ω; beneath thunderbolt, ΔΙ or ΔΙΟ. [Cf. VII. A 2. Insc. ΓΥƧΩƧΤΡΑΤΟƧ and thunderbolt; and VII. A 1; inser. ΔΙ and elephant.]

Obv.	Rev.
7. Head of Pallas, as No. 1. Car. cxv. 223; and cf. 224 (? ΦΙ for ΔΙ).	Owl seated, facing with expanded wings, both fully visible, on a serpent. Above **ΤΑΡΑΝΤΙΝΩΝ**. In f. to r., ⋛Ω⋛ or ⋛Ω; in f. to l. ΔΙ.

TARENTUM AS A *CIVITAS FŒDERATA*.

It is the currently received opinion that the Roman occupation of 272 B.C. put an end to the Tarentine coinage until at least the date of Hannibal's entry into the city, and the short space of revived independence under his protection between the years 212 and 207 B.C. But it may with good reason be urged that historic evidences weigh rather in the opposite scale. The first entry of the Romans into Tarentum was, in fact, very different from their recovery of the city in 207, after its defection to Hannibal. From the beginning of the Pyrrhic epoch it had been obvious that Rome could count on a friendly faction within the walls, and the philo-Roman element in Tarentum had been largely reinforced by the oppressive dominion exercised in the city by Pyrrhus himself, and at a later period by his Governor, Milôn. It was as the champion of the exiled Tarentines who, under their leader Nikôn, had ineffectually revolted against Pyrrhus' lieutenant, that the Consul Papirius appeared beneath the walls, and it was yielding to internal pressure that Milôn made terms with the Romans. Plundering took place no doubt; ships and arms were surrendered, statues and paintings graced Papirius' triumph; the walls were dismantled, and a Roman garrison succeeded the Epirote. But the well-being of Tarentum was so little impaired that two generations later, at the time of the second capture, its riches were hardly inferior to those of Syracuse. The spoils carried off by Papirius were insignificant compared with what remained to adorn the later triumph of Q. Fabius. The walls were already repaired before the date of Hannibal's occupation, and in the first Punic War we find the Tarentines assisting the Romans with a squadron of their own. More than this, we are expressly told that the autonomy of the Tarentine Commonwealth was conceded. Tarentum remained a "Free and Allied City."[196]

It is worth observing, moreover, in this connexion, that to Hêrakleia, the colonial offshoot and intimate ally of Tarentum, the Romans granted terms of alliance so exceptionally favourable that Cicero[197] speaks of the treaty as "almost unique" in its character. The passage

---

[196] Zonaras, Liv. *Ep.* xv. Strabo says distinctly that it was only after the Hannibalic war that the Tarentines were deprived of their liberty (vi. 3, 4). There is indeed some colour for supposing that even after this date Tarentum, like Neapolis and Rhêgiôn, remained, in name at least, a *civitas fœderata*. Thus Antiochos, whom the Romans had accused of making Greek cities servile and tributary, is made by Livy (l. xxxv. 16) to retort through the mouth of his minister, " Qui enim magis Zmyrnæi Lampsacenique Græci sunt quam Neapolitani et Rhegini et Tarentini a quibus stipendium a quibus naves ex fœdere exigitis?" Sulpicius, while rejecting the parallel, lays stress on the uninterrupted character of the Roman claim to exact from Naples, Rhêgiôn, and Tarentum " quæ ex fœdere debent." In 193 B.C., therefore, there was still (if Livy is to be trusted) a treaty, though an unfavourable one.

[197] *Pro Balbo*, 22. " Quacum (*sc.* Heraclea) prope singulare fœdus Pyrrhi temporibus, C. Fabricio Consule, ictum putatur." It is true that this treaty was apparently concluded at a time when, in order to detach Hêrakleia from Pyrrhus, it was necessary for Rome to bid high. But its terms may well have been held out as an incentive to Tarentine repentance. We may be sure at least that this exceptional *fœdus Heracleense* was not concluded without an eye to its effect on the mother-city.

of Polybios, in which he describes the Romans as "borrowing" the Tarentine ships during the second Punic War,[198] implies that in theory at least they were free agents; and it is noteworthy that on this occasion they are placed in the honourable company of the exceptionally free cities of Locri, Velia, and Neapolis. It is probable, indeed, that by the date of this contribution the condition of the Tarentines had considerably deteriorated from that which they enjoyed in the earlier period of the Roman alliance. There is, as we shall see, good evidence that the autonomous coinage of the city ceased about the year 228, and it is evident that by the time of the Hannibalic struggle the Roman yoke had become intolerable. But Tarentum was, even then, in name at least, a "Civitas Fœderata."

These historical considerations must be certainly taken to favour the assumption that the Roman occupation of 272 did not at once put an end to the autonomous coinage of Tarentum. That as a matter of fact this coinage did continue during the first period at least of the enforced alliance with Rome is, I venture to think, conclusively established by the evidence of another large find of over fifteen hundred Tarentine silver coins discovered at Taranto itself in 1883.

The greater part of this hoard was acquired by the Italian Government and is now in the Taranto Museum. Being at Taranto myself, however, shortly after the discovery, I was fortunate enough to obtain some three hundred coins, mostly didrachms, belonging to the same deposit, and by the careful examination of these was able

---

[198] Polybius, *Hist.* l. 20. "ἀλλὰ παρὰ Ταραντίνων καὶ Λοκρῶν ἔτι δὲ Ἐλεατῶν καὶ Νεαπολιτῶν συγχρησάμενοι πεντηκοντόρους καὶ τριήρεις. . ."

to obtain an intimate acquaintance with its character. Subsequently, by the courtesy of Professor Viola, the Director of the Museum at Taranto, who proposes to publish a report on the discovery in the *Notizie dei Scavi*, I was enabled to examine that part of the hoard which had passed into official hands, and owing to his kind collaboration, it has been possible for me to give an analysis of the whole hoard, including my own specimens, under Appendix C.

All the coins of this hoard belong to the reduced standard, but the Pyrrhic types are much worn and but sparsely represented, and, from a comparison of this with the preceding Calabrian find, it results that the coins contained in it belong, as a whole, to a distinctly later date. Thus it appears that out of one thousand and thirty-two didrachms from this hoard, no less than nine hundred and eighty belonged to types entirely unrepresented in the Calabrian deposit, a clear indication that the issues most abundantly represented in this second hoard belong to the post-Pyrrhic period of Tarentine history. From the variety and profusion of these new types it becomes evident that, so far from the Tarentine coinage breaking off with the Roman occupation, it continued for a very considerable period after that event.

The hoard itself, as will be seen from the analysis given under Appendix C, was by no means confined to didrachms. It contained an extensive series of litræ and hêmilitra, drachms, diobols, obols and hêmiobolia, the bulk of which, both from their condition and from the signatures and symbols that appear upon them, must have been issued during the same post-Pyrrhic epoch as the didrachms with which they are associated. In the summary tables of these coins of minor denominations given in

Appendix C, references are given to the didrachm types with which the letters and symbols that appear upon them bring them into connexion. From this it appears that in the case of the silver coins of less denomination than a drachm the letters as a rule refer not to the magistrate who on the didrachms and drachms signs in full, but to the more abbreviated signatures that in the larger coins occupy a secondary position in the field, and belong in all probability to the actual moneyer.[199] The symbols, on the other hand, seem to answer to the magistrates' names.[200] It is noteworthy that diobols of the type presenting two horses' heads were absent from this find, though the corresponding obols with a single head occurred in sufficient abundance.

The only other mint represented in this find besides the Tarentine was that of Thurioi, of which city there occurred twenty-two didrachms of a late style and debased silver. Of these some of the most recent belonged to a rare and hitherto almost unknown type,[201] presenting on the ob-

---

[199] Thus the most abundant of the didrachm types of the Taranto find (VIII. A 9), reading ΛΥΚΙΝΟΣ on the obverse with ΣΥ in the field, and with an owl in the field on the reverse, answers to the litra (No. 2) and the diobol (No. 3), with ΣΥ and an owl; the next most abundant didrachm type (VIII. D 1), reading ΑΡΙΣΤΟΚΛΗΣ with ΔΙ in the field on the obverse, and a head of a nymph on the reverse, answers to the litra (No. 7) and the diobol (No. 3), with ΔΙ and the same symbol. The monogram ⚹ of the didrachm (IX. D 1) signed ΟΛΥΜΠΙΣ recurs on litræ, hemilitra, diobols, and obols.

[200] Thus the anchor, on didrachms and drachms solely associated with the full-length signature ΑΡΙΣΤΙΣ (or ΑΡΙΣΤΙC), is seen on the diobol, No. 15. The flower which appears on didrachms signed ϜΗΡΑΚΛΗΤΟΣ Ε, and on drachms with ϜΗΡΑΚΛΗΤΟΣ, occurs on the litra No. 6, associated with the monogram only, but from the analogy of the drachms must be taken to refer to Herakletos.

[201] No example exists in the British Museum.

verse the laureate head of Apollo. The Taranto hoard stands out in marked contrast to the Calabrian find, from the complete absence of the coins of Hêrakleia, so brilliantly represented in the other deposit. It would thus appear that at the date when the present hoard was withdrawn from circulation, which, as we shall see, may be approximately fixed as 228 B.C., the Hérakleians, in spite of their *singulare fœdus*, had ceased the issue of their silver coinage.

The later Tarentine didrachms, so fully represented in this find, show, for the most part, a marked falling off as compared with those of the Pyrrhic epoch. The earlier light-weight didrachms of Pyrrhus' time are distinguished from the succeeding class by their broad-spread character. It would seem, indeed, as if the moneyers had sought to render the reduction of the standard less patent by giving these issues a module if anything somewhat larger than that of the immediately preceding types of heavier weight. But the later didrachms, comprising the great majority of those represented in the Taranto find, show no longer this transitional trait. They are smaller for the most part, and of more careless workmanship.

It is only towards the close of this series that a marked reaction again sets in. In this great find, amongst hundreds of coins, alike of inferior fabric and preservation, there occurred a small but well-defined and brilliant group of didrachms, evidently fresh from the mint at the time the hoard was deposited, and displaying in their design and execution a marked contrast to the carelessly executed and monotonous designs of the preceding class.

The internal evidence supplied by this Taranto find thus enables us to divide the post-Pyrrhic issues of

Tarentum into an earlier and a later class, which I have therefore distributed into two corresponding Periods, VIII. and IX.

PERIOD VIII.—THE ROMAN ALLIANCE: I.
B.C. 272—c. 235.

In this Period, as already explained, I have comprised the types intermediate between those represented in the Calabrian hoard and that later group of coins which, from their exceptional preservation in the Taranto find, must have been but recently minted at the time of its deposit. It was of these intermediate types that the great bulk of the Taranto hoard itself was composed, and from the fact that they include among them over thirty varieties of coins, some of them ranking among the most abundant of the Tarentine issues, it becomes evident that the Period during which the present class was struck must have extended over a considerable space of years. If we allow for it a space of time proportionate to other well-represented classes of Tarentine coins, thirty-five years will hardly be considered an excessive estimate. Taking, then, the date 272 B.C. as our starting point, we may roughly fix the duration of the present Period as between that year and the approximate date of 235 B.C.

The abundance of these late types is a speaking proof that the enforced alliance with Rome had not, at least after the first excesses of the occupation, sensibly impaired the material prosperity of the Tarentines. Their condition was in all probability more flourishing than it had been in the time of what Livy describes [202] as their "miserable servitude" under Pyrrhus' governor. The types and symbols of some of the didrachms of this Period supply us, indeed, with a remarkable piece of evidence tending to prove that the Tarentine commerce was still in a position to dominate some of the South Italian markets.

There exists a well-known class of Tarentine didrachms which both in their standard and type deviate from the ordinary issues. On these the type of Taras on his dolphin is replaced by a female head bearing a great resemblance to the Parthenopê or Dia Hêbê of the Neapolitan series. The weight is that of the Campanian didrachms, and reference has already been made to the view that these coins were a peculiar class of Tarentine didrachms based on the Campanian monetary system and intended for circulation in the Samnian, Apulian, and other border districts dominated by it. The superior execution of a few exceptional pieces affords some ground for supposing that the earliest of these Campano-Tarentine types may already have been issued during the years that preceded Pyrrhus' expedition. But, as already pointed out, the fabric of the generality of these coins points to a distinctly later date; and a minuter examination of the evidence at our disposal seems to me to be conclusive in establishing the fact that the great bulk of them belong to the post-Pyrrhic Epoch of the Tarentine coinage.

It has hitherto been generally assumed, in conformity with the convenient theory that the independent silver coinages of Southern Italy were extinguished by the first

---

[202] *Hist.* lib. xxiii. 7.

emission of the Roman denarius in 268, that both these Campano-Tarentine types and their Neapolitan counterparts ceased to be issued after that date. There seems in fact to be even less historical warrant for supposing that the Free and Allied City of Neapolis suppressed its silver coinage as soon as the first denarii issued from the temple of Juno Moneta than for supposing that four years before that event the Roman alliance had put an end to the mintage of Tarentum. That the same unexplained inscription I⋛ appears accompanying the same type both on a late class of Neapolitan didrachms and on bronze coins of Æsernia, all of which were certainly struck after 262 B.C., is a coincidence hard to explain on the assumption that the issue of the latest Neapolitan silver coins had ceased six years before that date. With regard, however, to the date of a whole series of types belonging to the Campano-Tarentine class, the ordinary Tarentine didrachms belonging to the Period with which we are dealing supply some valuable indications.

The horseman type as it appears on the bulk of these Campano-Tarentine coins is of a late and monotonous character. The scheme is that of the boy rider crowning a stationary horse which lifts up its off fore-leg, while beneath the horse is seen almost invariably a small dolphin. This type of horse and rider appears indeed at an earlier period of the Tarentine coinage, but in a very different style. We have no longer here the noble steeds with their curling manes of that earlier epoch, the gracefully posed boy riders with their flowing tresses, often crowned by a flying Victory. The curious androgynous form of a somewhat similar horseman type of the last period of the full-weight issues is also wanting on the present class, nor is it till after Pyrrhus' date that we discover any real parallel in style and design to these Campano-Tarentine types in the ordinary didrachm series. It is only in Period VIII., that a wooden representation of horse and rider strikingly analogous to that on these latter coins becomes usual on the Tarentine dies, nor is it indeed till the beginning of the next Period that a coin appears (IX. F; Pl. X. 6) in the normal Tarentine series which not only reproduces this identical scheme of the horse and rider, but combines it with the dolphin below, thus affording an exact counterpart to the most typical of the Campano-Tarentine pieces. But this analogy, striking as it is, does not end here. The type of Period IX. referred to as presenting this identical design, and which shows together with the dolphin the signature ΦΙΛΟΚΛΗϹ beneath the horse, presents us on the reverse a figure of Taras on his dolphin holding out a rhyton, terminating in the protomê of an animal, one of the few symbols that appear on the Campano-Tarentine series. The same symbol in a similar conjunction occurs on another coin of the present Period signed ΞΕΝΕΑϚ, but it is otherwise unknown on the Tarentine dies.

Of the other symbols that appear on the Campano-Tarentine coins, one only, the dog[203], is confined to that class. The Ionic capital occurs once, indeed, in Period V., but is otherwise confined to Periods VII. and VIII. The anchor and the tripod are seen as symbols in the field both on types of the latest Period (VI.) of the full-weight didrachm issues and on others of

---

[203] Car. cviii. 93. It is possible, however, that this is only a misinterpretation of the doe, which occurs on a didrachm of Period VI. (F 1), signed ΝΙΚΟΔΑΜΟϚ - ΣΟΡ and on litræ of the same date.

Periods VIII. and IX.[204] The single eight-rayed star occurs on a Pyrrhic type.[205] In these cases we have an alternative connexion with the latest full-weight coinage of Tarentum, or the still later issues that date from the time of the Pyrrhic Hegemony or the Roman Alliance. For the remaining five symbols in the field, however, we have no such alternative. The only parallels that can be found to them on the regular didrachm series of Tarentum belong, as will be seen from the following table, exclusively to the post-Pyrrhic periods.

Lion passant	.	Period VIII.	[ΛΕΩΝ].
Bunch of grapes	.	,, VIII.	[ϝΙΣΤΙΑΡ(ΧΟϚ)].
Cornucopiæ	. .	,, VIII.	[ϝΑΓΕΑϹ].
Wreath	. .	,, IX.	[ΟΛΥΜΠΙϚ].
Crescent	. .	,, IX.	[ΚΑΛΛΙΚΡΑΤΗϚ].

It thus appears that the type and symbols as well as the generally inferior execution of the Campano-Tarentine coins link them in a peculiar way to the post-Pyrrhic periods of the Tarentine mintage. This parallelism becomes the more significant when it is realised that, as in the case of the Hêrakleian Tables,[206] many of the symbols that are found on Tarentine coins of the regular didrachm series belonging to these later Periods refer in fact to the magistrates whose signatures now appear at length beneath the horse on the obverse. That this is the case is rendered indeed almost certain by the remarkable coincidence of certain names and symbols. On one of the above

---

[204] The tripod occurs as a symbol in the field on coins of Period VI., signed ΦΙΛΙΑΡΧΟϚ; of Period VIII., signed ΦΙΛΙϹΚΟϹ; and IX., ΟΛΥΜΠΙϚ; for the anchor, see Period VI., ΑΝΘΡΩϚ; and Period VIII., ΑΡΙϚΤΙϚ.

[205] Signed ΘΕ ΑΛΕΞ.

[206] See p. 25.

list the signature ΛΕΩΝ is coupled on the reverse with the *type parlant* of a lion passant. The reappearance of the same lion badge on the Campano-Tarentine piece must therefore be regarded as an indication that it was struck under the magistracy of the same Leôn. In the same way the signature ΣΟΡ beneath a symbol of a doe on type of Period VI., contains a probable allusion to ΣΟΡΚΑΣ a dialectic form of ΔΟΡΚΑΣ, a deer. A coin of Period VIII. exhibits a torch-racer coupled with the signature ΔΑΙΜΑΧΟΣ, a mere translation of the name,[207] and ΟΛΥΜΠΙΣ with the wreath of an *Olympionika*. The rayed solar emblem on the shield of a horseman of Period VII., has in the same way a probable connexion with the name ΑΠΟΛΛΩΝ[ΙΟΣ] that appears below it, just as on the small gold piece of the Molossian Epoch we find the signature ΑΠΟΛ (probably an earlier Apollônios) associated with the radiated head of the Sun-God.[208]

Sometimes the fact that the symbol is connected with a special magistrate's name is brought out in other ways. The bunch of grapes, for instance, which appears on the reverse of a didrachm of Period VIII., cited above, bearing on its obverse the signatures ΗΙΣΤΙΑΡ, reappears on a contemporary drachm in direct association with the same name in its amplified form ΗΙΣΤΙΑΡΧΟΣ. The signature ΑΡΙΣΤΙΣ or ΑΡΙϹΤΙϹ is in the same way doubly coupled with the anchor, and ΑΡΙΣΤΟΚΡΑΤΗΣ with a Term. Two allied types (G 1 and 2) of Period VIII., signed ΗΗΡΑΚΛΗΤΟΣ, afford, moreover, interesting

---

[207] For the sense in which this is to be regarded as a *type parlant*, see p. 188, 189.

[208] Several of the *types parlants*, adduced by Fiorelli (*Osservazioni sopra talune monete rare di città greche*, Naples, 1843), must, however, be rejected as too fanciful.

proof that the symbols held in Taras' hand should also be taken as occasionally containing a reference to the magistrate. On one of these Taras holds a flower in his hand while a *thymiatèrion* appears in the field, on the other [209] the flower is in the field and the *thymiatèrion* in Taras' hand. On the corresponding drachm this flower, in which I have ventured to trace an allusion to the Hyakinthia,[210] is again associated with the name of Hêraklêtos.

These instances are sufficient to show that in many cases the symbols on these later didrachms contain a direct allusion to the names of the magistrates during whose period of office the types were issued. When, therefore, we find the same symbols as, for instance, the lion passant, the bunch of grapes, the wreath, and others reappearing on the Campano-Tarentine series, we are warranted in tracing a reference to names of magistrates who sign in full on the regular didrachm types of the later Periods, and thus gain a new evidence as to the contemporaneity of the two classes.

The fact that, in the middle of the third century B.C., a class of Tarentine coins should have continued to be issued with an exclusive view to the markets dominated by the Campanian monetary system, affords conclusive proof that the Roman alliance was not incompatible with extensive commercial relations with other Italian districts, and in a principal degree with Apulia and Samnium. The affinity of the obverse type, as well as the weight, to the Neapolitan didrachms, points at the same time to the traditional intimacy between Naples and Tarentum, which had already manifested itself at an earlier date in the issue by the

---

[209] Cf. Avellino, *Adnotationes in Carellii Tabulas*, p. 47.
[210] See p. 186, *seqq.*

Campanian city of small silver types of Tarentine and Hêrakleian character. At a time when Tarentum and Neapolis stood out as the chief remaining representatives of Hellenic life in Southern Italy, it was natural that they should have been drawn even more closely together, and it is by no means improbable that these Campano-Tarentine coins are the outcome of a definite monetary convention. That these pieces, in fact, formed part of a federal coinage is shown by the contemporaneous appearance at Teate in Apulia of some late didrachm types which, in both their obverse and reverse design, in their standard, and almost in their inscription, are identical with this Campano-Tarentine class.[211]

VIII. Type A.

Naked boy-jockey crowning horse, standing l. and lifting off fore-leg.

Obv.	Rev.
1. Type described. Beneath horse, ΑΡΙΣΤΙΣ and anchor. Car. cx. 128. [Pl. IX. 1.]	Taras astride, &c., to l., holding distaff in l. hand, and with r. receiving small Victory, who reaches out a crown.
2. Same; but in f. to r., ΦΕΙ. Beneath horse, ΙΩΠΥΡΟΣ. Car. cxi. 146.	Same.
3. In f. to r., ΓΥ. Beneath horse, ΙΩ-ΠΥΡΟΣ.	Same; but in f. to r., ΧΡΗ ?

---

[211] See Sambon, *Monnaies de la Presqu'île Italique*, p. 218 (Pl. XV. 7). Garrucci, T. xcii. 1—3. On many of these Teatine coins the inscription is simply ΤΙΑ; on the Campano-Tarentine, ΤΑ.

PERIOD VIII.

Obv. | Rev.

4. In f. to r., cornucopiæ. Beneath horse, ⊢ΑΓΕΑC.
A. J. E.

Taras astride, &c., to l., holding trident in l. hand, and with r. extending kantharos. In f. to r., ΠΟΛΥ.

5. In f. to r., cornucopiæ. Beneath horse, ΦΙΛΩΤΑξ.
Car. *Descr.* 354.

Taras astride, &c., to l., holding trident in l. hand, and with r. extending kantharos. In f. to r., ΠΟΛΥ.

6. In f. to r., ΝΚ Beneath horse, ΦΙ-ΛΟΚΡΑ.
Car. cxiv. 206.
[Pl. IX. 2.]

Same; but in f. to r., ΑΠΟΛ.

7. Same.
Car. *Descr.* 348.
A. J. E.

Same; but in f. to r., ΑΡΕΥ.

8. Same; but in f. to r., ξΥ. In front of horse, ΔΕ; and beneath, ΛΥΚΙ ΝΟξ.
Car. cxii. 165.

Taras astride, &c., to l., his back half-turned towards the spectator, holding chlamys on his l. arm, and with his r. hand brandishing a trident in a Poseidonian pose (cf. VII. E 2). In f. to r., an owl.

9. Same type and insc., but without ΔΕ.
[Pl. IX. 3.]

Same.

10. Same; but in f. to r., ΕΥ. Beneath horse, ⊢ΙξΤΙΑΡ.
Car. cxi. 157.

Taras astride, &c., to l., holding trident in l. hand, and with r. receiving small wreath-bearing Victory. In f. to r., bunch of grapes.

11. In f. to r., ΔΙ. Beneath horse, ΦΙΛΩΤΑC.
Car. cxiv. 211.

Taras astride, &c., to l., holding in l. hand distaff, and with r. extending kantharos. In f. to r., cock.

VIII. Type B.

Naked boy-jockey crowning stationary horse, which lifts its off fore-leg. As Type A, but horse to r.

a a

178   THE "HORSEMEN" OF TARENTUM.

Obv.	Rev.
1. Beneath horse, ΑΓΑΘΑ ΡΧΟΣ. Car. cx. 116.	Taras astride, &c., to l., holding cornucopiæ in l. hand, and with r. extending kantharos. In f. to r., a lighted torch.
2. In f. to l., ΦΙ. Beneath horse, ΙΩΠΥΡΟΣ. Car. cxi. 147.	Taras astride, &c., to l., holding trident in l. hand, and with r. extending cornucopiæ. In f. to r., a cicada.
3. Beneath horse, ΛΕΩΝ. Car. cxii. 164. [Pl. IX. 4.]	Taras astride, &c., to l., holding trident in l. hand, and with r. extending bunch of grapes. In f. to r., ΑΙ. Beneath dolphin, a lion passant.
4. In f. to l., ΑΡ. Beneath horse, bearded mask; under foreleg, ΚΥ ΝΩΝ. Car. cxii. 162.	Taras astride, &c., resting his l. hand on dolphin's back and with r. extending kantharos.

VIII. Type C.

As B, but horse does not lift fore-leg.

1. In f. to l., ΕΥ. In front of horse, ΦΙ; beneath, ΞΕΝΕΑΣ. A. J. E.	Taras astride, &c., to l., holding in l. hand trident, and with r. extending cornucopiæ. In f. to r., spike of corn.
2. In f. to l., ΦΙ-ΛΟΚΡΑ. Beneath horse, ΝΚ. A. J. E. Cf. Car. cx. 130, "ΗΡΑ ΝΚ."	Taras astride, &c., to l., holding in l. hand trident, and with r. receiving small wreath-bearing Victory. In f. to r., and below dolphin, ΑΡΙΣΤΟ.
3. Same. A. J. E.	Same; but in f. to r., ΑΠΟΛ.

VIII. Type D.

Naked horseman on prancing horse to r., lancing downwards. Behind him a large round shield and reserve of two lances.

PERIOD VIII.

Obv.

1. In f. to l., **ΔΙ**.
Beneath horse,
ΑΡΙΣΤΟ
ΚΛΗΞ.
Car. cx. 131.
[Pl. IX. 6.]

Rev.

Taras astride, &c., to l., holding trident in l. hand, and with r. extending kantharos. In f. to r., head of nymph.

2. Same; in f. to l., **Ν**. Beneath horse,
ΝΙΚΟ
ΚΡΑΤΗΞ.
Taranto find.

Taras astride, &c., to r., holding crested helmet between his hands. Below, Ionic capital.

VIII. Type E.

Boy-rider to r. on stationary horse, holding reins.

1. In f. to r., **ΗΙ**.
Beneath horse,
ΦΙΛΗΜΕΝΟΞ.
Car. cxiv. 200.
[Pl. IX. 7.]

Taras astride, &c., to l., holding trident in l. hand, and with r. extending tripod. In f. to r., bucranium.

VIII. Type F.

Naked youth, raising his l. hand, and with drapery about his loins, on stationary horse to r.

1. Beneath horse,
ΦΙΛΙCΚΟC.
Car. cxiv. 202.
[Pl. IX. 8.]

Taras astride, &c., to l., holding trident in l. hand, and with r. extending kantharos. Beneath dolphin, a tripod.

VIII. Type G.

Warrior in close-fitting lorica and crested helmet, holding in l. hand a lance, and with large round shield behind him, on horse standing r. and raising its off fore-leg.

1. Beneath horse,
ΗΡΑ
ΚΛΗΤΟΞ
Car. cxi. 152.
[Pl. IX. 9.]

Taras astride, &c., to l., holding in l. hand cornucopiæ, and with r. extending flower. In f. to r., **Ε** and thymiatérion.

Obv.	Rev.
2. In f. ΦΙ. ⊢ΗΡΑ ΚΛΗΤΟ϶. Mionnet, No. 406. [Pl. XI. 14, Cab. des Médailles, 1447.]	Taras astride, &c., to l., holding in l. hand cornucopiæ, and with r. extending thymiatêrion. In f. a flower and monogram Ɐ.

VIII. Type H.

Warrior, as Type G, but on cantering horse to r.

1. In f. to l., ΔΙ. Beneath horse, ΑΠΟΛΛ ΩΝΙΟ϶. Car. ex. 121.	Taras astride, &c., to l., half turned towards the spectator, with chlamys caught round his l. arm and flowing behind him, holding in r. hand a trident, while a small Victory flies forward to crown him. Beneath, waves.
2. In f. to l., ⊙Ι. Beneath horse, ΑΡΙ϶ΤΟΚ. B. M. Cat. 250. Cf. Car. ex. 122, "ΑΠΟΛΛΩ." [Pl. IX. 10. Taranto find.]	Same; but beneath dolphin, a rudder.

VIII. Type K.

Warrior in close-fitting thorax, raising r. hand behind him and galloping r.

1. Beneath horse, ⊢ΙΠΠΟΔΑ. Car. cxi. 156.	Taras astride, &c., to l., holding in l. hand cornucopiæ, and with r. extending kantharos. In f. to r., ΔΙ and amphora.

VIII. Type L.

Naked boy-rider crowning horse standing, or walking, r., while a small Victory flies forward to crown the jockey from behind.

1. In front of horse, ΦΙ; beneath, ΑΡΙ϶ΤΟ ΚΡΑΤΗ϶. Car. ex. 132. [Pl. IX. 11.]	Taras astride, &c., to l., holding trident and kantharos. In f. to l., ΠΙ; to r., Term.

Obv.	Rev.
2. In front of horse, ΦΙ ; beneath, **ΑΡΙΣΤΕΙΔ**. Car. cx. 124.	Taras astride, &c., to l., holding trident and corn-spike. In f. to r., ⊌ᴾ.
3. In front of horse, **ΕΥΝ** ; beneath, **ΔΑΜΟΚΡΙΤΟΣ**. Car. cxi. 140. [Pl. IX. 12.]	Taras astride to r., holding cornucopiæ and trident. In f. to l., 𝕏.

VIII. Type M.

Warrior in crested helmet and holding shield (seen sideways) behind him, on horse standing l., and holding up fore-leg.

1. Ornamental shield. In f. to l., **ΕΥΦ** in minute letters. Beneath horse, **ΑΡΙΣΤΩΝ**. [Pl. IX. 13. A. J. E.]	Taras astride, &c., to l., holding trident and hippocamp. In f. to r., **ΙΩΓ**.
2. Same; but plain shield and **ΕΥ**. B. M. Cat. 194. Car. cx. 138, "**ΑΡΙΣΤΙΩΝ**." A. J. E.	Same.

VIII. Type N.

Naked horseman holding palm-branch, on horse advancing to r.

1. To r., **Ν**. Beneath horse, **ΝΙΚΟΚ ΡΑΤΗΣ** B. M. Cat. 165. [Pl. IX. 14.]	Taras astride, &c., to l., chlamys flowing from his l. arm, and holding in his r. hand a trident.

VIII. Type O.

The two Dioskuri, clad in mantles and peaked helmets, cantering r. (The further horse is half a length ahead of the other.)

Obv.	Rev.
1. Beneath horses, **NIKYΛOϹ**. Car. cxii. 126. [Pl. IX. 5.]	Taras seated sideways on dolphin to l., holding trident in l. hand, and with r. extending kantharos. In f. to r., **Æ**

DRACHMS BELONGING TO PERIOD VIII.

1. Head of Pallas in Scylla helmet to r. Car. cxv. 230.	Owl seated to r. with closed wings on olive branch. In f. to l., **APIϹ-TOKPATHϹ**; to r., Term. [Cf. VIII. L 1, **APIΣTOKPATHϹ-ΓI**, Term.]
2. Same. Car. cxv. 231.	Same. In f. to l., **ͰHPAKΛHTOϹ**. A flower growing out of olive spray. [Cf. VIII. G 1 and 2, **ͰHPAKΛHTOϹ**, flower.]
3. Same, Car. cxv. 232.	Same; but the owl is seated on a thunderbolt. In f. to l., **ͰIϹTIAP-XOΣ**; to r., **EY** and bunch of grapes. [Cf. VIII. A 10, **EY ͰIϹTIAP**, bunch of grapes.]
4. Same. A. J. E.; (cf. Car. cxv. 225. No. insc.)	Same; but the owl is seated on an anchor. In f. to l., **APICTIC**; to r., **TA**. [Cf. VIII. A 1, **APIϹTIϹ**, anchor.]
5. Same. Car. cxv. 229.	Same; but the owl is seated on a bucranium. In f. to r., **TAP** and **ΛEΩN**. [Cf. VIII. B 3, **ΛEΩN**, lion.]
6. Same. Car. cxv. 235. Cf. *Descr.* 400.	Same; but the owl is seated on an Ionic capital. In f. to l., **NIKOK-PATHϹ**; to r., **TAP** and **AN**. [Cf. VIII. D 2, **NIKOKPATHϹ N**, Ionic capital.]
7. Head of Pallas to l. Car. cxv.	Same; but owl seated to l. on thunderbolt. In f. to l., lighted torch; to r., **TAP**. [Cf. VIII. B 1, **AΓAΘAPXOϹ**, lighted torch.]

PERIOD IX.—THE ROMAN ALLIANCE: II.
c. 235—228 B.C.

The great Taranto find is peculiarly valuable from the light which it throws on a late and well-marked class of didrachm types, which, with the aid of the evidence thus supplied, I have no hesitation in grouping in a class by itself, and which must be regarded as the immediate successor of those of Period VIII. In this find, besides a great abundance of coins belonging to Period VIII., and presenting, for the most part, the appearance of having been some time in circulation, was a small and brilliant group, evidently fresh from the mint, and displaying in their design and execution, as well as their condition, a marked contrast to the carelessly-engraved and monotonous designs of the preceding Period. The most typical specimens of this more recent group which evidences a distinct revival of the monetary art at Tarentum, are characterized by the animated figures they present of galloping *hippakontists* and torch-racers, of boy-jockeys in wild career literally hanging on their horses' necks, of Taras with a leafy crown about his head turning round on the back of his marine charger, and raising his flowing mantle like a sail behind him—a scheme, perhaps, more strictly picturesque in its composition than any other in the long Tarentine series [Pl. X. 7]. They display, one and all, a careful minuteness in the engraving which, though over elaborate, is worthy of a better age, and it was not without reason that Raoul Rochette, in his well-known letter to the Duc de Luynes,[212] was led to single out the small

---

[212] *Lettre à M. le duc de Luynes sur les graveurs des Monnaies Grecques*, p. 45 and Pl. IV. 35. He describes the coin as "une des plus rares de Tarente."

letters ϟΩ seen between the horns of a bucranium on a coin of this group [IX. B, Pl. X. 2] as a clear example of an artist's signature on a Tarentine coin. As to the origin of this remarkable artistic revival on the Tarentine coinage at this late period, we must be content to remain in ignorance. In any case, it is a most remarkable phenomenon.

Notwithstanding the great superiority of this group of coins to the bulk of those issued during Period VIII., there can be no doubt that they belong to a later date. The evidence of the great Taranto find is by itself decisive on this head, and the character of the epigraphy exhibited by the present series points to the same conclusion. A complicated style of monogram now makes its appearance in the field quite unknown to the earlier coinage, though a tendency to it is perceptible in the preceding Period VIII. Types A, G, and H of this series present in particular highly elaborate combinations very different from the simple linking together of a couple of letters, such as Ƌ or ⴒ on earlier issues. In the forms of the letters themselves a decided change is perceptible, and the chevroned type of Λ, ● for O, and C for ϟ,[213] now become frequent. A further indication of a late date is seen,

---

[213] The lunar form of ϟ makes its first appearance on four amongst the forty varieties of coins (including seven drachms) belonging to Period VIII. (ΑΡΙϹΤΙϹ, drachms only; ΗΑΓΕΑϹ, ΦΙΛΩΤΑϹ, ΦΙΛΙϹΚΟϹ). In the present Period it occurs on five out of the ten varieties (ΔΑΙΜΑΧΟϹ, ΟΛΥΜΠΙϹ, drachms only; ΑΡΙϹΤΙΠΠΟϹ, ΦΙΛΟΚΛΗϹ, ΞΕΝΟΚΡΑΤΗϹ), and in two cases (A 1 and E 1) we find for the first time the form ΤΑΡΑϹ. The lunar C makes its first isolated appearance on Rhodian coins of Alexandrine age. It only reached Sicily towards the end of the second century B.C. (See S. Reinach, *Traité d'Épigraphie Grecque*, p. 208.)

moreover, in the fact that Types C, D, and to a certain extent E, were copied in an inferior style at the time of the Hannibalic occupation.

Another feature to be observed in this class is the appearance of horsemen in full military costume. The thorax, in which a galloping hippakontist is clad, in Type C, with the signature ΟΛΥΜΠΙΣ, finds indeed its parallel in a horseman type of Period VIII., signed ͰΗΡΑΚΛΗΤΟΣ, but the scarce coin of the present group (Type H) signed ΚΑΛΛΙΚΡΑΤΗΣ, shows still greater elaboration of equipment. Upon it we see a bearded horseman completely uniformed in thorax and shoulder-pieces, and with his military mantle flowing behind him.

Besides the freshly-struck coins of the present class represented in the Taranto hoard, I have been able to add to it, on grounds of design, style, and signature, a few other rare types of Tarentine coins. The coin of this class with the galloping hippakontist, signed ΟΛΥΜΠΙΣ, finds its counterpart, so far as style and signature is concerned, in an almost unique piece of the same monetary magistrate in my own collection,[214] in which a naked youth appears on a stationary horse. The coin signed ΞΕΝΟΚΡΑΤΗC, bearing on its obverse the over-clad figure of a Dioskuros in tunic and mantle, and that already referred to with the name of ΚΑΛΛΙΚΡΑΤΗΣ display in a marked degree the characteristics of this late Period.

The horse-racing types, that now become so common on

---

[214] The only other example of this type that has come under my observation is in the Museo Nazionale at Naples (Fiorelli, *Catalogo, &c., Medagliere*, No. 1855), but without the monogram.

the Tarentine dies, certainly point to a great revival about this time of some religious celebration of an agonistic character, and a comparison of types and symbols seems to afford some clue as to the occasion of these equestrian contests. Reasons have been already given for connecting the hippic types of the Tarentine coinage with prevalent heroic cults of this city, in which Taras himself and Phalanthos, or those twin Lacedæmonian patrons, the Dioskuri, certainly participated. But amongst the local cults which Tarentum had inherited from its historic founder, the Amyklæan Phalanthos, one of the most ancient was that of Hyakinthos, or the Hyakinthian Apollo, whose tomb, originally perhaps one of the imposing prehistoric barrows still to be found in this old Sallentine region, occupied a conspicuous position outside the Têmenid gate.[215] There can be little doubt that, as the Duc de Luynes pointed out, one of the earliest incuse Tarentine coins representing a nude youthful figure holding a lyre under his left arm, and with his right raising a flower to his nostrils, refers to this Hyakinthian cult.[216] It

---

[215] It was from here that the pre-arranged fire-signal was given by Hannibal to the Tarentine conspirators within the walls (Polyb. *Reliquiæ*, lib. xiii. 30).

[216] *Annali dell Instituto di Corr. Archeologica*, VII., 337 *seqq*. The conclusion of the Duc de Luynes that the flower on these archaic Tarentine coins represents, in fact, the hyacinth of the local hero, receives striking corroboration from the observations of Panofka, who (*op. cit.*, p. 342 *seqq.*, and *tav. d'aggiunta*, 1830, M. 3) publishes a vase representing on one side the Amyklæan Apollo, and on the other a female figure holding the same flower represented as growing from a bulb. On vases this flower appears in a specially agonistic connexion as offered by the judge to the Ephêbos who had carried off the prize either in lyrical or gymnastic contests, *v*. Panofka *loc. cit.* No symbol could better indicate the *Hyakinthia*. A frequent characteristic of the flower is the trefoil arrangement of

is not, however, till Period IX. that the same hyacinthine flower as is seen in the hands of the Apollo-like figure of the earliest coinage reappears as a Tarentine monetary symbol. It is found on two closely allied didrachm types, in the one case in the outstretched hand of Taras, in the other as a symbol in the field, and in both instances associated with the signature ⱵHPAKΛHTOⱵ. On a drachm of the same Period it again appears coupled with the same signature. There can be little doubt that this Hêraklêtos whose name is thus markedly associated with the flower symbol of Apollo is the same monetary magistrate who signs ⱵHPA and ⱵHPAKΛHI on two of the latest pieces of the Pyrrhic Period, which have a special bearing on our present subject, as for the first time presenting us with the type of the torch-racer, and at the same time supplying the prototype of the coin of the present Period with the same device signed ΔAIMAXOC.

That the first appearance of the most characteristic of the horse-racing types of the later Tarentine series and the revival of the Hyakinthian symbol on the Tarentine coinage should connect themselves thus with the same name, is a fact of considerable significance, and leads to the conclusion that this Hêraklêtos, who seems to have held office at Tarentum about the time of the Roman occupation in 272, and again during the first period of the Roman alliance, was in some way associated with the re-

---

the leaves, which, as well as the veined petals on which were read the Υ of Ὑάκινθος and the ΑΙ ΑΙ of his mourners (cf. Pliny xxi. 11, Mosch. *Idyll* III. v. 6) suggests a flower of the iris kind. In its origin this Chthonic flower-cult had, no doubt, a wider and more general sepulchral application, and the flower itself is only a Greek transformation of the lotus seen in the hands of the heroized departed, as, for instance, on the Harpy tomb at Xanthos, in Lykia.

vival or special institution of an agonistic festival in honour of the Hyakinthian Apollo. That horse-races formed a leading feature of the Hyakinthia is well known, and it was apparently during a contest of this kind at Amyklæ that Phalanthos, according to the legend, had planned to put on his cap as the signal for the Parthenian rising.[217] The Chthonic and funereal side of the cult of Apollo, as assimilated to Hyakinthos, so different from the wonted aspect of the Light God's festival, sufficiently explains the prominence which the torch-race, or lampadêdromia, seems to have had in this Tarentine celebration.

These conclusions lead us to the elucidation of a singular point. The coin belonging to the short period, with which we are at present concerned, exhibiting the type of the torch-racer, has been cited as an example of a *type parlant*, the signature ΔΑΙΜΑΧΟC below standing apparently in obvious relation to the torch or δαίς in the rider's hand.[218] But it has been shown that the type of the torch-racer already appears at a distinctly earlier date associated with the signatures ΗΡΑ and ΗΡΑΚΛΗΙ. The obverse of the coin signed ΔΑΙΜΑΧΟC is simply a careful revival at a later date of the piece struck about the time of the Roman occupation with the signature of Hêraklêtos. It is evident, therefore, that in its origin at least this type cannot have been originally due to a play on the personal name of Daïmachos. But the large monogram, ⋈ for ΗΡΑ, which appears in the field of the later coin, affords at least a probable solution of the enigma. It looks as if in this case we had to do with a patronymic, and that Daïmachos

---

[217] Strabo, *Geogr.* vi. 3.
[218] See Avellino, *Ital. Vet. Num.* T. 1, p. 88; Suppl., p. 36. Cavedoni in Carelli, *op. cit.* p. 48.

may himself have stood in a filial relation to Hêraklêtos. If, as we have good reason to believe, this magistrate took an active part in an agonistic revival, of which torch-racing was a feature, he might have called his son ΔΑΙΜΑΧΟC, for the same reason that he placed a δαϊμάχος on his own coins. Daïmachos himself in this case chose a type which had supplied the religious occasion of his own name-giving. This is a *type parlant* with a difference.

The spirited series of types that characterize the present Period show that it was at this time, and perhaps owing to the family traditions of the magistrate above-named, that the agonistic revival already indicated reached its height. And that this revival, as commemorated for us by these Tarentine coin-types, was in fact connected with the cult of Apollo receives a remarkable confirmation from an unexpected quarter. These late Tarentine types of the horseman at full gallop, holding a torch or clinging to his horse's neck, or the kindred design, in which the boy-rider holds a palm with a fillet or lemniskos attached, served, in fact, as the prototypes of a well-known series of Roman denarii belonging to the Calpurnian family. In this later Roman series, in which the figures of the galloping torch-racers are specially prominent, the contests represented are connected in the most unmistakeable way with the cult of Apollo, whose head is represented on the obverse side of the coins. The historic event commemorated on these Calpurnian types is indeed well known.[219] After the battle of Cannæ attention was called to the prophetic lays of the Seer Marcius, who had foretold the disaster, and had warned the Romans that if they wished to expel the enemy from their territory they should insti-

---

[219] Eckhel, *Doctrina Numorum*, II. 158.

tute annual games in honour of Apollo, to be celebrated "according to the Greek rite." The "Ludi Apollinares," first held in obedience to this sibyllic warning in 212 B.C., were in the succeeding year made perpetual on the motion of the Prætor Calpurnius, upon whom, in virtue of his office, the superintendence of the ceremony had devolved.[220] If the Prætor to whom the organization of these games was due is to be identified with the Calpurnius who was taken prisoner at Cannæ in 216, he may himself, while serving in Southern Italy, have been a witness to the agonistic revival at Tarentum, of which the didrachms before us afford such striking evidence. The types of the Roman denarii struck by L. Calpurnius Piso Frugi in 89 B.C., and again by the later C. Calpurnius Piso in 64, show at least that the "Ludi Apollinares" as celebrated in Rome "according to the Greek rite" were framed on a Tarentine model. The dolphin which appears beside Apollo's head on some of these Calpurnian pieces may point in the same direction, and the flower, which also occurs in the same juxtaposition, as well as the prominence given to the lampadêdromoi, or ἑαϊμάχοι, seems to show that the Chthonic and Hyakinthian aspects of the Tarentine cult were not without their influence on the Roman celebration. This parallel is further borne out by some denarii of the Gens Marcia, commemorating the part played by the Seer Marcius in introducing the same games at Rome. On these is seen another agonistic type, that of the *desultor*, or ἄμφιππος, leading a second horse,[221] a representation, which though it does not occur on the didrachms of this Period, still finds its nearest

---

[220] Cf. Livy, xxv. 12, and xxvi. 23; Macrobius, *Saturnal.*, I. 17.

[221] This type also occurs on coins of the Sepullia family.

parallel on a Tarentine coin. Thus, together with the importation of this Hellenic festival, the old traditions of the turf, which the Tarentines themselves had in great part derived from the horse-loving Iapygian and Messapian indigenes, were transferred to Roman soil.

The conclusion arrived at from the internal evidence supplied by the present group of Tarentine coins, that a great agonistic revival had lately taken place in honour of the local Apollo, which reached its height soon after the approximate date of 235 B.C., fits in well so far as chronology is concerned with the introduction at Rome in 212 of the "Ludi Apollinares," after a Tarentine model. The enthusiasm of which these highly animated Tarentine types are the abiding record, seems to have infected its Roman observers, and in view of the interesting numismatic parallels before us, we may be allowed to trace the first appearance of these games at Rome, more than to the fortuitously discovered verses of the Seer Marcius, to the contagious example of the great Greek city of the South.

The comparative rarity of the types of the class with which we are dealing forbids us to suppose that their issue extended over any length of time. There are, moreover, special considerations which make it improbable that any didrachms of the present standard were struck after the year 228. Between the coins of this Period and the latest class of Tarentine coins which seem to have been issued during the time of the Hannibalic occupation, there is a break in style and a break in standard, best explicable on the supposition that for a short period at least the Tarentine coinage itself had broken off.

Of this interruption of the autonomous mintage of Tarentum, we have in fact direct evidence in a hoard of coins discovered in 1880 at a spot called Pizzone, at Taranto.[222] This find consisted entirely of Roman Victoriati of full weight, averaging about 3·30 grammes, and its deposit was therefore not later than 217, the date of the reduction of weight of Victoriatus to 2·92 grammes in conformity with that of the reduced denarius. It follows then that already before that date the native Tarentine coinage must have been superseded by the new international currency of Rome.

The occasion of this monetary revolution at Tarentum may with great probability be sought in the events of the year 228 B.C. Rome had about this time adopted as a convenient medium of external exchange the originally Capuan *Victoriatus*, being the half of the old Phocæo-Campanian stater as harmonized with the Roman metric system by its reduction to three scruples.[223] But the rise of the Illyrian maritime power, which might at any time become still more formidable as an instrument in Macedonian hands, the fall of Corcyra and the siege of Epidamnos or Dyrrhachium, had led the Romans to secure a firmer foothold on the shores of the Adriatic and Ionian seas. The successful campaign of 229 against the Illyrian pirate state, and the establishment of a Roman protectorate over Dyrrhachium, Apollonia, and Corcyra, brought with them monetary arrangements, the chief object of which was to secure the wider extension of the

---

[222] This find was described by Prof. de Petra in a communication to the Accademia Pontaniana of Naples, September 2nd, 1881. A summary account of it, with de Petra's conclusions, is given by Prof. Viola, *Notizie dei Scavi*, 1881, p. 408 *seqq.*

[223] For the Campanian origin of the *Victoriatus*, see M. Zobel's remarks in the Duc de Blacas' translation of Mommsen's History of the Roman Coinage, II. 104.

newly adopted Victoriate currency. The two Illyrian cities, admitted to the Roman connexion on terms of freedom and alliance, henceforth begin to coin their well-known drachms on the Victoriate standard, and the Corcyræans followed the same example.

But while these extra-Italian dependencies were allowed to adapt their indigenous coinages to the Roman system, there is evidence that within the limits of Italy itself Rome seized every occasion of imposing, at least so far as the silver currency was concerned, her own official issues, so much so that shortly after this date Roman *Victoriati* began to be struck at Krotôn, Luceria, and other cities of Southern Italy.[224] What the immediate pretext may have been for depriving the Tarentines of their right of coinage we do not know, but we have good reason for believing that before the outbreak of the second Punic War the Romans had laid a heavier hand on Tarentine liberties. On the eve of the final struggle against the Carthaginians there was less room for those milder considerations of policy, such as seemed to have prevailed during the earlier period of the enforced alliance of Tarentum with Rome. In

---

[224] A *Victoriatus*, with the mint-mark **CROT**, in the Blacas Collection (Blacas, *op. cit.* iv. p. 30) weighs 3·49 grammes, and was therefore struck before 217 B.C. Lucerian Victoriati of the full weight are also found. The Victoriate Mint, established in Corcyra, seems to have been late, as the monogram of Agésandros which occurs on its issues is common to quinarii from the same mint, and must therefore have been struck about 104 B.C. Mommsen (*op. cit.* ii. 93) assumes that the Romans immediately after their occupation of Corcyra in 229 suppressed the native silver coinage, and established a Victoriate mint of their own. But there can be no doubt that the autonomous silver coinage of Corcyra continued to a much later date (see Gardner, *B. M. Cat., Thessaly to Epirus*, p. xix. and 135 *seqq.*), though the standard adopted was partly at least that of the Roman Victoriatus.

view of a possible diversion on the Macedonian side it was moreover specially necessary to secure a firm hold on the city which as past history had shown was the first objective of hostile enterprise from the Epirote shore. When the Tarentines turned to Hannibal for deliverance the Free City had already been practically reduced to the position of a Roman garrison town.

IX. Type A.

Naked youth at full gallop to l., holding torch behind him.

Obv.
1. In f. to l., ⊌𝐏. Beneath horse, ΔΑΙΜΑΧ●C. Car. cxi. 137. [Pl. X. 1.]

Rev.
Taras astride, &c., to l., holding trident in l. hand, and with r. extending kantharos. In f. to r., ⌫. Beneath, ΤΑΡΑC.

IX. Type B.

Boy-jockey, clad in short tunic, at full gallop to r.; his body is thrown back, and with his l. hand he seems to cling to the horse's mane.

1. Beneath horse, ΞΩΠΥΡΙΩΝ and bucranium, between the horns of which in minute letters, ≶ Ω. Car. cx. 129. ("ΑΡΙ≶ΤΙΩΝ.") B. M. Cat. 189. [Pl. X. 2.]

Taras astride, &c., to l., holding trident in l. hand, and with r. extending hippocamp. In f. to r., head of bearded Pan seen sideways, and ꟼ.

IX. Type C.

Hippakontist in close-fitting thorax galloping r., and hurling short javelin.

1. In f. to l., wreath. Beneath horse, ΟΛΥΜΠΙ≶. Car. cxiii. 181. [Pl. X. 3.]

Taras astride, &c., to l., holding in l. hand cornucopiæ, and with r. extending kantharos. In f. to r., tripod. Beneath, ΤΑΡΑΣ.

IX. Type D.

Naked boy-jockey to r., crowning stationary horse.

Obv.
1. In f. to l., Amazonian shield. In front of horse ♠. Beneath horse, **ΟΛΥΜ-ΠΙ§**.
[Pl. X. 4. A. J. E.]

Rev.
Taras astride, &c., holding trident in l. hand, and with r. extending rhyton terminating in protomê of a horse. Beneath dolphin, a cuttlefish.

IX. Type E.

Naked boy-jockey, holding palm bound with fillet, cantering r.

1. In f. to l., **Æ**. Beneath horse, **ΑΡΙϹΤΙΠΠΟϹ**.
Cf. Car. ix. x. 125.
[Pl. X. 5.]

Taras astride, &c., to l., crowned with a wreath. He rests his l. hand on the dolphin's back, and with r. extends a kantharos. In f. to r., ᴧ. Beneath dolphin, **ΤΑΡΑϹ**.

IX. Type F.

Naked boy-rider to r., crowning stationary horse, which lifts up its off fore-leg.

1. In f. to l., ⚓. In f. to r., **Æ**. Beneath horse, **ΦΙΛΟ ΚΛΗϹ** and small dolphin.
Car. cxiv. 204.
[Pl. X. 6.]

Taras astride, &c., to l., his left leg drawn back, his l. hand resting on dolphin's back and holding trident, his r. extending rhyton, terminating in protomê of an animal. In f. to r., two amphoras.

IX. Type G.

Single figure of a Dioskuros in short tunic and chlamys, raising further arm. The horse stands l., and raises off fore-leg.

1. In f. to r. **Ƙ**, and pileus. Beneath horse, **ΞΕΝΟΚ ΡΑΤΗϹ**.
Car. cxiii. 180.
[Pl. X. 7.]

Taras with a leafy crown on his head turning round on dolphin, with left hand raising his chlamys, and with r. holding trident, which rests on his shoulder. Beneath dolphin, cuttlefish, and waves. In f. to r. ✕.

IX. Type H.

Warrior bareheaded to r., in full military costume, with tunic, thorax, shoulder-pieces, and mantle, on horse cantering r. He turns his face to the spectator, and holds out his right hand behind him to receive small wreath-bearing Victory.

Obv.	Rev.
1. In f. to l. ⸌ER and crescent. Beneath horse, ΚΑΛΛΙΚΡΑ-ΤΗΣ. Car. T. cxii. 158. B. M. 277. [Pl. X. 8.]	Taras astride, &c., to l., holding trident in l. hand, and extending r. to receive small wreath-bearing Victory. In f. to l., NE.
2. Same, without the crescent. Mon. ⸌Ek B. M. 276.	Same.

To Period IX. must be referred the following drachms :—

1. Head of Pallas in Scylla helmet to r., K on flap. [B. M. Cat. 815; Sambon, op. cit., Pl. XVIII. 27.]	Owl seated to r., with closed wings, on an olive spray. In f. to l. ΟΛΥΜΠΙΣ, to r. ⸎. [Cf. IX. D 1, ΟΛΥΜΠΙΣ, ⸎.]
2. Same. Taranto find.	Same ; but in f. to r., wreath.
3. Head of Pallas, three-quarters facing, in triple-crested helmet. To l. ⸌ΒΚ. Car. cxv. 236.	Owl as No. 1; uncertain inscription. [? cf. Mon. ⸌ΒΡ on IX. A. The form here is variant, but the character of the monogram answers best to the didrachms of this late period.]

PERIOD X.—THE HANNIBALIC OCCUPATION.
c. 212—209 B.C.

The remarkable class of coins with which we have now to deal stands apart both in standard and fabric from all other Tarentine issues. The traditional didrachm type is preserved, but the full weight of the highest denomination of coin now issued, 3·46 grammes (53½ grs.), is less than half that of the earlier **full-weight** didrachms of 7·90 grammes (122 grs.), and at the same time nearly three grammes lower than the average weight of the reduced coinage belonging to the post-Pyrrhic Periods that immediately precede them in date. Sambon [225] regarded these coins as representing the drachms of the Tarentine series before the reduction of the didrachm standard, but though their weight possibly admits of such a conclusion, their fabric and the types that they represent are absolutely fatal to it. Mr. Head, who rightly recognised their late date, **was misled**, perhaps by an error of Carelli, into believing **that didrachms of full-weight existed belonging to this class.**[226] Such, however, are not forthcoming.

On the other hand, the type itself is that hitherto almost exclusively set apart for the Tarentine didrachms. But it has been already shown that from about the year 228 onwards there was a break in the Tarentine coinage, and it need hardly surprise us therefore that, when a brief

---

[225] *Recherches sur les anciennes Monnaies de l'Italie Méridionale*, p. 118.

[226] *Historia Numorum*, p. 54. The usually accurate Carelli figures on Pl. CXIII. two coins of different denominations, with the signature, ϹΩΚΡΑΤΗϹ. The first (No. 196) seems to be a didrachm of full weight, belonging to Period VI. The legend on the second, however, is simply a misreading for ϹΩΚΑΝΝΑϹ of the present Period; and by a further erroneous interpretation of the design, the palm-branch and fillet in the horseman's hand is converted into a laurel-branch, similar to that held by Taras on another full-weight didrachm described under Period VI., also with the legend, ϹΩΚΡΑΤΗϹ (Car. cx. 135, without the inscription). Such an erroneous engraving is therefore fertile in confusion.

return of more favourable circumstances gave occasion for a temporary revival of the coinage, the standard of the new issue should present an abrupt contrast to that of the preceding class.

The view expressed in the *Historia Numorum* that the present class of coins belongs to the Hannibalic period of Tarentine history, is entirely corroborated by my own researches. The previous interruption of the Tarentine mintage is naturally accounted for by the tightening of the Roman hold on the eve of the final struggle against Carthage. The nominally free city lived under martial law imposed upon her by her too powerful ally. Under such circumstances the Carthaginian appeared as a deliverer, and the Tarentines, in virtue of the favourable convention concluded with Hannibal,[227] gained a new lease of their civic liberties, which had been reduced to a dead letter by the suspicious tyranny of Roman commandants. That the privilege of striking their own coins was now exercised once more can hardly be doubted.

The past period of depression, however, had inevitably left its mark. The circumstances of the times had changed, and it would be useless to expect that the standard of the new coinage should come up to that observed in the earlier issues from Pyrrhus's time onwards. The desperate finan-

---

[227] Livy, xxv. 8. "Congressi cum Hannibale rursus fide sanxerunt liberos Tarantinos leges suas suaque omnia habituros neque ullum vectigal Pœno pensuros præsidiumve invitos recepturos." Polybius, *Rel. Lib.* viii. c. 27, "Ταραντίνους ἐλευθερώσειν καὶ μήτε φόρους πράξασθαι κατὰ μηδένα τρόπον μήτ' ἄλλο μηδὲν ἐπιτάξειν Ταραντίνοις Καρχηδονίους." The suppression of the native coinage was no doubt enumerated amongst the "πολλὰς καὶ ποικίλας κατηγορίας" made against the Romans by the Tarentine conspirators in their interview with Hannibal (Polybius, l. viii. c. 26).

cial expedients to which Rome herself had been reduced by the stress of the Hannibalic war had revolutionized the conditions of the Italian money-markets. In 217 the value of the originally libral As, which had already in practice fallen to two ounces, was reduced in virtue of the *Lex Flaminia* to a single ounce. At the same time the weight of the Roman denarius had fallen from about 4·55 grammes to 3·90,[228] and that of the Victoriatus to 2·92. Tarentine commerce must have felt the full effect of this depreciation, since, as already remarked in the preceding section, the find of early Victoriati within the ancient walls of Tarentum tends to show that these Romano-Capuan coins had by this time entirely displaced the native Tarentine.

It does not seem, however, that the new Tarentine coinage had any direct relation to the Roman currency which it temporarily displaced. The average weight of seven Tarentine pieces of the present class of which I have a personal knowledge is 3·46 grammes. As compared with the contemporary Victoriatus, which since 217 had fallen to 2·92 grammes, this indicates a very considerable rise in the weight of the principal monetary unit. The weight, however, is still too low to be confounded with that of the reduced denarius of 3·90 grammes.

It is clear, however, that in the interests of their prospective commerce, the Tarentines when adopting a new standard for their staters, must have endeavoured as far as possible to conform to one or other of the monetary

---

[228] Mommsen, *op. cit.* (ed. Blacas, ii. 22 and 77), who, while admitting his inability to decide whether the reduction of the denarius weight had been gradual or the result of a special law, points out that the reduced weight becomes permanent about the year 217 B.C.

systems then in vogue. And as a matter of fact the weight of the Tarentine coins of the present class presents a striking conformity with that of the pieces struck on the old Victoriate system as it still existed in the great Illyrian staples of the opposite Adriatic shore. When in 228 B.C., after the first Illyrian war, Dyrrhachium and Apollonia entered into perpetual alliance with Rome, it was found possible in their new drachm coinage to harmonize their traditional monetary system with the new Victoriate currency of Rome. The average weight of the earliest class of Dyrrhachian and Apolloniate drachms now issued, about 3·47 grammes,[229] not only agrees with that of the early Victoriatus of three Roman scruples, but represents, nearly enough, a third of the old Corinthian tridrachms[230] of the same cities, the issue of which had for some time been discontinued, but which still no doubt formed the norm of official reckoning.

It will be seen that this system reconciled in a singularly felicitous manner the old traditions of Illyrian commerce with the new unit of calculation which was gaining such rapid vogue not only throughout Italy but in the Gaulish and Spanish staples of the far West. East of the Adriatic it was by no means confined to Dyrrhachium and Apollonia. It was shared, as we have seen, by Corcyra, and found

---

[229] Mommsen, *op. cit.* (ed. Blacas, ii. 91). "Les pièces dont le style et les légendes moins complètes prouvent une plus grande ancienneté (Mionnet, T. ii. p. 43, du No. 148 au No. 152) sont les plus fortes : elles pèsent 3 gr. 52 (= 66½), 3 gr. 48 (= 65¼, trois exemplaires), 3 gr. 40 (= 64)." A well-preserved Dyrrhachian piece, of a slightly later type, with the names ΑΛΚΑΙΟΣ and ΑΡΙΣΤΗΝΟΣ, which occurred in the Selci find, deposited c. 190 B.C., weighed 3 gr. 42. (See *Num. Chron.*, 1880, p. 272.)

[230] Their weight is c. 11 grammes 14; and the full weight of the corresponding drachm would have been c. 3 gr. 71.

besides a wide extension throughout Epirus and Thessaly. The Dyrrhachian and Apolloniate drachms were, however, especially abundant, and their acceptance by Rome indifferently with its own Victoriati as a medium of exchange [231] is a tribute to the commercial prosperity at this time enjoyed by the two Illyrian cities. Their monetary system, indeed, though adopted under Roman influence, had such independent vitality that, when Rome herself fell away from the original Victoriate standard, Dyrrhachium and Apollonia continued to uphold it for long with scarcely appreciable diminution. East of the Adriatic and far away to the Dacian gold-fields, these Illyrian drachms, and not their depreciated Roman representatives, continued for over a hundred years to be the principal medium of exchange. Nothing under the circumstances was more natural than for the Tarentines to revert to the old Victoriate system as still preserved by their commercial neighbours of Illyricum, and as a matter of fact the average weight of the early Illyrian drachms is practically identical with that of the Tarentine pieces of the present class.

The reproduction by the Tarentines of their old monetary types, both on the obverse and reverse of these late pieces, shows that they were still intended to represent the earlier silver staters of the city, although their weight had now sunk to that of contemporary drachms. As if, indeed, to emphasize the fact that the new coin was still regarded

---

[231] This seems to be the reasonable interpretation of Pliny's confused statement, xxxiii. 3, 46, in which he mixes up the later quinarius with the original Victoriatus, and confounds the latter with the Illyrian drachms. "Qui nunc Victoriatus appellatur lege Clodia percussus est. Antea enim hic nummus ex Illyrico advectus mercis loco habebatur."

as the legitimate representative of the Tarentine silver
stater, one magistrate, Sókannas, struck a half, weighing
about 1·70 grammes. It presents the same obverse and
reverse types as the larger piece, an unusual but not altogether unexampled repetition. On the other hand, halves
of the usual kind, such as are still found in the preceding
Period, with the head of Pallas on the obverse and her
owl on the reverse, are at this time wholly wanting;
another proof of the break of continuity in the Tarentine
coinage.

The types of the coins with which we are dealing
themselves afford certain evidence that many of them
belong to a later date than the issues of Period IX. The
remarkable piece (Type D, Pl. X. 12) signed ΦΙΛΙΑΡΧΟϹ,
now for the first time published, presents us with the
obverse device of the galloping hippakontist, which,
except that in this instance the warrior is bearded, is
simply an inferior copy of the coin with the same type
signed ΟΛΥΜΠΙϹ, of Period IX. Another piece of that
Period, in which the same signature is associated with a
standing horse, has, in like manner, served as prototype
both in the obverse and reverse design for a coin of this
inferior standard, signed by ϹΗΡΑΜΒΟϹ (Type A;
Pl. X. 9). The coin signed ϹΩΓΕΝΗϹ (Type B;
Pl. X. 10), on the other hand, which, from its superior
execution, may be one of the earliest of the present class,
reproduces as its obverse design one of the most familiar
schemes of the preceding Period IX.; and Type C again
(Pl. X. 11), in which the rider holds a palm, displays a
reminiscence of Type E 1, of the same Period. It is remarkable, however, that the epigraphy of these late coins
is in some cases more conservative of older forms than
that of the prototypes of the preceding Period. C for Ϲ

and A for A are no longer found. On the other hand, the form A for A now makes its appearance.

The break of continuity exemplified by the weight and fabric of these coins is further illustrated by the character of the signatures which they display. While in the preceding Periods a certain proportion of the signatures of one class are common to that which succeeds it, in the present case there is no overlapping of this kind, and we have to deal with a total divergence of nomenclature as regards the preceding post-Pyrrhic Periods. The name ΦΙΛΙΑΡΧΟΣ, indeed, is the only one that occurs on any of the earlier Tarentine types. But the earlier piece that bears this signature belongs to the last issue of the full-weight didrachms, and is separated, therefore, from the coin of the present class (which, if fabric is to count for anything, must be reckoned amongst the very latest products of the Tarentine mint) by the whole series of the reduced-weight coinages.

Nothing, on the whole, is more suggestive of altered political conditions in the present group of coins than the character of some of the signatures. Names now appear of distinctly non-Hellenic origin, and certainly of no aristocratic ring. The signature ΣΗΡΑΜΒΟΣ recalls the ΣΑΡΑΜΒΟΣ mentioned in Plato's Gorgias[232] as celebrated in the wine trade. ΣΩΚΑΝΝΑΣ, another personal name that now appears, has an equally foreign sound. We should naturally look for parallels in that old Messapian stock which supplied the præ-Hellenic ingredients of the Tarentine population, and which has left its

---

[232] Ed. Steph. p. 518. "Σάραμβος ὁ κάπηλος." Referred to by Avellino (*Adnotationes in Carellii Num. Vet. It. Descr.* p. 11), who also connects the form *Exærambus* of Plautus.

traces among the magistrates' names in the Tarentine colonial foundation of Hêrakleia.[233] As a matter of fact, moreover, the indigenous elements of South-Eastern Italy had at this time gained new prominence in league with the Carthaginian, and at Brundisium, at Arpi, at Salapia, three chiefs of the typically Messapian name of Dasius[234] had stood forth at the head of the national party against Rome. These Tarentine names, however, do not fit in with any known personal names belonging to this Italo-Illyric group. Their nationality remains obscure, but the appearance now, for the first time, on the Tarentine dies, of such non-Hellenic[235] forms, is itself an unmistakeable indication of political change, and of the coming to the fore of new elements. In default of Greek or Italic comparisons we have at least to face the possibility that Hannibal, whose fiscal needs were pressing, secured, as a kind of financial guarantee, the nomination of some of his own officers as monetary magistrates. In that case it may even happen that the origin of these

---

[233] *Tabulæ Heracleenses* (ed. Mazochii, p. 257, 259), ΔΑΖΙ-ΜΟΣ ΓΥΡΡΩ (Δάζιμος Πύρρου).

[234] See Mommsen, *Die Unteritalienischen Dialekte*, p. 72. Under the form Dassius the same name had also a wide trans-Adriatic extension amongst the kindred Illyrian tribes of Dalmatia, &c.

[235] Lenormant (*La Grande Grèce*, i. 27) speaks of "la proportion des noms Messapiques qui figurent parmi ceux des magistrats qui ont inscrit leur signature sur les monnaies de Tarente." But the only other clear example of a non-Hellenic form on Tarentine coins, besides the two cited above, is the remarkable inscription INVANIΩ or YNVANIΩ coupled with ΞΩ on a drachm. See Avellino, *Bull. Arch. Napoletano*, T. 11, p. 100. [It may be suggested that this inscription is only a barbarous rendering of the name NEYMHNIOΞ, which occurs on other similar drachms, sometimes in a corrupt form; one in my possession reads NIYIHIZIO . . . This coin has been plated.]

strange sounding names should be sought in a Semitic quarter.

A negative phenomenon presented by the signatures of the short Hannibalic period of the Tarentine coinage is also of considerable interest. The names of the principal heroes of the Tarentine Revolution, Philêmenos, Nikôn, and Dêmokrates, are conspicuous by their absence. We are left, therefore, to infer that the signatures on the group of coins do not relate to the actual *Stratêgoi*, but to magistrates fulfilling more civil functions, as masters of the mint. It is possible that we have here a symptom of a more democratic spirit in the Tarentine polity. It was in the aristocratic party at Tarentum that the Romans had found their chief support, and it was the alienation of an influential part of this, occasioned by the pitiless execution of the Tarentine hostages when recaptured after an attempted escape, which had prepared the way for the final triumph of the anti-Roman elements in the city. The younger nobles, chief among whom were Nikôn and Philêmenos, the grandsons, it may be, of the Tarentine magistrates of the same names, who sign on coins of Pyrrhus' time and Period VIII., made common cause with the Tarentine Plebs, and the success of the conspiracy seems to have been due to the union of these *Junkers* with the popular party.[236] The otherwise plebeian character of the Revolution is clearly indicated in the passage of Livy, which describes this alliance, and the non-aristocratic and

---

[236] Cf. Livy, xxiv. 13. " Ad Hannibalem . . . quinque nobiles juvenes ab Tarento venerunt . . . . Ei memores beneficiorum ejus perpulisse magnam partem se juventutis Tarentinæ referunt ut Hannibalis amicitiam ac societatam quam populi Romani mallent . . . . *in potestate juniorum plebem, in manu plebis rem Tarentinam esse.*"

even non-Hellenic character of some of the signatures of this period may well be due to the democratic lines on which the Tarentine commonwealth was now re-constituted.

That the issue of these late Tarentine coins, of the same standard as the original Victoriatus and the Illyrian drachms, corresponds with the Hannibalic Period at Tarentum, is corroborated by another remarkable coin, that seems to have been struck under the same auspices by the neighbouring city of Metapontion. This city, like Tarentum, became, after Pyrrhus' time, a dependent ally of Rome, and from the fact that no ordinary didrachms of the reduced weight were struck there, it would seem that the silver coinage of Metapontion had ceased entirely during this period of Roman connexion. On the removal, however, of half the Roman garrison from Metapontion to the beleaguered citadel of Tarentum, the inhabitants at once went over to Hannibal; and there exists a small Metapontine silver piece, Fig. 3, in weight and fabric closely recalling the Tarentine coins of this Period, which must certainly be also referred to the short interval of revived independence between the date of the defection in 212 and 207, when Hannibal not only withdrew his garrison, but at the same time removed the Metapontines themselves to escape the Roman chastisement.[237] The coin in

Fig. 3.

---

[237] Livy, l. xxvii. 51. "Hannibal . . . Metapontinos, civitatem universam, excitos sedibus suis, et Lucanorum qui suæ ditionis erant, in Bruttium agrum traduxit."

question, of which I procured a fine specimen at Taranto, presents as its obverse type the helmeted head of Pallas, in a very late style, with loose flowing tresses, and on the reverse the usual corn-spike with an owl seated on the spray, and the legend **META** in punctuated characters.[238] Both the obverse and reverse designs are degenerate versions of those that occur on one of the latest of the full-weight issues.[239] The weight, however, of the present piece is 3·65 grammes, answering with sufficient approximation to that of the contemporary Tarentine pieces.

The attribution of this late Metapontine piece to the Hannibalic Period entails with it a further conclusion. Another silver coin exists, in its obverse and reverse type (including the owl symbol) identical with that described above but with the legend ΛOYKA in place of **META**, showing that it was struck by the Lucani in close alliance with the Metapontines. Its weight, 3·13 grammes,[240] is probably intended to tally with the contemporary Metapontine standard; and there can be no reasonable doubt that this alliance coin belongs to the period when the Lucanians and Metapontines threw off the Roman yoke and passed together under Hannibal's protection. Livy mentions the defection of the Lucani along with that of so many of the Italiote Greeks as a consequence of Cannæ,[241] and the extent to which their fortunes were linked to

---

[238] A specimen of a very similar type, in which the owl is more clearly represented, is engraved in Garrucci, *Monete dell' Italia Meridionale*, T. civ. 18; but the late character of the style is not sufficiently indicated, and the weight, as usual, is omitted.

[239] Carelli, *N. I. V.* clvi., 125, 127.

[240] Sambon, *Recherches sur les anciennes Monnaies de l'Italie Meridionale*, p. 131.

[241] Livy, xxii. 61.

those of the Metapontines appears from the subsequent notice of the same historian, according to which Hannibal, unable any longer to protect them at home, transported the inhabitants of Metapontion and the Lucanians subject to his dominion at one and the same time to the Bruttian territory.[242]

It thus appears that the existence at Tarentum of a class of coins minted during the period of the Hannibalic alliance is by no means an isolated phenomenon. It stands to reason moreover that whatever the nominal ἀτέλεια of Tarentum, Hannibal must have drawn largely on the resources of the great Greek city to pay his mercenaries, and the constant demand for pecuniary aid could only have been supplied by a sufficiently abundant mintage. Lenormant, indeed, has suggested that the appearance of a type of Gaulish gold coin, characteristic of the Amiens district, imitated from a Tarentine gold stater, was due to the return of Gaulish mercenaries from Hannibal's army, who in payment for their services at Tarentum had received gold pieces recently struck by the mint of that city. The theory here advanced that the prototypes of these Gaulish pieces, which are, in fact, no other than the beautiful gold staters of Tarentum representing the Dioskuri, and ranking among the finest products of the Tarentine mint, were issued during the Hannibalic period is too grotesque to need refutation;[243] but in view of the

---

[242] xxvii. 51.

[243] *La Grande Grèce*, p. 60 : " Comment les statères tarentins ont ils pu parvenir jusque sur les bords de la Somme vers ce moment, et cela en quantité assez abondante pour y servir de prototype à la fabrication monétaire indigène ? C'est ce qui ne peut pas absolument s'expliquer que par le retour dans ses foyers d'une troupe de ces mercenaires gaulois qui formaient une grande partie de l'armée d'Hannibal, troupe qui aura reçu le

late character of some other Tarentine gold types, the possibility of some of these having been struck at this epoch cannot be safely left out of sight.

Mr. Head [244] has already pointed out the propriety of referring to the Hannibalic Period the gold stater (Pl. X. 15), representing a very late version of the head of the youthful Hêraklês, and on the reverse Taras driving a biga; and I have ventured to add to this the smaller coin (Pl. X. 16), exhibiting on the obverse a head of Pallas of a very late and degenerate type and on the reverse Taras again driving a biga, the horses of which show great analogy to those of the stater. This coin weighs 44·2 grains, and must thus be regarded as a third of a stater, a wholly abnormal division in the Tarentine gold series, in which, however, sixths are of frequent occurrence. The head of Pallas on this coin presents so strong a resemblance to the same head on the silver coins struck, as we have seen, by the Metapontines and Lucanians on the occasion of the Hannibalic alliance, that it is impossible not to refer it to the same period.

The 83,000 lb. of gold looted by Fabius, on his capture of Tarentum, shows that the mint could not at least have lacked bullion. With regard, however, to the silver booty taken, the historian is more explicit, and Livy's allusion

---

payement de ses services à Tarente en monnaies nouvellement frappées de la ville." That these coins may have reached North-Western Gaul through the hands of mercenaries is always possible; but these mercenaries must have belonged to a period long anterior to Hannibal's time if the payment they received was, as is probable, in current coin.

[244] *Hist. Num.*, p. 48. The coin weighs 135 grs., and bears the signature ΑΙ on the reverse, with a thunderbolt symbol.

to the amount of coined as well as of wrought silver may be regarded as an additional testimony to the revived activity of the Tarentine mint.[245]

PERIOD X.

X. Type A.

Naked boy-rider crowning horse, standing r.

Obv.

1. In f. to l., KΛH. Beneath horse, ⋛HPAMBO⋛. Car. cxiii. 191. [Pl. X. 9.]

Rev.

Taras astride, &c., to l., holding trident in l. hand, and with r. extending akrostolion. Beneath dolphin, TA-PΑΣ. In f. to r., ⋈.

X. Type B.

Naked boy-rider crowning horse standing l. and lifting off fore-leg.

1. In f. to r., ΣΩ. Beneath horse, ⋛ΩΓΕ ΝΗ⋛. Car. cxiii. 195. [Pl. X. 10.]

Taras, astride, &c., to l., holding cornucopiæ in l. hand, and with r. receiving wreath-bearing Victory.

X. Type C.

Naked boy-rider holding *palma lemniscata*, crowning horse standing r., and lifting off fore-leg.

1. Beneath horse, KPITO⋛. [Pl. X. 11.]

Taras astride, &c., to l., holding trident in r. hand, and with l. receiving wreath-bearing Victory. In f. to l., EK; in f. to r., ⳨.

X. Type D.

Bearded hippakontist in cuirass on galloping horse to r., aiming dart.

---

[245] Livy, lib. xxvii., c. 16. "Argenti vis ingens facti signatique."

Obv.	Rev.
1. In f. to l., ΦΙ. Beneath horse, ΦΙΛΙΑΡΧΟϟ. [Pl. X. 12. A. J. E.]	Taras astride, &c., to r., a diadem round his head, and a chlamys flowing from his l. arm, aiming a trident with his r. hand.

X. Type E.

Horseman in crested helmet and cuirass, holding *palma lemniscata* on horse standing r. and lifting fore-leg.

1. Beneath horse, ϟΩΚΑΝΝΑϟ Cf. Car. cxiii. 197. " ϟΩΚΡΑΤΗϟ." [Pl. X. 13.]	Taras astride, &c., to l., holding trident in l. hand, and with r. extending kantharos. In f. to r., an eagle with expanding wings. Beneath dolphin, ΤΑΡΑϟ.

X. Type F. (Half of Unit.)

Naked boy-rider crowned by small Victory flying behind and crowning his horse, which is stationary to r.

1. Beneath horse, ϟΩΚΑΝ ΝΑϟ. B. M. Cat. App. 3. Sambon, *Mon. de la Presqu'ile Italique*, Pl. xviii. 26. [Pl. X. 14.]	Taras astride, &c., to l., holding trident in l. hand, and with r. extending kantharos; a chlamys on his l. arm.

APPENDIX A.

COINS FROM THE BENEVENTAN FIND.

Tarentum.

Obverse.	Reverse.	Fully described under	Weight in Grains.
1. Boy-rider, &c., with boy picking pebble out of hoof. ΦΙ. (Somewhat worn.)	Taras holding kantharos, trident, and small round shield. Waves and E.	IV. C 1	120
2. Lancer cantering r. ΦΙΛΙ. (Fresh condition.)	Infantile Taras, with distaff and small dolphin. Vine-leaf. Waves and ΦΙ.	V. B 3	122
3. Same. Beneath horse, ΞA. (Fresh condition.)	Infantile Taras holding distaff and extending hand. Prow.	V. B 2	119
4. Same; but horseman helmeted. ΔΑΙ. (Fresh condition.)	Taras astride, &c., with hippocamp, shield and trident. Murex and ΦΙ.	V. B 5	121½

Neapolis.

Weights in Grains.

5. *Obv.* Head of Parthenopé to r., four dolphins around. **ΝΕΟΠΟΛΙΤΩΝ.**

   Rev. Man-faced bull crowned by Niké to r.; head turned towards spectator. Below bull, **ΘΕ.** (Car., T. lxxix. 11) 113

6. *Obv.* Same.

   Rev. Same, but no letters under bull . . . 112½

7. *Obv.* Same, but different arrangement of the hair, the fillet that confines it completely circling the head. No dolphins. In f. to l., **X**.

		Weights in Grains.
Rev. Same, but the legend **NEOΓOΛITΩN** is on a base on which the bull stands. Under bull, ☉. (Car., T. lxxiv. 18)		112
(Fresh condition.)		

8. *Obv.* Same as last, but in f. to l. club.
    Rev. Same. (Cf. Car., lxxv. 3) 118½

9. *Obv.* Same as last, but in f. to l. bunch of grapes.
    Rev. Same, but no letter under bull . . . 110
    (Fresh condition.)

10. *Obv.* Same, but smaller head. In f. to l., Artemis holding a torch in either hand. Under neck, **APTEMI**.
    Rev. Same, but **N** beneath bull (Car., T. lxxv. 6) . 114
    (*Fleur de coin.*)

11. *Obv.* Same, but to l. astragalus (?). Beneath head, part of inscription, **APTEMI**.
    Rev. Same, but beneath bull, **ΘE**. (Car., T. lxxv. 9) 113
    (Fresh condition.)

12. *Obv.* Same, but to l. figure of Artemis advancing to r., and holding transverse torch. Under neck, **ΓAPME**.
    Rev. Same, but beneath bull, a bee. (Car., T. lxxvi. 2) 110½
    (Fresh condition.)

NOLA.

13. *Obv.* Head of Pallas in crested helmet to r. On helmet, owl and olive wreath. Behind, under crest, apparently **ξ**.
    Rev. **NΩΛAIΩN** in f. above; man-faced bull to l., face in profile. Under bull, **ΛE** in mon. (Cf. Car., T. lxxxiv. 4) . . . 110½
    (Well-preserved.)

14. *Obv.* Head of nymph to r., hair bound with fillet.

Rev. Same, but NΩΛΑΙΩΝ in ex. No letters under bull. (Car., T. lxxxiv. 8) . . 106¼

Hyrina.

15. *Obv.* Head of Pallas, as No. 13.
Rev. YPINA in f., above man-faced bull; head in profile 115

(Somewhat worn.)

16. *Obv.* Three-quarters facing head of Hèra wearing stephanos.
Rev. ΑΝΙ ¶Y, man-faced bull, head in profile to r.

(A good deal worn.)

Velia.

17. *Obv.* Head of Pallas to l., in crested helmet, ornamented with Pegasos and palmetto. In f. above, A; to l., Φ; to r. in small square, IE.
Rev. YE[ΛΗΤΩΝ]. Lion tearing down stag; both animals in profile 112½

(Fresh condition.)

18. *Obv.* Same, Φ to l., K to r.
Rev. Same insc. Lion walking l. Above, Φ 1 and triquetra.

(*Fleur de coin.*)

19. *Obv* Head of Pallas to l., in crested Phrygian helmet adorned with Sphinx. Under crest behind in minute letters, ϪE.
Rev. Lion to l., tearing prey; on base inscribed YEΛΗΤΩΝ. In f. above, ϪE . . 112

(*Fleur de coin.*)

APPENDIX A. 215

METAPONTION.

Weights in Grains.

20. *Obv.* Head of Dēmēter to l., with wreath of corn-spikes.

 Rev. **META**. Barley spike in f. to l., caduceus and **ΛΥ**. (Cf. Car., T. clii. 24) . . . 119

21. *Obv.* Head of Dēmēter to l., with wreath of corn-spikes and veil falling from back hair.

 Rev. Same, but on blade of spike a mouse, and in f. below **Φ**. (Car., T. clii. 6) . . . 118½
  (Fresh condition.)

CAPUA IN THE ROMAN NAME.

22. *Obv.* Bearded heroic head to l., in crested Corinthian helmet.

 Rev. Horse's head to r. on base, upon which **ROMANO**. In f. to l., barley spike . 111½
  (Somewhat worn.)

23. *Obv.* Youthful head of Hēraklēs to r.; lion's skin and club on shoulder.

 Rev. Wolf and twins. In ex. **ROMAN[O]** . . 108½
  (*Fleur de coin.*)

24. Another specimen 109
  (Fresh condition.)

216   THE "HORSEMEN" OF TARENTUM.

APPENDIX B.—CALABRIAN FIND.

	Obverse.	Reverse.	Reference for Full Description.	No. of Coins in Hoard.	Weight of Selected Coins.
					Grains.
1.	ϵΙ ΔΕΙΝΟΚΡΑΤΗϵ	ΔΙ, elephant	VI. D 2	1	123
2.	ΓΥ ΑΡΙϵΤΙΓ, horseman	ΠΟΛΥ, thunderbolt	VII. A 1	6	98
3.	ΓΥ ϵΩϵΤΡΑΤΟϵ	ΠΟΛΥ	VII. A 2	9	100
4.	ΕΥ ϵΩϵΤΡΑΤΟϵ	ΠΟΛΥ, prow	VII. A 3	24	101
5.	ΕΥ ΦΙΝΤΥΛΟϵ	ΓΥ or ΥΓ	VII. A 4	16	99½
6.	ϵΙ ΛΥΚΩΝ	ΔΙ, elephant	VII. A 6	21	101
7.	ΓΥ ΑΡΙϵΤΙΓ, standing figure	ΑΡΙϵ, two stars	VII. B 1	10	98
8.	ΗΩ ΝΕΥΜΗ, stationary horse	ΠΟΛΥ "	VII. C 2	7	102¼
9.	ΗΩ ΝΕΥΜΗ	Hippocamp on shield	VII. C 3	33	101¼
10.	Æ ΔΑΜΟΚΡΙ	ΘΙ	VII. C 4	1	99
11.	ΕΥ ΑΠΟΛΛΩ, two amphoras	ΘΙ Β	VII. C 5	7	100¼
12.	ΕΥ ΑΠΟΛΛΩ " "	ΘΙ	VII. C 6	2	99½
13.	ΕΥ ΑΠΟΛΛΩ " "	Ӿ	VII. C 7	1	98
14.	ΗΙ ΙΩΠΥ, squatting figure	ΓΥ	VII. C 8	1	99
15.	Φ ϵΑΛΩΝΟϵ, Dioskuri	ΓΥ	VII. D 1	12	100½
16.	Æ ϵΑΛΩΝΟϵ, Dioskuros	ΓΥ, Poseidonlike Taras	VII. E 1	5	102
17.	Uncertain Sig. "	ΑΝΘ or ΑΝ	VII. E 2	1	100½
18.	ΗΩ ΗΙ ΑΠΟΛΛΩ	ΑΝΘ or ΑΝ	VII. F 1	48	102
19.	ΗΩ ΑΠΟΛΛΩ	ΑΝΘ, spray	VII. F 2	17	99½
20.	ΗΩ ΑΠΟΛΛΩ	ΑΝΘ, serpent	VII. F 3	8	101¼
21.	ΗΩ ΑΠΟΛΛΩ	ΑΝΘ or ΑΝ	VII. F 4	1	—
22.	ΗΩ ϵΑΛΟ, Ionic capital	ΧΙ and diota	VII. G 1	79	100½
23.	⊥ΗΡΑ, Torch-racer	ΑΠΟΛ	VII. L 1	2	100½
24.	ΙΚ ΦΙΛΟΚΡΑ	ΑΡΙϵΤΟ	VIII. A 6	17	99
25.	ΦΙΛΟΚΡΑ ΙΚ		VIII. C 2	14	98½
				313	

APPENDIX B.

CALABRIAN FIND—(*continued*).

TARENTINE DRACHMS.

Obverse.	Reverse.	No. of Coins.	Weight in Grains.
Helmeted head of Pallas to l.	TAPANTINΩN ⋚Ω⋚, owl on bolt.	26	50
Same	Same, but ⋚Ω	10	49
Same	Same, but ⋚Ω⋚, beneath bolt ΔIO.	12	48½
Same	Same, but ⋚Ω, beneath bolt ΔIO.	6	—
Same, but head to r.	Owl on olive-spray, NEYMHNIO⋚ ΓOΛY.	7	49¼
Same	Same, NEYMHNIO⋚ API.	6	49½
Same	Same, but TAPA ℈ N.	1	48
	Total Drachms	68	

HÊRAKLEIA.—DIDRACHMS.

Obverse.	Reverse.	No. of Coins.	Weight in Grains.
1. Head of Pallas r., in Corinthian helmet, on which is a hippocamp. Above, ⊦HPAKΛEIΩN. Behind, ⊦H.	Hêraklês sacrificing. In f. to r., thunderbolt.	2	99
2. Head to l., griffin on helmet. Above, ⊦HPAKΛEIΩN.	Hêraklês facing, looking r. at small Victory flying towards him. In f. to l. ΦIΛO.	7	99½
3. Head r., plain helmet. ΑΛΕ above, EY behind, ⊥ beneath.	Hêraklês facing, owl flying l.	4	—
	Total Hêrakleia	13	

ff

CALABRIAN HOARD.—THURIAN DIDRACHMS.

Obverse.	Reverse.	
1. Helmeted head of Pallas to r.	Bull butting; beneath, Φ? N?	2
2. Same.	Same, Δ Φ, between legs of bull	1
	Total Thurian	8

SUMMARY OF COINS IN CALABRIAN HOARD.

Tarentine Didrachms	348
,, Drachms	68
Herakleian Didrachms	13
Thurian ,,	8
Total	427

APPENDIX C.
TARANTO FIND—TARENTINE DIDRACHMS.

	Obverse.	Reverse.	Reference for full Description.	No. of Coins in Hoard.	Average Weight.
					Grs.
1.	ΓΥ ΑΡΙΣΤΙΠ, horseman	ΔΙ, elephant	VII. A 1	3	98¼
2.	ΓΥ ΑΡΙΣΤΙΠ, male figure	ΔΙ, elephant	VII. B 1	1	93
3.	ΓΥ ΣΩΣΤΡΑΤΟΣ	ΠΟΛΥ, thunderbolt	VII. A 2	2	98½
4.	ΕΥ ΦΙΝΤΥΛΟΣ	ΠΟΛΥ, prow	VII. A 4	4	99
5.	ΗΙ ΣΩΓΥ, squatting figure	✶	VII. C 8	8	99½
6.	ΗΩ ΝΕΥΜΗ	ΠΟΛΥ, two stars	VII. C 9	1	101
7.	Υ ΑΠΟΛΛΩ	Β ΘΙ	VII. C 6	1	100
8.	ΗΩ ΣΑΛΟ, Ionic capital	ΑΝΘ	VII. G 1	1	99
9.	ΗΩ ΑΠΟΛΛΩ	ΑΝΘ	VII. F 2	9	100¼
10.	ΗΩ ΗΙ ΑΠΟΛΛΩ	ΑΝΘ	VII. F 1	8	100½
11.	ΣΙ ΛΥΚΩΝ	ΓΥ	VII. A 6	2	102
12.	ΦΥ ΣΑΛΩΝΟΣ, Dioskuri	ΓΥ	VII. D 1	8	100
13.	ΑΡΙ ΣΤΙΣ, anchor	T. holds Victory	VIII. A 1	1	97½
14.	ΣΥ ΛΥΚΙΝΟΣ	Owl	VIII. A 9	19	99¾
15.	ΣΥ ΔΕ ΛΥΚΙΝΟΣ	Owl	VIII. A 8	227	102¼
16.	ΕΥ ΗΣΤΙΑΡ	Bunch of grapes	VIII. A 10	2	99½
17.	ΦΙΛΩΤΑΣ, cornucopiæ	ΠΟΛΥ	VIII. A 5	20	97½
18.	ΔΙ ΦΙΛΩΤΑΣ	Cock	VIII. A 11	5	99½
19.	ΑΓΑΘΑΡΧΟΣ	Torch	VIII. B 1	60	99¾
20.	ΦΙ ΣΩΓΥΡΟΣ	Cicada	VIII. B 2	45	97½
21.	ΗΑΓΕΑΣ	ΠΟΛΥ	VIII. A 4	17	97
22.	ΛΕΩΝ, cornucopiæ	Α′, lion	VIII. B 3	5	99
23.	ΚΥΝΩΝ, mask	T. holds kantharos	VIII. B 4	14?	98¾
				23	
		Carried forward		484	

APPENDIX C (*continued*).

TARANTO FIND—TARENTINE DIDRACHMS.

	Obverse.	Reverse.	Reference for full Description.	No. of Coins in Hoard.	Average Weight.
					Grs.
		Brought forward .	. . . .	484	
24.	ΕΥ ΦΙ ΞΕΝΕΑΣ	Corn-spike	VIII. C 1	19	100¼
25.	ΔΙ ΑΡΙΣΤΟΚΛΗΣ . . .	Head of nymph . . .	VIII. D 1	152	100¼
26.	ΑΥ ΝΙΚΟΚΡΑΤΗΣ . . .	Ionic capital . . .	VIII. D 2	1	101½
27.	ΝΙΚΥΛΟΣ Dioskuri . . .	₳	VIII. O 1	2	100¾
28.	ͰΙ ΦΙΛΗΜΕΝΟΣ . . .	Bucranium	VIII. E 1	16	98½
29.	ΦΙΛΙCΚΟC	Tripod	VIII. F 1	9	98¾
30.	ͰΗΡΑΚΛΗΤΟΣ	ΕΠ, thymiatêrion . .	VIII. G 1	60	100
31.	ΔΙ ΑΠΟΛΛΩΝΙΟΣ . . .	T. with chlamys . .	VIII. H 1	69	99¼
32.	ΘΙ ΑΡΙΣΤΟΚ	Rudder	VIII. H 2	34	98¾
33.	ͰΙΠΠΟΔΑ	ΔΙ and amphora . .	VIII. K 1	38	99
34.	ΑΡΙΣΤΟΚΡΑΤΗΣ	ΠΙ and term . . .	VIII. L 1	22	98¾
35.	ΑΡΙΣΤΕΙΔ	ΗΡΑ	VIII. L 2	11	99¾
36.	ΕΥ ΔΑΜΟΚΡΙΤΟΣ . . .	Ӿ	VIII. L 3	31	99¼
37.	ΕΥ ΑΡΙΣΤΩΝ	ΣΩΠ	VIII. M 2	16	100
*38.	ΗΡΑ ΔΑΙΜΑΧοC	ΔΓ	IX. A 1	5	100¼
*39.	ΣΩΠΥΡΙΩΝ ΣΩ	ΕΠ, head of Pan . .	IX. B 1	5	99½
*40.	ΟΛΥΜΠΙΣ	Tripod	IX. C 1	26	100
*41.	ΑΡ ΑΡΙΣΤΙΠΠΟΣ . . .	ϒ	IX. E 1	11	101
*42.	ΦΙΛΟΚΛΗC ⚓ Æ . . .	Two amphoras . . .	IX. F 1	5	98¼
	Uncertain	. . . . . .	. . . .	16	
		Total Tarentine Didrachms .	. . .	1032	

* Fleur de Coin.

APPENDIX C (*continued*).

TARANTO FIND—TARENTINE DRACHMS.

Obverse.	Reverse.	Reference for full Description.	No. of Coins in Hoard.	Average Weight.
				Grs.
1. Head of Pallas in crested helmet, on which Scylla	NEYMHNIOΣ API .	VII. 1	4	48
2. Same	NEYMHNIOΣ ΠOΛY	VII. 2	2	47
3. Same; Ⅎ on helmet	⅁ N	VII. 5	1	49
4. Same (flowing hair)	ΣΩΣ (or ΣΩ), ΔIO (or ΔI)	VII. 6	2	48¼
5. Same as 1.	ⱵHPAKΛHTOΣ, flower	VIII. 2	1	
6. Same	ⱵIΣTIAPXOΣ EY, grapes.	VIII. 3	1	48½
7. Same	NIKOKPATHΣ N	VIII. 6	2	49¼
8. Same	APICTIC, anchor	VIII. 4	1	50¼
9. Same	OΛYMΠIΣ, wreath	IX. 2	2	50¼
	Total Tarentine Drachms .		16	

APPENDIX C (*continued*).

TARANTO FIND—TARENTINE LITRÆ.

Obverse.	Reverse.	Compare Didrachms.	No. of Coins in Find.	Average Weight.
				Grs.
1. Cockle shell	Dolphin; beneath, owl	VIII. A 7	12	$10\frac{7}{10}$
2. Same	Same; owl and ΕΥ	VIII. A 7	2	$8\frac{1}{2}$
3. Same	Same; thunderbolt	VII. A 2	25	$9\frac{22}{25}$
4. Same	Same; Ε	{ VIII. G 1 / IX. B 1 }	7	$9\frac{1}{2}$
5. Same	Same; Ε and flower	VIII. G 2	1	$9\frac{1}{4}$
6. Same	Same; Α and doe	IX. E 1	10	$9\frac{3}{4}$
7. Same	Same; ΔΙ, head of nymph	VIII. D 1	2	$9\frac{1}{2}$
8. Same	Same; ΦΙ		4	$9\frac{3}{4}$
9. Same	Same; rudder	VIII. H 2	1	9
10. Same	Same; Α	IX. D 1	3	$9\frac{1}{2}$
11. Same	Same; in f. above, Victory flying		4	$9\frac{1}{2}$
12. Same	Same; in f. above, rhyton	IX. F 1	2	$8\frac{3}{4}$
13. Uncertain, or with no symbol or letter			15	$9\frac{7}{10}$
		Total Tarentine Litræ	88	

APPENDIX C (*continued*).

TARANTO FIND—TARENTINE HÊMILITRA.

Obverse.	Reverse.	Compare Didrachms.	No. of Coins in Hoard.	Average Weight.
				Grs.
1. Cockle . .	Dolphin ; beneath, owl . . .	VIII. A 8, 9	1	4
2. Same . .	Same ; beneath, thunderbolt . .	VII. A 2	3	$4\frac{1}{2}$
3. Same . .	Same ; Ε	VIII. G 1, 2	8	$4\frac{1}{3}$
4. Same . .	Same ; flower ?	VIII. G 2 ?	1	5
5. Same . .	Same ; doe	. . .	13	$5\frac{1}{13}$
6. Same . .	Same ; [illegible]	IX. D 1	6	$4\frac{11}{12}$
7. Same . .	Same ; ΘΙ	{ VII. C 6 / VIII. H 2 }	1	$4\frac{1}{4}$
8. Same . .	Same ; Τ	. .	3	$4\frac{2}{3}$
9. Same . .	Same ; ΦΙ	. . .	2	$4\frac{1}{2}$
10. Same . .	Same ; Victory flying . . .	. . . .	1	$4\frac{1}{2}$
Uncertain, or without letters or symbol		. . .	7	$5\frac{1}{7}$
	Total Tarentine Hêmilitra . .		46	

APPENDIX C (*continued*).

TARANTO FIND—TARENTINE DIOBOLS (Pallas Type).

Obverse.	Reverse.	Compare Didrachms.	No. of Coins in Hoard.	Average Weight.
				Grs.
1. Head of Pallas to r. in crested helmet, on which Scylla.	Héraklês standing, facing l., and strangling lion. In f. to r., cicada.	VIII. B 2	3	16¾
2. Same . . .	Same; but facing r. In f. to l., club; between legs, R.	IX. E 1?	3	16⅔
3. Same . . .	Same. In f. to l., doe; between legs, R.	IX. E 1?	7	17¼
4. Same . . .	Same. In f. to l., doe and club; between legs, R.	IX. E 1?	5	17½
5. Same . . .	Same. Inscr., TAPANTINΩN; between legs, ΦΙ.	. . .	8	16½
6. Same . . .	Same. In f. to l., bucranium; between legs, ΦΙ.	VIII. E 1	2	16
7. Same . . .	Same; but in f. to l., thunderbolt; between legs, ΦΙ.	. . .	11	15₁₁⁄₁₂
8. Same . . .	Same. In f. to l., club; between legs, ΔΙ.	. . .	2	17
9. Same; but hippocamp on helmet.	Same. In f. to l., club and owl above; in f. to r., ϟΥ.	VIII. A 8, 9	2	16
10. As 1; but head to l. .	Héraklês facing r., grappling with lion, and with r. raising club. Beneath, bow.	. . .	2	14¾

APPENDIX C.

11. Same as 1—8	As 1—7; but uncertain or without symbols or letters.	.	19	16¾
12. Same	Infant Héraklès strangling serpents. In f. to l., **TA** and **Υ**. In ex. thunderbolt.	VII. A 2	11	16¼¼
13. Head of Pallas in triple-crested helmet, three-quarter facing to l.	Héraklès strangling lion, as 2, &c. In f. to l., club and Amazonian shield; between legs, **Ɑ**.	IX. E 1?	7	17
14. Same	Same; club to l. Insc., **TAPANTI**·**ΝΩΝ**; between legs, **Ɑ**.	IX. E 1?	3	15½
15. Same, to r.	Héraklès kneeling on lion and raising club to strike it. In f. to r., tripod.	(VIII. F 1) (IX. C 1)	32	15¾
16. Same	Same. In f. to r., anchor	VIII. A 1	1	14¾
17. Head of Pallas to l. in Corinthian helmet.	Same as 11, &c. In f. to l., club; between legs, **ΙΗ**.		2	16
18. Same	Same; between legs, **ΦI**		4	16⅜
19. Same	Same; but **Ɑ**		1	16¼
20. Same	Same; but **ΔΙ**	IX. D 1	1	16
21. Same	Same as 13. Beneath, owl and uncertain object.	VIII. A 8, 9	9	16⅔
22. Same	Same; but uncertain letters			16¾
			26	
Total Tarentine Diobols (Pallas Type)			161	

APPENDIX C (continued).
TARANTO FIND—TARENTINE OBOLS (Diota Type).

Obverse.	Reverse.	Compare Didrachms.	No. of Coins in Hoard.	Average Weight. Grs.
1. Diota and three pellets	Diota and three pellets; thunderbolt	VII. A 2	5	$7\frac{1}{10}$
2. Same	Same; owl	VIII. A 8, 9	10	$7\frac{7}{10}$
3. Same	Same; ΔI and head of nymph	VIII. D 1	3	$6\frac{1}{2}$
4. Same	Same; doe and R	IX. E 1	17	$8\frac{6}{17}$
5. Same	Same; Φ	IX. D 1	5	$7\frac{3}{5}$
6. Same	Same; ΦI	.	6	$8\frac{1}{3}$
7. Same	Same; ΦI and bucranium	VIII. E 1	1	$7\frac{1}{2}$
8. Same	Same; E	{VIII. G 1—2} {IX. B 1}	6	7
9. Same	Same; grapes	VIII. A 10	1	8
10. Same	Same; cicada	VIII. B 2	1	$8\frac{1}{2}$
11. Same	Same; Δ	.	1	8
12. Same	Same; ⊢ and uncertain symbol	.	1	8
13. Same	Same; but ∴ and Φ	.	1	.
14. Same	Same as 1—12, but no letter or symbol	.	34	$8\frac{3}{34}$
	Total Tarentine Obols (Diota Type)		92	

APPENDIX C (continued).

TARANTO FIND—TARENTINE OBOLS (Horse's Head).

	Obverse.	Reverse.	Cognate Didrachms.	No. of Coins in Hoard.	Average Weight.
					Grs.
1.	Horse's head	Horse's head; thunderbolt	VIII. A 2	3	6½
2.	Same	Same; N	VIII. B 8 ?	1	5
3.	Same	Same; E	VIII. G 1—2	1	6½
			IX. B 1		
4.	Same	Same; ΦI		1	7¼
5.	Same	Same; tripod	VIII. F 1	3	6
			IX. C 1		
			IX. D 1		
6.	Same	Same; ⋆	.	6	6½
7.	Same	Same; Δ	.	1	7
8.	Same	Same; doe	.	22	7½
9.	Same	Same; grapes	VIII. A 10	4	6⅞
10.	Same	Same; A	IX. E 1 ?	1	7
11.	Same	Same; A and club	IX. E 1 ?	1	8
12.	Same	Same; owl	VIII. A 8, 9	1	6½
13.	Same	Same; uncertain or no letter or symbol	.	23	
		Total Tarentine Obols (Horse's Head)		68	

TARANTO FIND—HÊMIOBOLIA.

			Av. weight.
Two crescents and four pellets on *obverse* and *reverse*	.	33	3 4/5 grs.

APPENDIX C (continued).

TARANTO FIND—THURIAN DIDRACHMS.

Obverse.	Reverse.	No. of Coins in Hoard.
1. Head of Pallas to l., in crested Athenian helmet, on the fore-part of which is a griffin.	Bull butting r., the head turned towards the spectator. In f. above, owl flying. In ex., ΘΟΥΡΙΩΝ.	5
2. Head of Pallas to r., in helmet with wreath.	Same, but legend in f. above. In ex. flying bird.	4
3. Same.	Same, but floral device in ex.	1
4. Same.	Same, but without symbol.	1
5. Head of Pallas to r., in Corinthian helmet.	Same.	3
6. Laureate head of Apollo to r.	Same type. ΘΟΥΡΙΩΝ in ex. No symbol.	6
7. Same.	Same. In ex. flying bird.	1
Total Thurioi (Average weight $98\frac{1}{2}$ grs.) .		22

SUMMARY OF COINS IN TARANTO HOARD.

Tarentum	didrachms	1,032
,,	drachms	16
,,	litræ	88
,,	hêmilitra	46
,,	diobols (Pallas type)	161
,,	obols (diota type)	92
,,	obols (horse's head)	68
,,	hêmiobolia	33
	Total Tarentine .	1,536
Thurioi didrachms		22
	Total coins in hoard .	1,558

INDEX I.

Attributes and Symbols in Taras' Hands.

Akrostolion. II. H. 1, p. 45; II. L 1, p. 45; III. A 3, p. 58; III. B 1, 2, p. 58; X. A, p. 210.

Bow and arrows. IV. L, p. 80; V. B 17—19, p. 103; VII. A 1, p. 157; VII. B, p. 158; VII. C 1, p. 158.

Chlamys. VIII. A 8, 9, p. 177; VIII. H 1, 2, p. 180; VIII. N, p. 181; IX. G, p. 195; X. D, p. 211.

Club. VI. D 4, p. 134.

Corn-spike. VI. E 2, p. 135; VIII. L 2, p. 181.

Cornucopiæ. VII. A 2, p. 157; VII. B 4, p. 158; VIII. B 1, 2, p. 178; VIII. G 1, p. 179; VIII. G 2, p. 180; VIII. K, p. 180; VIII. L 3, p. 181; X. B, p. 210.

Cup (or vase), one-handled. III. G 4, p. 60; III. N, p. 62; IV. F 2—5, p. 78; V. A 1, p. 88; V. F 2, p. 105.

Dart (or harpoon). II. D 3, p. 43; II. E 5, p. 44; III. E, p. 59; VII. L, p. 161.

Distaff. V. A 2—8, pp. 88, 89; V. B 1—4, 10, pp. 101, 102; V. C 1—4, p. 104; VI. A 5, p. 133; VI. F 1, 2, p. 135; VI. G, p. 135; VII. D 8, p. 159; VII. F 1—6, p. 160; VII. G, p. 161; VIII. A 1—3, 11, pp. 176, 177. (Cf. p. 90 *seqq.*)

Dolphin (small). V. B 1, p. 101; VI. D 2, p. 134.

Fish, held by tail. L. V 2, p. 61.

Flower (hyacinth). VIII. G 1, p. 179. (Cf. pp. 186, 187.)

Grapes, bunch of. III. S, p. 63; VI. A 3, p. 132; VI. F. 2, p. 135; VII. F. 1—6, p. 160; VIII. B. 3, p. 178.

Helmet, crested. II. C 1, p. 43; IV. H 1—5, p. 79; VIII. D 2, p. 179.

Helmet, horned. VII. C 2, 3, p. 158.

Hippocamp. IX. B, p. 194.

Hippocamp, on round shield. IV. H 6, p. 79; IV. K, p. 79; V. B 5—8, p. 102; VII. B 4, p. 158; VII. D, p. 159.

Hyacinth. VIII. G 1, p. 179. (Cf. pp. 186, 187.)

Kantharos—*passim.*

Oar. II. D 1, 2, p. 43; V. B 20, 21, p. 103.

Œnochoē. III. H 1, p. 61.

Olive-branch. VI. A 2, p. 132.

Palma lemniscata. V. D, p. 104; VII. H, p. 161.

Rhyton. VIII. C 1, p. 178;
IX. D, p. 195; IX. F, p. 195.
Shield, oval. II. C 1, p. 48.
Shield, round. IV. B, p. 76;
IV. C 1—5, p. 77; IV. D, p. 77; V. B 9, p. 102.
Shield, ditto, with hippocamp. See above.
Shield, ditto, with E. VI. B 1, 2, p. 133.
Spears (or lances), two. IV. K, p. 79; VI. B 1, 2, p. 133;
VI. E 1, p. 134; VII. B, p. 159; VII. L, p. 161.
Thymiatèrion. VIII. G 2, p. 180.
Torch, lighted. VI. H, p. 135.
Trident—*passim*.
Tripod. VI. A 1, p. 132; VIII. E, p. 179.
Watersnake. V. E, p. 105.
Wreath. III. Q, p. 63; VI. C 3, p. 134; VII. A 5, p. 157.

INDEX II.

Symbols and Objects in the Field.

Amazonian shield. IX. D, p. 195; diobol, p. 225, No. 13.
Amphora, single. VIII. K, p. 180.
Amphoræ (two). VII. C 5—7, p. 159; IX. F, p. 195.
Amphoræ (two) and twin stars of Dioskuri, gold stater, p. 140; ¼ stater, p. 141.
Anchor. VI. D, p. 134; cf. pp. 145—147 and 172; VIII. A 1, p. 176; p. 182; diobol, p. 225, No. 16.
Anchor and wreath, p. 146, 147.
Athêna Alkis, gold stater, p. 139; litra, p. 140.
Bow. Diobol, p. 223, No. 10.
Bucranium. VIII. E, p. 179; drachm, p. 182; diobol, p. 224, No. 6; obol, p. 226, No. 7.
Caduceus (Kêrykeion). II. E, p. 44; V. G, p. 105.
Capital (Ionic), p. 19; V. E, p. 104; VIII. D 2, p. 179; p. 172; p. 182.
Cicada. VIII. B 2, p. 178; diobol, p. 224, No. 1; obol, p. 226, No. 10.
Club. IV. B 1, p. 76; diobols, p. 224, 225; obols, p. 227, No. 11.
Cock. VI. G 135; VIII. A 11, p. 177.
Convolvulus leaf (?). V. B 4, p. 102.

Corn-spike. VII. F 5, p. 160; VIII. C 1, p. 178.
Cornucopiæ. VIII. A 4, 5, p. 177; p. 173.
Crescent. IX. H 1, p. 196; p. 173.
Cuttlefish (or sepia). II. B. p. 43; III. F 1, p. 59; III. F 3, p. 59; IX. G, p. 195.
Diota. VII. L, p. 161; VII. M, p. 162.
Doe, looking back. VI. F 1, p. 135; litra, p. 128, 222, No. 6; hêmilitron, p. 223, No. 5; diobols, p. 224, Nos. 3, 4; obol, p. 227, No. 8.
Dog, p. 172.
Dolphin. V. B 2, p. 101; p. 172; IX. F, p. 195.
Eagle, with folded wings. V. A, pp. 88, 89; see p. 87.
Eagle, with expanding wings. X. E, p. 211.
Elephant, p. 139; p. 145, litra; VII. A 1, p. 157; VII. B, p. 158; VII. C 1, p. 158.
Fillet (and uncertain object). VII. K 2, p. 161.
Fish (uncertain). III. D 1, p. 59.
Flower (hyacinth). VIII. G 2, p. 180; p. 182; litra, p. 222, No. 5; hêmilitron, p. 222, No. 4.
Grapes, bunch of. VIII. A 10, p. 177; drachm, p. 182; litra, p. 128; obols, p. 226, No. 10; p. 227, No. 9.
Helmet (Corinthian). V. D, p. 104; VII. H, p. 161; on Kylix, III. E 1, p. 59.
Helmet, with cheek pieces; gold stater, p. 141.

Helmet, horned, pp. 148, 149; VII. C 2, p. 158.
Herm (Ithyphallic). III. H 1, 2, p. 61.
Hippocamp. VI. E 1, p. 134; on shield, V. B 5—8, p. 102; litra, p. 128.
Hyacinth. VIII. G 2, p. 180; drachm, p. 182; pp. 186, 187; litra, p. 222, No. 5; hêmilitron, p. 223, No. 5.
Ionic capital, p. 19; V. E, p. 104; VII. G, p. 161; VIII. D 2, p. 179; p. 182; p. 172.
Ivy-leaf. V. B 1, V. B 3, p. 101; V. B 10, p. 102.
Kantharos, p. 18; III. O 3, p. 62.
Kylix, p. 18; III. R, p. 63.
Kylix, with representation of Corinthian helmet. III. E 1, p. 59.
Laurel-branch. VII. F 3, p. 160.
Lion, passant. VIII. B 3, p. 178; p. 173.
Mask, bearded. VIII. B 4, p. 178.
Murex (purple-shell), gold stater, p. 66; V. B 5, 6, 8, p. 102.
Nikê, flying; litra, p. 222, No. 11; hêmilitron, p. 223, No. 10.
Nymph's head. VIII. D 1, p. 179; diobols and litras, p. 167.
Owl, flying. V. F, p. 105.
Owl, seated. VIII. A 8, 9, p. 177; diobols and litras, p. 167 and p. 222 *seqq.*; gold stater, p. 140; hêmilitron, p. 223, No. 1; obol. p. 226, No. 2.

Pallas Promachos gold stater, p. 139; litra, p. 140.
Pan's head, bearded. IX. B, p. 194.
Prow. V. B 2, p. 101; p. 148; VII. A 4, p. 157.
Purple-shell (murex) gold stater, p. 66; V. B 5, 6, 8, p. 102.
Rhyton, p. 172; litra, p. 222, No. 12.
Rudder. VIII. H 2, p. 180; gold stater, p. 66; litra, p. 222, No. 9.
Scallop. I. C, p. 35; II. A, p. 43; II. F, p. 44; II. G, p. 44; II. E 1, p. 44; IV. F 5, p. 78.
Serpent, coiled, raising head. VII. F 4, p. 160.
Shield, Amazonian. IX. D, p. 195; diobols, p. 225, No. 13.
Shield, round, gold stater, p. 66.
Spearhead. VI. E 2, p. 135; quarter stater, p. 141; litra, p. 143. (See pp. 142, 143.)
Star, single. VII. A 5, p. 157; p. 173.
Stars, twin (eight-rayed) of Dioskuri. IV. H, p. 79.
Stars, twin (twelve-rayed) of Dioskuri. VII. C 2, 3, p. 158.
Stars, twin, of Dioskuri, over Amphoras, gold staters, pp. 140, 141.
Tablet or Tessera. III. F 8, p. 59; III. G 2, p. 60; IV. F 1, 2, 4, p. 78. See pp. 50, 52, 70, 106. On diobol, p. 50.
Term. VIII. L, p. 180.
Thunderbolt gold stater, pp. 85, 140, 141, 148; VII. A 2, 3, p. 157; litra, p. 222, No. 3; hemilitron, p. 223, No. 2; diobols, p. 224, No. 7, 225, No. 12; obols, p. 226, No. 1, p. 227, No. 1.
Thymiaterion. VIII. G 1, p. 179.
Torch, lighted. VIII. B 1, p. 178; drachm, p. 182.
Tripod, p. 172; VIII. F, p. 179; IX. G, p. 194; obol, p. 227, No. 5; diobol, p. 225, No. 15.
Tunny-fish. III. F 2, p. 59; IV. A 2, p. 76; IV. H 6, p. 79.
Wreath. IX. C, p. 194; p. 173.

INDEX III.

SIGNATURES.[1]

A.

—A—. III. T, p. 64.
—A. II. 4, p. 44.
A—(A or Λ). V. B, 22, p. 104.
—A (⊢). IV. D, p. 77; III. N 2, p. 62.
—A ✗ (⊢HPAKΛHI). VII. M, p. 162.
— AΓA (ΦIΛIAPXOΣ ΣA). VI. A, 3, p. 132.
—AΓA (NIKOΔAMOΣ EY). VI. G, p. 135.
AΓAΘAPXOΣ—. VIII. B 1, p. 178.
AΓΩ KPATINOΣ— (ΙΩP). VI. A 4, p. 133.
AΛ—. II. E 3, p. 44.
AΛEΞ ΘE— (ΣI). VII. A 5, p. 161.
AΛEΞAN ΘE—. VI. D 4, p. 134.
—ANΘ or AN (AΠOΛ ΛΩ). VII. F 2, p. 160.
—ANΘ or AN (AΠOΛΛΩ ΙΩ H). VII. F 1, p. 160.
—AN ΙAΛO (Ι). Drachm, p. 162.
—ANΘ or AN (ΙΩ ΙA ΛO). VII. G, p. 161.
—ANΘ (ΙΩ "ЄIC"). VII. F 6, p. 160.
—N Ƌ (Ι). Drachm, p. 162.
—N (ΛEΩN). VIII. B 3, p. 178.
— N NIKOKPATHΣ. VIII. D 2, p. 179; VIII. N, p. 181.
AN NIKOKPATHΣ. Drachm, p. 182.
ANΘPΩΣ—(EY AP). VI. D 1, p. 134.
AΠH Λ Ι Λ— (ΣOI). V. C 2, p. 104.
AΠH — (Φ). V. F 1, p. 105.
AΠ, AΠOΛ. On gold hemilitra, p. 84.
AΠ, AΠOΛ. On gold staters, p. 85.
AΠOΛ (K or NK). Gold stater, p. 141.

---

[1] The signature on the opposite side of the coin to that specially cited is placed in brackets. The — after a signature indicates that it occurs on the obverse (horseman) side. The — before a signature indicates that it occurs on the reverse. Unless otherwise specified, the coins enumerated are silver staters.

h h

—ΑΠΟΛ (ΦΙΛΟΚΡΑ ΝΚ).
VIII. A 6, p. 177; VIII C
3, p. 178.
ΑΠΟΛΛΩ ΕΥ—(ΘΙ). VII.
C 5, p. 159.
ΑΠΟΛΛΩ ΕΥ— (Β ΘΙ).
VII. C 6, p. 159.
ΑΠΟΛΛΩ Η— (ΘΙ). VII.
C 7, p. 159.
ΑΠΟΛΛΩ— (ΑΝΘ or
AN). VII. F 2—5, p.
160.
ΑΠΟΛΛΩ ΙΩ Η—(ΑΝΘ
or AN). VII. F 1, p. 160.
—Ϸ Ν (Ι). Drachm, p.
162.
ΑΠΟΛΛΩΝΙΟΣ ΔΙ—.
VIII. H 1, p. 180.
ΑΡΕΘΩΝ ΣΑ— (ΣΑΣ).
VI. A 1, p. 132.
—ΑΡΕΥ (ΝΚ ΦΙΛΟΚΡΑ).
VIII. A 7, p. 177.
ΑΡΙΣΤΕΙΔ ΦΙ— (ΗΡ).
VIII. L 2, p. 181.
ΑΡΙΣΤΙΑΣ ΕΥ— (ΚΑΗ
or ΚΑΝ). VI. F 4, p.
135.
ΑΡΙΣΤΙΠ ΓΥ— (ΔΙ). VII.
A 1, p. 157.
ΑΡΙΣΤΙΠ ΓΥ— (Δ). VII.
B, p. 158.
—ΑΡΙΣ (ΙΩ ΝΕΥΜΗ).
VII. C 2, p. 150.
ΑΡΙ ΝΕΥΜΗΝΙΟΣ.
Drachm, p. 162.
—Ϸ (ΙΩ ΝΕΥΜΗ). VII.
C 1, p. 158.
ΣΑΛΩΝΟΣ (?) —(ΓΥ).
VII. E 1, p. 159.
—Ϸ ΙΑ (ΝΚ). Gold ¼ sta-
ter, p. 141.
—Ϸ Σ (ΝΚ). Gold stater, p.
141.
Ϸ ΣΩΚΡΑΤΗΣ—(ΙΟΡ).
VI. A 2, p. 132.

—ΑΡΙ (ΝΙΚΩΝ ΕΥ). VI.
E 2, p. 135.
ΑΡΙΣΤΙΠΠΟC Ϸ—(Υ).
IX. E, p. 195.
ΑΡΙΣΤΙΣ—. VIII. A 1,
p. 176.
ΑΡΙCΤΙC. Drachm, p.
182.
—ΑΡΙΣΤΟ (ΦΙΛΟΚΡΑ
ΝΚ). VIII. C 2, p. 178.
ΑΡΙΣΤΟΚΛΗΣ ΔΙ—.
VIII. D 1, p. 179.
ΑΡΙΣΤΟΚ ΘΙ—. VIII.
H 2, p. 180.
ΑΡΙΣΤΟΚΡΑΤΗΣ ΦΙ—
(ΠΙ). VIII. L 1, p. 180.
ΑΡΙΣΤΟΚΡΑΤΗΣ.
Drachm, p. 182.
[ΑΡΙΣΤΟΞΕΝΟΣ]. (See
pp. 54, 55, 78, &c.)
—ΑΡΙ (ΚΑΛ Α Ϝ Α). IV.
H 2, p. 79.
ΑΡΙ Ε Π Α—(ΚΛ). V. B 20,
p. 103.
ΑΡΙ Ι—(ΚΛ Ε Π Α). V.
B 21, p. 103.
—ΑΡΙ (ΕΥ ΝΙΚΩΝ). VI.
E 2, p. 135.
ΑΡ—. IV. A 1, p. 76.
ΑΡ—(Χ). III. K 2, p. 61.
Ϸ ΦΙ—. V. A 1, p. 88.
Ϸ ΦΙ (Φ). V. A 2, p. 88.
Ϸ ΦΙ (ΦΙ). V. A 4, p. 89.
Ϸ ΦΙ (ΦΙΛΙΣ). V A 3, 5,
pp. 88, 89.
—Ϸ (ΣΑ). V. B 11, p. 102.
—|Α
 |Ρ(ΣΑ). V. B 16, p.
103.
—Ϸ ϜΗΡ (ΣΑ). V. B 19,
p. 103.
—ΑΡ ΕΥ (ΑΝΘΡΩΣ).
VI. D 1, p. 134.
Ϸ ΚΥΝΩΝ—. VIII. B 4,
p. 178.

ΑΡΙΣΤΩΝ ΕΥ—(ΙΩΓ).
VIII. M 2, p. 181.
ΑΡΙΣΤΩΝ ΕΥΦ—
(ΙΩΓ). VIII. M 1, p. 181.

B.

—Β ΘΙ (ΕΥ ΑΠΟΛΛΩ).
VII. C 6, p. 159.

Γ.

ΓΥ ΑΡΙΣΤΙΓ—(ΔΙ). VII.
A 1, p. 157.
ΓΥ ΑΡΙΣΤΙΓ—(Δ). VII.
B, p. 158.
ΓΥ   ΙΩΓΥΡΟΣ—
(ΧΡΗ?). VIII. A 3, p. 176.
ΓΥ   ΣΩΣΤΡΑΤΟΣ—
(ΠΟΛΥ). VII. A 2, p. 157.
—ΓΥ (Ϙ ΣΑΛΩΝΟΣ).
VII. D, p. 159.
—ΓΥ (Ϙ ΣΑΛΩΝΟΣ?).
VII. E 1, p. 159.
—ΓΥ (ΣΙ ΛΥΚΩΝ). VII.
A 6, p. 157

Δ.

Δ— (Κ). III. L 5; III. M, p. 62.
Δ Ϝ ΚΑΛ— (ΦΙ). IV. L, p. 80.
ΔΑΙ — (Ϝ). IV. E, p. 77.
ΔΑ[Ι] — (Ε). V. B 8, p. 102.
ΔΑΙ — (ϜΗ). V. B 7, p. 102.
ΔΑΙ — (ΦΙ). V. B 5, p. 102.
ΔΑΙ — (ΦΗ). V. B 6, p. 102.
ΔΑΙΜΑΧΟC ΚΡ —(ΖΥ). IX.
A, p. 194.

ΔΑΜΟΚΡΙ Æ—. VII. C 4, p. 158.
ΔΑΜΟΚΡΙΤΟΣ ΕΥΝ—
(Ζ). VIII. L 3, p. 181.
ΔΕ ΣΥ ΛΥΚΙΝΟΣ—.
VIII. A 8, p. 177.
ΔΕΙΝΟΚΡΑΤΗΣ ΣΙ—.
VI. D 2, p. 134.
—ΔΙ (ΓΥ ΑΡΙΣΤΙΓ). VII.
A 1, p. 157.
—Δ (ΓΥ ΑΡΙΣΤΙΓ). VII.
B, p. 158.
ΔΙ. Litra, p. 222, No. 7;
obol, p. 226, No. 3.
—ΔΙ or ΔΙΟ (ΕΥ). Drachms, p. 162.
—ΔΙ (ΣΩΣ). Drachms, p. 163.
ΔΙ   ΑΠΟΛΛΩΝΙΟΣ—.
VIII. H 1, p. 180.
ΔΙ ΑΡΙΣΤΟΚΛΗΣ. VIII.
D 1, p. 179.
—ΔΙ (ϜΙΠΠΟΔΑ). VIII.
K, p. 180.
ΔΙ ΦΙΛΩΤΑΣ—. VIII.
A 11, p. 177.
ΔΟΡ—. III. Q, p. 64.

E.

E, on shield. VI. B 1, 2, p. 133.
E, on dolphin. (See p. 119.)
—Ǝ (Λ). III. D 1, p. 59.
—E (Φ). IV. C 1, IV. C 3, p. 77.
—E (ΔΑ[Ι]). V. B 8, p. 102.
ΕΙC, on shield. VII. F 6, p. 160.
—Ɛ (ϜΗΡΑΚΛΗΤΟΣ).
VIII. G 1, p. 179.
—Ɛ (ϜΗΡΑΚΛΗΤΟΣ
ΦΙ). VIII. G 2, p. 180.
—Ɛ (ΙΩΓΥΡΙΩΝ ΣΩ).
IX. B, p. 194.

Ǝ. Litra, p. 222, Nos. 4, 5;
hêmilitron, p. 223, No. 3;
obols, p. 226, No. 8; 227,
No. 3.
ΕΓΑ ΑΡΙ — (ΚΛ). V.
B 20, p. 103.
—ΕΓΑ ΚΛ (ΑΡΙ Σ). V.
B 21, p. 103.
ΕΥΑΡΧΙΔΑ Ϛ ΕΥ—. VI.
H, p. 135.
ΕΥ ΑΡΙ Ϛ ΤΙΑ Ϛ — (ΚΛΗ or ΚΑΝ). VI. F 4, p. 135.
—ΕΥ ΑΡ (ΑΝΘΡΩ Ϛ). VI.
D 1, p. 134.
ΕΥ ΣΕΝΕΑ Ϛ ΦΙ. VIII.
C 1, p. 178.
ΕΥ ΝΙΚΟΔΑΜΟ Ϛ —
(ΑΓΛ). VI. G, p. 135.
ΕΥ ΝΙΚΩΝ — (ΑΡΙ). VI.
E 2, p. 135.
ΕΥ ΝΙΚΩΤΤΑ Ϛ —
(ΣΟΡ). VI. E 1, p. 134.
ΕΥ Ϛ Ω Ϛ ΤΡΑΤΟ Ϛ —
(ΓΟΛΥ). VII. A 3, p. 137.
ΕΥ ΦΙΛΩΝ —. VI. C 1, 2, p. 133.
ΕΥ ΦΙΝΤΥΛΟ Ϛ — (ΓΟΛΥ). VII. A 4, p. 157.
ΕΥ ΦΙΛΟΚΛΗ Ϛ (ΛΥ). VI.
C 3, p. 134.
ΕΥΝ ΔΑΜΟΚΡΙΤΟ Ϛ —
(Σ). VIII. L 3, p. 181.
ΕΥΦ ΑΡΙ Ϛ ΤΩΝ —
(ΣΩΓ). VIII. M 1, p. 181.
ΕΥ ΑΡΙ Ϛ ΤΩΝ — (ΣΩΓ).
VIII. M 2, p. 181.

Ϛ.

—Ϛ (Σ). IV. F 1, p. 78.
—ϚΑ Ϛ (ϚΛ ΑΡΕΘΩΝ).
VI. A 1, p. 132.

—ϚΟΙ (ΑΓΗ Λ Σ Λ). V.
C 2, p. 104.
—ϚΟΙ (ΚΑΛ Α). V. C 1, p. 104.

Σ.

Σ—. III. E, p. 59.
Σ— (Κ). IV. F 3, p. 78.
—Σ (Κ). IV. F 2, p. 78.
Σ— (Ϛ). IV. F 1, p. 78.
Σ ΑΡΙ— (ΕΓΑ ΚΛ). V.
B 21, p. 103.
—Σ Α Ʀ (ΝΚ). Gold staters, p. 141.
ΣΑΛΟ ΣΩ — (ΑΝΘ or AN). VII. G, p. 161.
ΣΑΛΟ Σ —(ΑΝ). Drachm, p. 162.
Σ—(Ϡ Ν). Drachms, p. 162.
ΣΕΝΕΑ Ϛ ΕΥ ΦΙ. VIII.
C 1, p. 178.
ΣΕΝΟΚΡΑΤΗ Ϛ Ƙ —(✶).
IX. G, p. 195.
ΣΟΡ. Drachms, p. 126.
ΣΟΡ. Gold staters, p. 130.
—ΣΟΡ (ΚΡΑΤΙΝΟ Ϛ ΑΓΩ). VI. A 4, p. 133.
—ΣΟΡ (ΛΥΚΙΑΝΟ Ϛ).
VI. B 1, p. 133.
—ΣΟΡ. VI. B 2, p. 133.
—ΣΟΡ (ΝΙΚΟΔΑΜΟ Ϛ).
VI. F 1, p. 185.
—ΣΟΡ (ΝΙΚΩΤΤΑ Ϛ ΕΥ). VI. E 1, p. 134.
ΣΩΓΥ Η — (✶). VII. C 8, p. 159.
ΣΩΓΥ ΕΥ— (ΘΙ). VII.
H, p. 161.
ΣΩΓΥ Σ— (ΘΙ). VII.
K 1, p. 161.
ΣΩΓΥ Σ. VII. K 2, p. 161.

INDEX. 237

ΙΩ ͰΑΠΟΛΛΩ—(ΑΝΘ or ΑΝ). VII. F 2—5, p. 160.
ΙΩ "ΕΙC" — (ΑΝΘ). VII. F 6, p. 160.
ΙΩ ΝΕΥΜΗ—(Ρ). VII. C 1, p. 158.
ΙΩ ΝΕΥΜΗ— (ΑΡΙϚ). VII. C 2, p. 150.
ΙΩ ΝΕΥΜΗ— (ΠΟΛΥ). VII. C 3, p. 150.
ΙΩΠΥΡΙΩΝ ϚΩ— (Ε). IX. B, p. 194.
ΙΩΠΥΡΟϚ ΓΥ— (ΧΡΗ ?). VIII. A 3, p. 176.
ΙΩΠΥΡΟϚ ΦΕΙ. VIII. A 2, p. 176.
—ΙΩΠ (ΕΥ ΑΡΙϚΤΩΝ). VIII. M 2, p. 181.
—ΙΩΠ (ΕΥΦ ΑΡΙϚΤΩΝ). VIII. M 1, p. 181.
ΙΩ ϚΩΓΕΝΗϚ. X. B, p. 210.

H.

H on dolphin. III. Δ 2, p. 58 (and see p. 120).
—ΗΡ ͰΗΡ (ϚΑ). V. B 18, p. 103.
ΗϚ—. III. H 2, p. 61.

Ͱ.

Ͱ— (Α). III. N 2, p. 62; IV. D, p. 77.
Ͱ— (Ι). III. L 3, p. 61.
—ͰΑ. III. 5, p. 62.
ͰΑ ΚΑΛ Μ— (ΚΑΛ). IV. G, p. 78.
Ͱ ΚΑΛ Α— (ΦΙ). IV. H 1, p. 79.
—Ͱ (ΔΑΙ). IV. E, p. 77.
Ͱ— (Π). III. N 1, p. 62.

ͰΑΓΕΑC—(ΠΟΛΥ). VIII. A 4, p. 177.
ͰΕ—. III. H 1, p. 61.
ͰΗ. V. F 2, V. 9, p. 105.
—ͰΗΡ Ρ (ϚΑ). V. B 19, p. 103.
—ͰΗΡ ΗΡ (ϚΑ). V. B 18, p. 103.
—ͰΗΡ (ϚΑ). V. B 17, p. 103.
—ͰΗΡ (ϚΙΜ). IV. A 2, p. 76.
ͰΗΡΑ—(ΧΙ). VII. L, p. 161.
ͰΗΡΑΚΛΗΙ — (ΧΔ). VII. M, p. 162.
ͰΗΡΑΚΛΗΤΟϚ — (Ε). VIII. G 1, p. 179.
ͰΗΡΑΚΛΗΤΟϚ ΦΙ—(Ε). VIII. G 2, p. 180.
ͰΗΡΑΚΛΗΤΟϚ. Drachm, p. 182.
ͰΡ ΔΑΙΜΑΧΟC — (ΑΡ). IX. A, p. 194.
—ͰΡ (ΦΙ ΑΡΙϚΤΕΙΔ). VIII. L 2, p. 181.
ͰΡ. Drachm, p. 196.
ͰΙ (ΚΛΗ ϚΗΡΑΜΒΟϚ). X. A, p. 210.
ͰΙ ΑΠΟΛΛΩ—(ΘΙ). VII. C 7, p. 159.
ͰΙ ΙΩ ΑΠΟΛΛΩ — (ΑΝΘ or ΑΝ). VII. F, p. 160.
ͰΙ ΙΩΠΥ—(*). VII. C 8, p. 159.
ͰΙ ΦΙΛΗΜΕΝΟϚ—. VIII. E, p. 179.
ͰΙΠΠΟΔΑ—(ΔΙ). VIII. K, p. 180.
ͰΙϚΤΙΑΡ ΕΥ—. VIII. A 10, p. 177.
ͰΙϚΤΙΑΡΧΟϚ. Drachm, p. 182.

Θ.

Θ—. III. O 3, p. 62; III. R, p. 64.
Θ—(Θ). III. P, p. 64; III. O 1, p. 62.
Θ—(Γ). I. B, p. 35.
ΘΕ ΑΛΕΞΑΝ—. VI. D 4, p. 134.
ΘΕ ΑΛΕΞ—(Ϛ I). VII. A 5, p. 157.
ΘΙ. Hémilitron, p. 223, No. 7.
—ΘΙ (ΕΥ ΑΓΟΛΛΩ). VII. C 5, p. 159.
—ΘΙ (ϜΙ ΑΓΟΛΛΩ). VII. C 7, p. 159.
—ΘΙ Β (ΕΥ ΑΓΟΛΛΩ). VII. C 6, p. 159.
—ΘΙ (ΕΥ ΣΩΓΥ). VII. H, p. 161.
—ΘΙ (Σ ΣΩΓΥ). VII. K 1, p. 161.
ΘΙ ΑΡΙϚΤΟΚ—. VIII. H 2, p. 180.
ΘΡΑ—(ΘΡΑ). III. F 1, p. 59.

I.

—Ι (Ϝ). III. L 3, p. 61.

K.

—Κ (Δ). III. L 5, p. 62; III. M, p. 62.
Κ—Σ). IV. F 2, p. 78.
Κ ΦΙ—(Κ). III. G 4, p. 60.
Κ ΦΙ—(Ϟ). III. G 3, p. 60.
Κ ΦΙ—(Α). III. G 1, p. 60.
Κ—(Ω). IV. B, p. 76.
ΚΑΛ—(ΚΑΛ). IV. K, p. 79.
ΚΑΛ Α Ϝ Α—(ΦΙ). IV. H 1, p. 79.
ΚΑΛ Α Ϝ Α—(ΑΡΙ). IV. H 2, p. 79.
ΚΑΛ Α Ϝ Α—(ΚΑΛ). IV. H 3, p. 79.
ΚΑΛ Α Ϝ Α—(ΟΝΑ). IV. H 4, p. 79.
ΚΑΛ ϜΑ Μ—(ΚΑΛ). IV. G, p. 78.
ΚΑΛ Χ Α Ν—(ΚΑΛ). IV. H 5, p. 79.
ΚΑΛ Ν Ν—(Κ). IV. H 6, p. 79.
ΚΑΛ Ϝ Δ—(ΦΙ). IV. L, p. 80.
ΚΑΛ Α—(ϹΟΙ). V. C 1, p. 104.
ΚΑΛΛΙΚΡΑΤΗϚ — (ΝΕ ΈΡ). IX. H, p. 196.
—ΚΛ (ΑΡΙ Ε Γ Α). V. B 20, p. 103.
—ΚΛ Ε Γ Α (ΑΡΙ Σ). V. B 21, p. 103.
—ΚΛΗ (or ΚΑΝ) (ΕΥ ΑΡΙϚΤΙΑϚ). VI. F 4, p. 135.
ΚΛΗ ϚΗΡΑΜΒΟϚ— (Ν). X. A, p. 210.
ΚΟΝ. Gold stater, p. 99.
—ΚΟΝ (ϚΑ). V. E, p. 104.
ΚΡΑΤΙΝΟϚ ΑΓΩ— (ΣΟΡ). VI. A 4, p. 133.
ΚΡΙΤΟϚ—(Σ). X. C, p. 210.
ΚΥΛΙΚ. Gold stater, p. 66.
ΚΥΝΩΝ Æ—. VIII. B 4, p. 178.

Λ.

Λ—II. H, II. L 1, p. 44; III. B 1, III. C 1, p. 58.
—Λ. III. A 1, p. 58.
Λ—(Λ). II. H; II. L 1, p. 45; III. A 3, p. 58.

Λ (or Γ) — (A). III. L 1, p. 61.
Λ—(Ⅎ). III. D 1, p. 59.
Λ—(P). III. A 2; III. C 2, p. 58; III. K 3, p. 61.
ⴷΛ—. II. L 2, p. 45.
ΛΕΩΝ—(Ν). VIII. B 3, p. 178.
ΛΕΩΝ. Drachm, p. 182.
ₑ ΦΙΛΟΚΛΗϹ ẃ—. IX. F, p. 195.
ΛΥ. Gold staters, p. 99.
—ΛΥ (ΦΙΛΟΚΛΗϚ ΕΥ). VI. C 3, p. 134.
ΛΥΚΙΑΝΟϚ — (ΙΟΡ). VI. B 1, p. 133.
ΛΥΚΙΝΟϚ ϚΥ—. VIII. A 9, p. 177.
ΛΥΚΙΝΟϚ ϚΥ ΔΕ. VIII. A 8, p. 177.
ΛΥΚΩΝ Ϛl. VI. D 3, p. 132.
ΛΥΚΩΝϚI—(ΓΥ). VII. A 6, p. 157.

M.

M ΚΑΛ ⊦Α—(ΚΑΛ). IV. G, p. 78.

N.

N A X ΚΑΛ—(ΚΑΛ). IV. H 5, p. 79.
N N ΚΑΛ— (K). IV. H 6, p. 79.
ΝΕΥΜΗ ΙΩ— (Ɑ). VII. C 1, p. 151.
ΝΕΥΜΗ ΙΩ — (ΑΡΙϚ). VII. C 2, p. 158.
ΝΕΥΜΗ ΙΩ— (ΓΟΛΥ). VII. C 3, p. 158.
ΝΕΥΜΗΝΙΟϚ ΑΡΙ. Drachm, p. 162.
ΝΕΥΜΗΝΙΟϚ ΓΟΛΥ. Drachm, p. 162.
—ℕΕ (ΚΑΛΛΙΚΡΑΤΗϚ Ɛk). IX. H 1, p. 196.
ΝΙ—. III. S, p. 63.
ΝΙΚΑΡ (ℕΚ). Gold staters, pp. 140, 141.
ΝΙΚΟΔΑΜΟϚ —(ΙΟΡ). VI. F 1, p. 135.
ΝΙΚΟΔΑΜΟϚ ΕΥ— (ΑΓΑ). VI. G, p. 135.
ΝΙΚΟΚΡΑΤΗϚ Ν—. VIII. N, p. 181.
ΝΙΚΟΚΡΑΤΗϚ — (ΑΝ). Drachm, p. 182.
ℕΚ — (Ɑ). Gold stater, p. 141.
ℕΚ —(Ɑ Ϛ). Gold stater, p. 141.
ℕΚ—(Ɑ ΙΑ). Gold ½ stater, p. 141.
ℕΚ — (ϚΩΚ). Gold stater, p. 140.
ℕΚ (ΦΙ). Gold stater, p. 141.
ℕΚ (or K)—(ΑΓΟΛ). Gold stater, p. 141.
ℕΚ ΦΙΛΟΚΡΑ— (ΑΠΟΛ). VIII. A 6, p. 177; VIII. C 3, p. 178.
ℕΚ ΦΙΛΟΚΡΑ — (ΑΡΕΥ). VIII. A 7, p. 177.
ℕΚ ΦΙΛΟΚΡΑ — (ΑΡΙϚ- ΤΟ). VIII. C 2, p. 178.
ΝΙΚΥΛΟϚ — (Ɑ). VIII. O, p. 182.
ΝΙΚΩΝ ΕΥ—(ΑΡΙ). VI. E 2, p. 135.
ΝΙΚΩΤΤΑϚ ΕΥ— (ΙΟΡ). VI. E 1, p. 134.

O.

ΟΛΥΜΓΙϚ. IX. C, p. 194.
ΟΛΥΜΠΙϚ. Drachm, p. 196.

ΟΛΥΜΠΙΣ ⚹ —. IX. D, p. 195.
—ΟΝΑ (ΚΑΛ Α ⊢ Α). IV. H 4, p. 78.

Γ.

—Π. II. B, p. 43.
Γ—. III. O 2, p. 62.
—Γ (Θ). I. B, p. 35.
—Γ (⊢). III. N 1, p. 62.
—Γ (Φ). IV. C 2; IV. C 5, p. 77.
ᚷ ΚΑΛΛΙΚΡΑΤΗΣ — (ΝΕ). IX. H 1, p. 196.
—ΓΙ (ΑΡΙΣΤΟΚΡΑΤΗΣ ΦΙ). VIII. L 1, p. 180.
—ΠΟΛΥ (ΓΥ ΣΩ-ΤΡΑΤΟΣ). VII. A 1, p. 157.
ΠΟΛΥ (ΕΥ ΣΩ-ΤΡΑΤΟΣ). VII. A 2, p. 157.
—ΠΟΛΥ (ΕΥ ΦΙΝΤΥ-ΛΟΣ). VII. A 3, p. 157.
—ΠΟΛΥ (⊢ΑΓΕΑΣ). VIII. A 4, p. 177.
ΠΟΛΥ ΝΕΥΜΗΝΙΟΣ. Drachm, p. 162.
ΠΟΛΥ ΣΩΣΤΡΑΤΟΣ. Drachm, p. 162.
—ΠΟΛΥ (ΦΙΛΩΤΑΣ). VIII. A 5, p. 177.

Ρ.

—Ρ. III. K 3, p. 61.
—Ρ (Λ). III. A 2, III. C 2, p. 58; III. L 2, p. 61.

Σ.

—Σ. II. C 1, p. 43.
Σ—(Σ). II. C 2, p. 43.
ΣΑ. Gold stater, p. 99.
ΣΑ. V. B 2, p. 101.
ΣΑ—(Ρ). V. B 11, p. 102.
ΣΑ—(Α/Ρ), V. B 16, p. 103.
ΣΑ—(Α/Κ). V. B 13, p. 103.
ΣΑ ΑΡΕΘΩΝ — (ΣΑΣ). VI. A 1, p. 132.
ΣΑ—(⊢ΗΡ). V. B 17, p. 103.
ΣΑ— (⊢ Η Ρ). V. B 19, p. 103.
ΣΑ—⊢ΗΡ ΗΡ). V. B 18, p. 103.
ΣΑ—(Κ). V. B 12, p. 103.
ΣΑ—(ΚΟΝ). V. E, p. 104.
ΣΑ— (ΣΥΜ). V. D, p. 104.
ΣΑ— (ΣΩ). V. B 14, p. 103.
ΣΑ—(ΦΙ). V. B 1, p. 101; V. B 10, p. 102.
ΣΑ ΦΙΛΙΑΡΧΟΣ — (ΑΓΛ). VI. A 3, p. 132.
ΣΑ—(Ω/Σ). V. B 15, p. 103.
ΣΑΛΩΝΟΣ (?) Ρ— (ΓΥ). VII. E 1, p. 159.
ΣΑΛΩΝΟΣ ⚹ — (ΓΥ). VII. D, p. 159.
ΣΗΡΑΜΒΟΣ ΚΛΗ— (Η). X. A, p. 210.
ΣΙ ΔΕΙΝΟΚΡΑΤΗΣ—. VI. D 2, p. 134.
—ΣΙ (ΘΕ ΑΛΕΞ). VII. A 5, p. 157.
ΣΙ ΛΥΚΩΝ—. VI. D 3, p. 134.
ΣΙ ΛΥΚΩΝ— (ΓΥ). VII. A 6, p. 157.
ΣΙ ΦΙΛΟΚΛΗΣ — (ΛΥ). VI. C 3, p. 134.
ΣΙ— (ΦΙ). VI. A 8, p. 89.

INDEX.

ΣΙΜ— (ϜΗΡ). IV. A 2, p. 76.
ΣΙΜ— (ΦΙ). V. A 6, 7, p. 89.
ΣΥ ΛΥΚΙΝΟΣ. VIII. A 9, p. 177.
ΣΥ ΔΕ ΛΥΚΙΝΟΣ—. VIII. A 8, p. 177.
ΣΥ—. Litra, p. 222, No. 2; diobol, p. 224, No. 9.
ΣΩ (on tessera). Diobol (see p. 50).
ΣΩ ΣΩΓΥΡΙΩΝ — (E). IX. B, p. 194.
ΣΩΓΕΝΗΣ ΣΩ. X. B, p. 210.
ΣΩΚΑΝΝΑΣ—. X. E, F, p. 211.
ΣΩΚΡΑΤΗΣ Α— (Κ). VI. A 5, p. 133.
ΣΩΚΡΑΤΗΣ Ρ— (ΣΟΡ). VI. A 2, p. 132.
ΣΩΚ (on tablet)— (ΣΩΚ, on tablet). III. F 3, p. 59.
—ΣΩΚ (ΝΚ). Gold stater, p. 140.
ΣΩΣΤΡΑΤΟΣ ΓΥ— (ΠΟΛΥ). VII. A 2, p. 157.
ΣΩΣΤΡΑΤΟΣ ΕΥ— (ΠΟΛΥ). VII. A 3, p. 157.
ΣΩΣΤΡΑΤΟΣ ΠΟΛΥ. Drachm, p. 162.
ΣΩΣ ΔΙ. Drachm, p. 163.

T.

—T. I. A 1, p. 85.

Y.

Y—. III. C 3, p. 59.

Φ.

Φ—. IV. C 4, p. 77.
—Φ (ΑΠΗ). V. F 1, p. 105.
Φ— (E). IV. C 1, IV. C 3, p. 77.
Φ— (Π). IV. C 2, IV. C 5, p. 77.
ΦΕΙ ΣΩΓΥΡΟΣ. VIII. A 2, p. 176.
—ΦΗ (ΔΑΙ). V. B 6, p. 102.
—ΦΙ (ϜΗΡΑ). V. B 9, p. 102.
—ΦΙ (ΚΑΛ Α Ϝ Α). IV. H 1, p. 79.
—ΦΙ (ΚΑΛ Ϝ Δ). IV. L, p. 80.
ΦΙ Κ — (Α). III. G 1, p. 60.
ΦΙ Κ — (Ж). III. G 3, p. 60.
ΦΙ Κ — (Κ). III. G 4, p. 60.
—ΦΙ (ΔΑΙ). V. B 5, p. 102.
—ΦΙ (ΣΑ). V. B 1, p. 101; V. B 10, p. 102.
—ΦΙ (ΣΙ). V. A 8, p. 89.
—ΦΙ (ΣΙΜ). V. A 6, 7, p. 89.
ΦΙΛΙ— (ΦΙ). V. B 3, p. 101; V. B 4, p. 102.
ΦΙ Ρ — (ΦΙ). V. A 4, p. 89.
ΦΙ Ρ — (Φ). V. A 2, p. 88.
ΦΙ Ρ —. V. A 1, p. 88.
—ΦΙΛΙΣ (ΦΙ Ρ). V. A 3, p. 88; V. A 5, p. 89.
[ΦΙΛΙΣΤΙΩΝ. See p. 110, 111 seqq.]
ΦΙ ΑΡΙΣΤΕΙΔ—(ϜΡ). VIII. L 2, p. 181.

ΦΙ ΑΡΙΣΤΟΚΡΑΤΗΣ —
(ΓΙ). VIII. L 1, p. 180.
ΦΙ ΗΡΑΚΛΗΤΟΣ – (Ε).
VIII. G 2, p. 180.
ΦΙ ΕΥ ΞΕΝΕΑΣ—. VIII.
C 1, p. 178.
ΦΙ ΞΩΠΥΡΟΣ—. VIII.
B 2, p. 178.
ΦΙ (ΝΚ). Gold stater, p. 141.
ΦΙΛΗΜΕΝΟΣ ΗΙ—. VIII.
E, p. 179.
ΦΙΛΙΑΡΧΟΣ   ΣΑ —
(ΑΓΑ). VI. A 3, p. 182.
ΦΙΛΙΑΡΧΟΣ ΦΙ. X. D, p. 211.
ΦΙΛΙCΚΟC. VIII. F, p. 179.
ΦΙΛΟΚΛΗC ⚚ Æ—. IX. F, p. 195.
ΦΙΛΟΚΡΑ ΝΚ — (ΑΠΟΛ). VIII. A 6, p. 177; VIII. C 3, p. 178.
ΦΙΛΟΚΡΑ ΝΚ — (ΑΡΕΥ). VIII. A 7, p. 177.
ΦΙΛΟΚΡΑ ΝΚ — (ΑΡΙΣΤΟ). VIII. C 2, p. 178.
ΦΙΛΩΝ ΕΥ—. VI. C 1, 2, p. 184.
ΦΙΛΩΤΑΣ — (ΠΟΛΥ). VIII. A 5, p. 177.

ΦΙΛΩΤΑΣ ΔΙ—. VIII. A 11, p. 177.
ΦΙΝΤΥΛΟΣ ΕΥ — (ΓΟΛΥ). VII. A 4, p. 157.
⚚ ΣΑΛΩΝΟΣ — (ΓΥ). VII. D, p. 159.

X.

—X (ΑΡ). III. K 2, p. 61.
X ΚΑΛ Α Ν — (ΚΑΛ). IV. H 5, p. 79.
—ΧΡΗ (?) (ΞΩΠΥΡΟΣ · ΓΥ). VIII. A 3, p. 176.
—⚚ (ΞΩΠΥ ΗΙ). VII. C 8, p. 159.
—⚚ Ξ (ΗΗΡΑ). VII. L, p. 160.
—⚚ Α (ΗΗΡΑΚΛΗΙ). VII. M, p. 162.

Ω.

Ω (Κ). IV. B, p. 76.
'Ω (ΣΑ). V. B 15, p. 103.
(Σ)
⚚ (ΞΕΝΟΚΡΑΤΗC Κ). IX. G, p. 195.

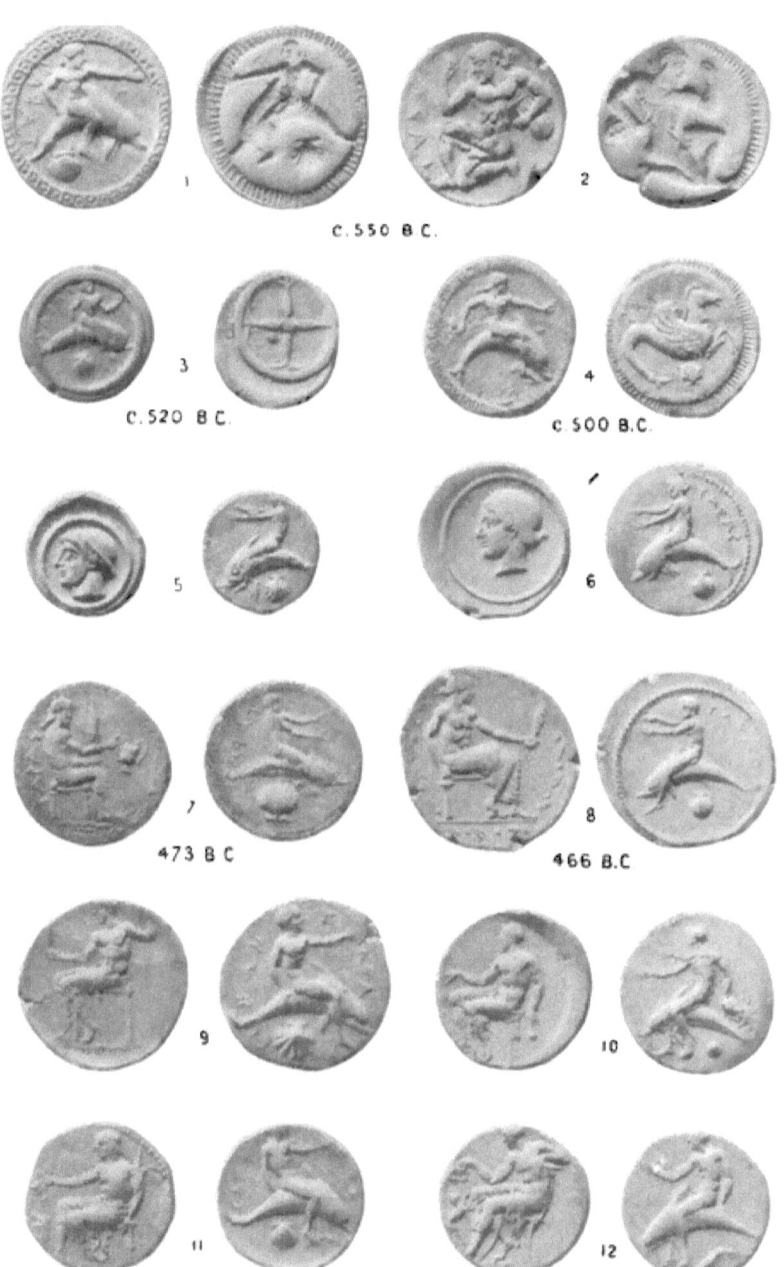

Early Didrachm Types to c. 420 B.C.

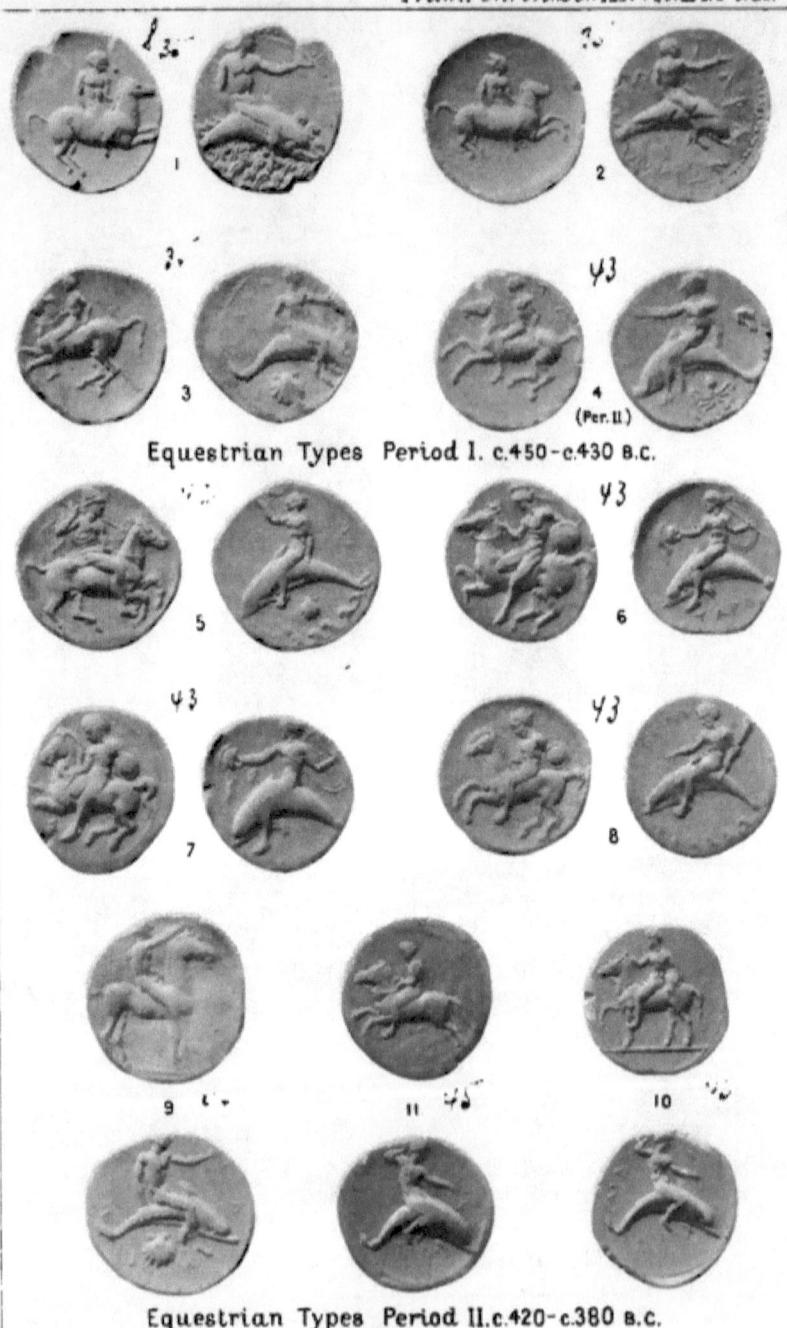

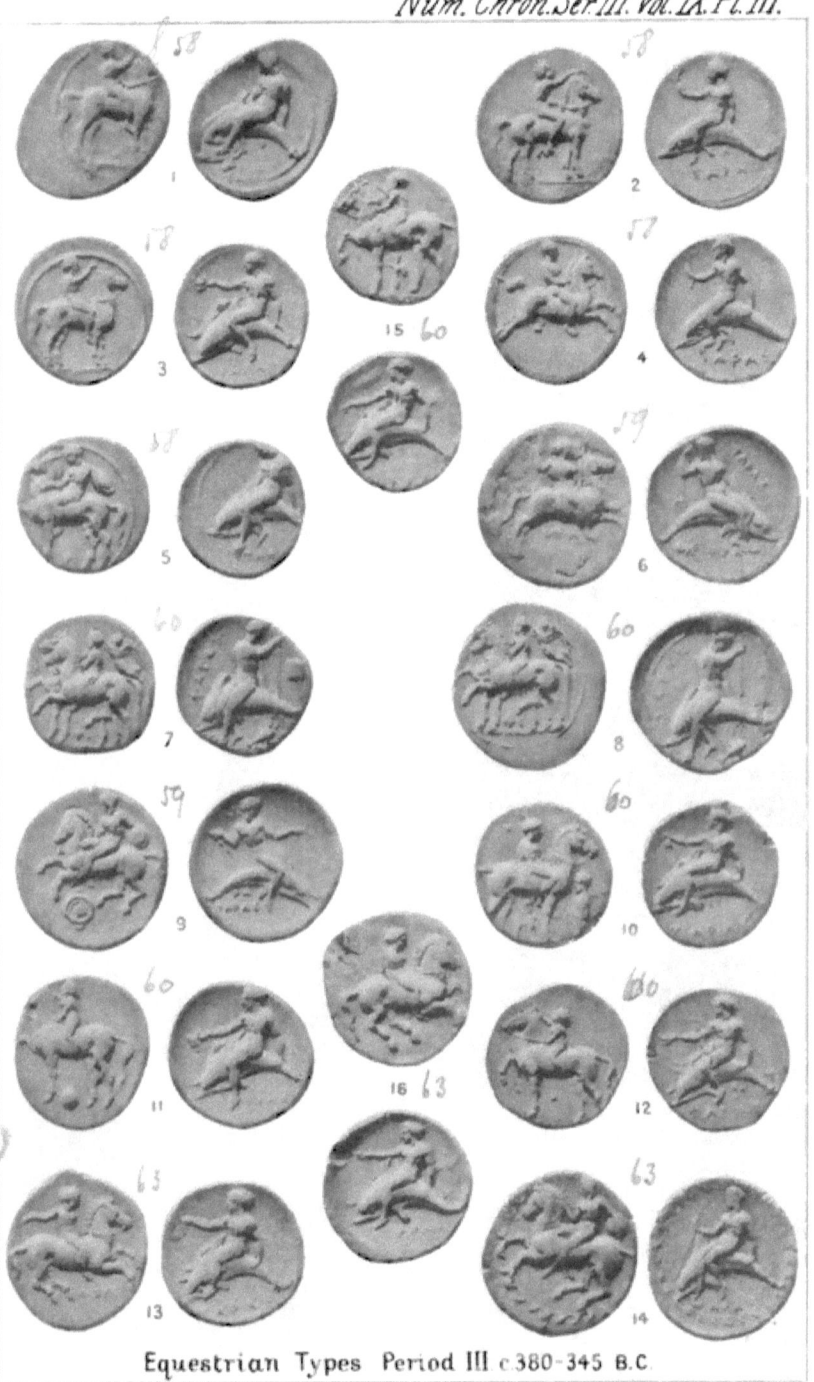

Equestrian Types   Period III c.380-345 B.C.

TARENTUM, PLATE III.

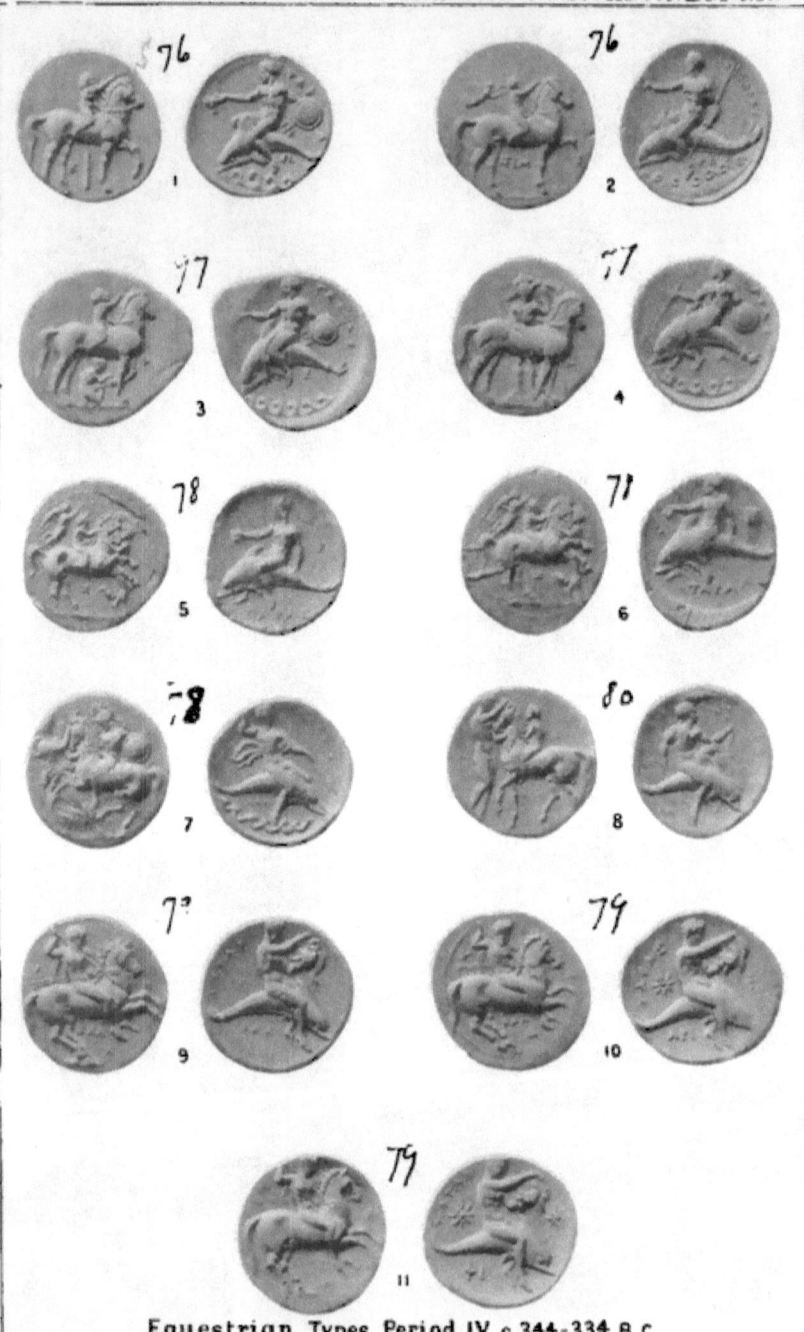

Equestrian Types Period IV c. 344-334 B.C.

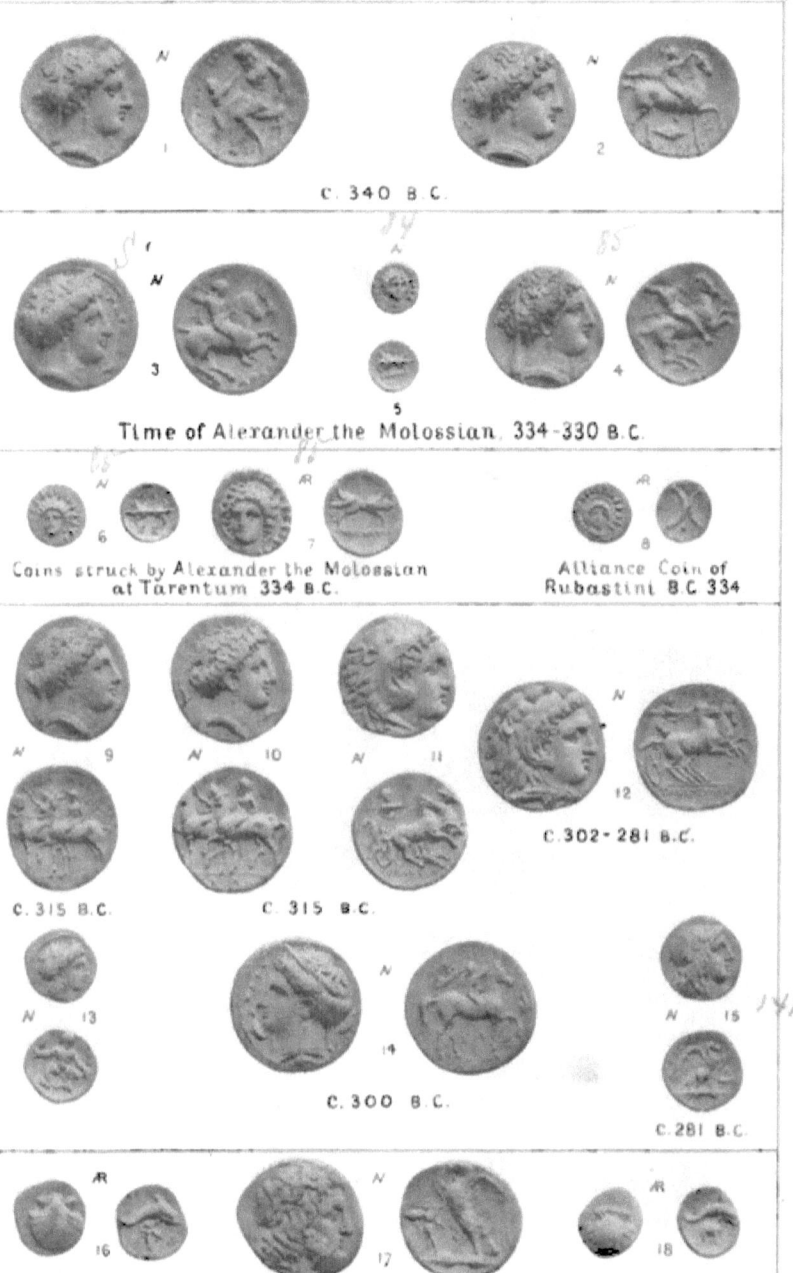

Molossian Types 334–330 B.C.

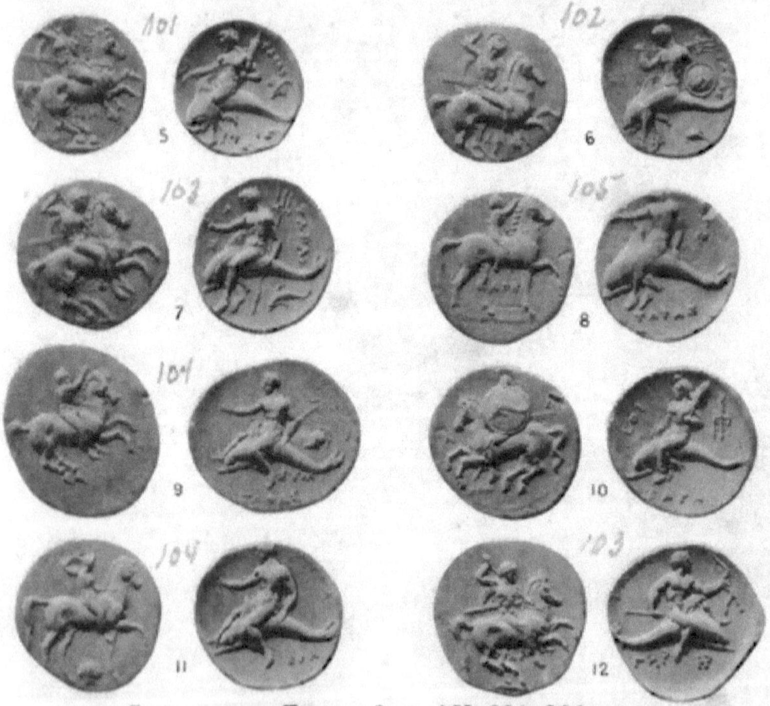

Equestrian Types, Period V. 334–302 B.C.

Campano-Tarentine Types.

www.ingramcontent.com/pod-product-compliance
Lightning Source LLC
Chambersburg PA
CBHW021353230426
43666CB00006B/514